MEMORY VISION

BOOKS, VIDEOS AND AUDIO TAPES
BY TONY BUZAN

Books
Speed Reading
Master your Memory
Use Your Head
Use Your Memory
The Brain User's Guide
Make the Most of Your Mind
Harnessing the ParaBrain
(Business version of *Make the Most of Your Mind*)
Spore One (poetry – Limited Edition)

Video Tapes
Use Your Head
The Enchanted Loom
Buzan Business Training
Family Genius Training

Audio Tapes
Learning and Memory
The Intelligence Revolution
Make the Most of Your Mind
Supercreativity and Mind Mapping

Other Works
The Universal Personal Organiser
'*Body and Soul*' (Master Mind Map poster)
The Mind Map Kit
Master Your Memory Matrix (SEM³) 0–10,000

see Appendix for more information
including how to order these items

MEMORY VISION

Tony Buzan

DAVID & CHARLES
Newton Abbot   London

External editor-in-chief: Vanda North

British Library Cataloguing in Publication Data

Buzan, Tony
    Memory vision.
    1. Man. Memory. Training
    I. Title
    153.1'4

    ISBN 0-7153-9393-6

Phototypeset by Typesetters (Birmingham) Ltd
Smethwick West Midlands
and printed in Great Britain
by Billings & Sons Ltd, Worcester
for David & Charles Publishers plc
Brunel House   Newton Abbot   Devon

CONTENTS

INTRODUCTION

'Welcome to the World of Memory!

Memory Vision is an introduction to the greatest of the oldest systems – the Major System devised in the mid-seventeenth century by Stanislaus Mink von Wennsshein – and the first major expansion of this system in 400 years, the Self-Enhancing Master Memory Matrix (SEM[3]) devised by the author.

Von Wennsshein's objective was to create a memory system that would alternately allow the user to translate any number into any letter, and any letter into any number, thus allowing the memoriser to use numbers to make words, and to use words as recording devices for numbers.

One reported significant result of Von Wennsshein's work was the creation of the Major Memory Peg System of one to 100 items, in order, reverse order and by rhyme. Von Wennsshein's system was slightly modified and adjusted in the eighteenth century by an Englishman, Dr Richard Grey. In converting numbers to letters, the Major System has a specific code devised so that by its own nature it allows itself to be memorised by itself! The code is as follows:

Numbers		Associated Letters
0	=	s, z, soft c
1	=	d, t, th
2	=	n
3	=	m
4	=	r
5	=	l
6	=	j, sh, soft ch, dg, soft g
7	=	k, hard ch, hard c, hard g, ng, qu
8	=	f, v
9	=	b, p

The vowels a, e, i, o, u and the letters h, w and y do not have numbers associated with them and are used simply as 'blanks' or fillers in the Key Memory Image Words you will soon be creating.

The Major System's special code can be memorised by applying the Mnemonic Principles to themselves in the following way:

Memorising the Major System Code

0 The letter s, or z, is the first sound of the word zero; o is the last letter.
1 The letters d and t have one downstroke.
2 The letter n has two downstrokes.
3 The letter m has three downstrokes.
4 The letter r is the last letter in the word four.
5 The letter l can be thought of as either the Roman numeral for 50 or a hand with five spread fingers, the index finger and thumb forming an L shape.
6 The letter j is the mirror image of 6.
7 The letter k, when seen as a capital, contains two number 7s.
8 The letter f, when handwritten, has two loops, similar to the number 8.
9 The letters b and p are the mirror image of 9.

Once you have grasped the Special Code, it is possible to translate any number into any word.

For example, the number 43 translates to the letters r and m. Using one of the vowel 'fillers' (and in devising the system it is always best to try 'a' before 'e', 'e' before 'i', etc) discover the word 'ram', which immediately translates back to the number 43.

Similarly, the number 82 translates to the letters 'f' and 'n'. Again using the vowel 'filler' you immediately have the word 'fan', which itself translates back to the number 82.

Using this approach it is easy to develop the Basic System of 100 previously described. Following for your convenience, is a 'Base 100' Key Memory Words, constructed by using the Major System Special Code.

The Major System One Hundred

It is important that you practise memorising them by referring in your Mind's Eye back to the Special Code, and that you have each word clearly *imaged* in your mind in order that it

	0	1	2	3	4	5	6	7	8	9
0–9	Zoo	Day	Noah	Ma	Rah	Law	Jaw	Key	Fee	Bay
10–19	Daze	Dad	Dan	Dam	Dare	Dale	Dash	Deck	Daffy	Dab
20–29	Nasa	Net	Nan	Name	Nero	Nail	Nash	Nag	Navy	Nab
30–39	Mace	Mat	Man	Ma'am	Mare	Mail	Mash	Mac	Mafia	Map
40–49	Race	Rat	Rain	Ram	Rare	Rail	Rash	Rack	Rafia	Rap
50–59	Lace	Lad	Lane	Lamb	Lair	Lily	Lash	Lake	Laugh	Lab
60–69	Chase	Chat	Chain	Chime	Chair	Chill	Chacha	Check	Chaff	Chap
70–79	Case	Cat	Can	Cameo	Car	Call	Cash	Cake	Café	Cab
80–89	Face	Fat	Fan	Fame	Fair	Fall	Fish	Fake	Fife	Fab
90–99	Base	Bat	Ban	Bam!	Bar	Ball	Bash	Back	Beef	Baby

will be ready to latch on to any new information you wish to recall.

If you wish to substitute your own words for any words suggested, feel free to do so as long as your substitutions use the appropriate letters.

If you wish to draw little images, or make any key word notes around any of the Key Memory Words in the Basic One Hundred, this will enhance your memory.

From 100 to 10,000 in One Easy Bound!

The Self-Enhancing Master Memory Matrix (SEM^3) was developed by the author in 1987 to enable the memoriser to go from 100 to 10,000 and more, using a new approach which allows the system not only to 'memorise itself' but to enhance the user's overall power of memory while both practising and using the system.

The Self-Enhancing Master Memory Matrix (SEM^3) is explained as follows.

The Self-Enhancing Master Memory Matrix (SEM^3)

The Self-Enhancing Master Memory Matrix allows you, by using the very principles of Mnemonic Techniques themselves, to expand from 100 to 10,000 as quickly as you can visualise!

Using the Basic One Hundred from the Major System, you multiply this system by 10 (1,000) and then by 10 again (10,000).

To do this you use both synaesthesia and basic knowledge grids as follows:

0– 999	Vision	5,000–5,999	Sensation
1,000–1,999	Sound	6,000–6,999	Animals
2,000–2,999	Smell	7,000–7,999	Birds
3,000–3,999	Taste	8,000–8,999	The Rainbow
4,000–4,999	Touch	9,000–9,999	The Solar System

For example, from zero to 999 you use **VISION** – in other words, you focus on your *seeing* the image you wish to remember as your key memory image. For 1,000 to 1,999 you use **SOUND**, focussing on your *hearing* for each image. From 2,000 to 2,999 you use your sense of **SMELL**, focussing your

Thousands		0–99	100–199	200–299	300–399	400–499	500–599	600–699	700–799	800–899	900–999
100– 999	**Vision**	–	Dinosaur	Nobility	Moonlight	Ravine	Lightning	Ocean	Concorde	Fire	Paintings
1,000–1,999	**Sound**	Sing	Drum	Wind	Moan	Roar	Lap	Shh	Gong	Violin	Brook
2,000–2,999	**Smell**	Sea-Weed	Tar	Nutmeg	Mint	Rose	Leather	Cheese	Garlic	Flowers	Pine
3,000–3,999	**Taste**	Spaghetti	Tea	Nuts	Mango	Rhubarb	Liver	Jam	Clove	Fudge	Banana
4,000–4,999	**Touch**	Sand	Damp	Honey	Mud	Rock	Oil	Jelly	Grass	Velvet	Bark
5,000–5,999	**Sensation**	Swimming	Dancing	Energy	Mingling	Warm	Loving	Shaking	Climbing	Flying	Peacefulness
6,000–6,999	**Animals**	Zebra	Dog	Newt	Moose	Rhinoceros	Elephant	Chimpanzee	Kangaroo	Fawn	Bear
7,000–7,999	**Birds**	Seagull	Duck	Nightingale	Magpie	Rooster	Lapwing	Chaffinch	Eagle	Flamingo	Peacock
8,000–8,999	**Rainbow**	Red	Orange	Yellow	Green	Blue	Indigo	Violet	Black	Grey	White
9,000–9,999	**Solar System**	Sun	Mercury	Venus	Earth	Mars	Jupiter	Saturn	Uranus	Neptune	Pluto

memory images on this sense. And so on, for each thousand, using consequently, **TASTE, TOUCH, SENSATION, ANIMALS, BIRDS, THE COLOURS OF THE RAINBOW** and **THE SOLAR SYSTEM**.

For each separate 100 of each 1,000, you have a specific Vision, a specific Sound, a specific Smell, etc. Thus, referring to the Matrix on page 10, your specific visions for the separate 100s from 100 to 999 are Dinosaur, Nobility, Moonlight, Ravine, Lightning, Ocean, Concorde, Fire and Paintings.

For example, keeping 0–99 as your Basic One Hundred Matrix, and using nine Vision-images to get you from 100 to 999, you would do the following:

101 might simply be a giant dinosaur with its head rising above the horizon next to the sun at the beginning of a new *day*; 140 would be a giant dinosaur leading an incredibly noisy, thundering and exciting dinosaur *race*. Whatever you wish to memorise as your 101st or 140th item would be attached to these SEM^3 images using the Basic Memory Principles.

Moving up in the first 1,000, all still related to the first of your synaesthesia elements, Vision, all items from 700 to 799 would still be the basic code items, but in this instance connected to the image of Concorde. Thus 706 might be Concorde with its bent nose as a giant jaw; 795 might be Concorde with a giant ball for its wheels. Again, any item you wish to attach to these images would be attached using the Memory Principles.

Similarly, for 3000 to 3999, each separate hundred in the progression would have a Taste image attached to the basic hundred: in this instance Spaghetti, Tea, Nuts, Mango, Rhubarb, Liver, Jam, Clove, Fudge, and Banana.

Each of the Sound, Smell, Taste, Touch and Sensation, etc, ten Key Words applies to the hundred items within its Matrix.

If, for example, you wanted to remember item 3,655, your Key Memory Image would be a Lily (55) covered with Jam (3,600), and you would imagine the Taste of that combination, and the image, connected to whatever you wished to remember.

When creating your images, which you should do as a game, as well as a mental exercise and mental brain training, make sure that in your key images for each of the different senses, you emphasise the sense. Thus, for 4,143, touch combined with dampness combined with ram, you obviously see the image of the wet ram, but your main memory device here is to *feel* the wetness of its fur, its horns, its muzzle, and the smell of damp fur.

By using this Self-Enhancing Master Memory Matrix, you will not only be developing a system that enables you to memorise 10,000 items with the ease of Haber and Nickerson's experimental subjects, but you will also be training each one of your sensory areas, which will have a profound and positive influence on all other aspects of your life. This will include a positive influence on your health. Inability to remember, and subsequent frustration and annoyance at that inability, is often a major cause of stress and disease. This in itself creates a worsening memory. By using SEM[3], you will be reversing the trend.

You will be creating a positive spiral in which the more you practise your memory techniques, the more your general memory will improve; the more you add your knowledge lists to your memory Matrix, the more you will be increasing the probability of automatic learning; and the more you do all this, the more automatically *all* of your various intelligences and mental skills will be improved.

The recommended approach is to categorise all the items you wish to remember in either hundreds or thousands, and use the appropriate parts of SEM[3] for that memorisation.

For a comprehensive compilation of Artists, Composers, Writers, the Plays of Shakespeare, Vocabulary improvement, ten basic Languages, Countries and their Capitals, Kings and Queens of England, the Musculature of the Body, the complete range of chemical Elements, the best red Wines, the Planets and Moons of our Solar System, and methods for memorising your life, see the author's *Master Your Memory*.

SEM[3] can be used for memorising literally *any* lists of data you wish, including not only the areas mentioned above, but the main elements on each page of books such as *War and Peace*, the entire outline of school and university courses, and *all* the significant dates and anniversaries of everyone close to you.

Using SEM[3], even if only as a mental gymnasium in which to stretch your memory and imagination, will enhance your entire range of mental skills, and also enhance your entire life!

12

CHAPTER ONE

VISION

NUMBER	SEM³	KEY WORD	IMAGE
0	Zoo	....	....
1	Day	....	....
2	Noah	....	....
3	Ma	....	....
4	Rah	....	....
5	Law	....	....
6	Jaw	....	....
7	Key	....	....
8	Fee	....	....
9	Bay	....	....
10	Daze	....	....
11	Dad	....	....
12	Dan	....	....
13	Dam	....	....
14	Dare	....	....
15	Dale	....	....
16	Dash	....	....
17	Deck	....	....
18	Daffy	....	....
19	Dab	....	....
20	Nasa	....	....
21	Net	....	....
22	Nan	....	....
23	Name	....	....
24	Nero	....	....
25	Nail	....	....
26	Nash	....	....
27	Nag	....	....
28	Navy	....	....
29	Nab	....	....
30	Mace	....	....
31	Mat	....	....
32	Man	....	....
33	Ma'am	....	....
34	Mare	....	....
35	Mail	....	....
36	Mash	....	....
37	Mac	....	....
38	Mafia	....	....
39	Map	....	....
40	Race	....	....
41	Rat	....	....

NUMBER	SEM[3]	KEY WORD	IMAGE
42	Rain	....	....
43	Ram	....	....
44	Rare	....	....
45	Rail	....	....
46	Rash	....	....
47	Rack	....	....
48	Rafia	....	....
49	Rap	....	....
50	Lace	....	....
51	Lad	....	....
52	Lane	....	....
53	Lamb	....	....
54	Lair	....	....
55	Lily	....	....
56	Lash	....	....
57	Lake	....	....
58	Laugh	....	....
59	Lab	....	....
60	Chase	....	....
61	Chat	....	....
62	Chain	....	....
63	Chime	....	....
64	Chair	....	....
65	Chill	....	....
66	Chacha	....	....
67	Check	....	....
68	Chaff	....	....
69	Chap	....	....
70	Case	....	....
71	Cat	....	....
72	Can	....	....
73	Cameo	....	....
74	Car	....	....
75	Call	....	....
76	Cash	....	....
77	Cake	....	....
78	Café	....	....
79	Cab	....	....
80	Face	....	....
81	Fat	....	....
82	Fan	....	....
83	Fame	....	....
84	Fair	....	....
85	Fall	....	....
86	Fish	....	....
87	Fake	....	....
88	Fife	....	....
89	Fab	....	....
90	Base	....	....
91	Bat	....	....
92	Ban	....	....
93	Bam!	....	....
94	Bar	....	....
95	Ball	....	....

NUMBER	SEM³	KEY WORD	IMAGE
96	Bash	....	....
97	Back	....	....
98	Beef	....	....
99	Baby	....	....
100	Dinosaur Zoo	....	....
101	Dinosaur Day	....	....
102	Dinosaur Noah	....	....
103	Dinosaur Ma	....	....
104	Dinosaur Rah	....	....
105	Dinosaur Law	....	....
106	Dinosaur Jaw	....	....
107	Dinosaur Key	....	....
108	Dinosaur Fee	....	....
109	Dinosaur Bay	....	....
110	Dinosaur Daze	....	....
111	Dinosaur Dad	....	....
112	Dinosaur Dan	....	....
113	Dinosaur Dam	....	....
114	Dinosaur Dare	....	....
115	Dinosaur Dale	....	....
116	Dinosaur Dash	....	....
117	Dinosaur Deck	....	....
118	Dinosaur Daffy	....	....
119	Dinosaur Dab	....	....
120	Dinosaur Nasa	....	....
121	Dinosaur Net	....	....
122	Dinosaur Nan	....	....
123	Dinosaur Name	....	....
124	Dinosaur Nero	....	....
125	Dinosaur Nail	....	....
126	Dinosaur Nash	....	....
127	Dinosaur Nag	....	....
128	Dinosaur Navy	....	....
129	Dinosaur Nab	....	....
130	Dinosaur Mace	....	....
131	Dinosaur Mat	....	....
132	Dinosaur Man	....	....
133	Dinosaur Ma'am	....	....
134	Dinosaur Mare	....	....
135	Dinosaur Mail	....	....
136	Dinosaur Mash	....	....
137	Dinosaur Mac	....	....
138	Dinosaur Mafia	....	....
139	Dinosaur Map	....	....
140	Dinosaur Race	....	....
141	Dinosaur Rat	....	....
142	Dinosaur Rain	....	....
143	Dinosaur Ram	....	....
144	Dinosaur Rare	....	....
145	Dinosaur Rail	....	....
146	Dinosaur Rash	....	....
147	Dinosaur Rack	....	....
148	Dinosaur Rafia	....	....
149	Dinosaur Rap	....	....

NUMBER	SEM[3]	KEY WORD	IMAGE
150	Dinosaur Lace	....	....
151	Dinosaur Lad	....	....
152	Dinosaur Lane	....	....
153	Dinosaur Lamb	....	....
154	Dinosaur Lair	....	....
155	Dinosaur Lily	....	....
156	Dinosaur Lash	....	....
157	Dinosaur Lake	....	....
158	Dinosaur Laugh	....	....
159	Dinosaur Lab	....	....
160	Dinosaur Chase	....	....
161	Dinosaur Chat	....	....
162	Dinosaur Chain	....	....
163	Dinosaur Chime	....	....
164	Dinosaur Chair	....	....
165	Dinosaur Chill	....	....
166	Dinosaur Chacha	....	....
167	Dinosaur Check	....	....
168	Dinosaur Chaff	....	....
169	Dinosaur Chap	....	....
170	Dinosaur Case	....	....
171	Dinosaur Cat	....	....
172	Dinosaur Can	....	....
173	Dinosaur Cameo	....	....
174	Dinosaur Car	....	....
175	Dinosaur Call	....	....
176	Dinosaur Cash	....	....
177	Dinosaur Cake	....	....
178	Dinosaur Cafe	....	....
179	Dinosaur Cab	....	....
180	Dinosaur Face	....	....
181	Dinosaur Fat	....	....
182	Dinosaur Fan	....	....
183	Dinosaur Fame	....	....
184	Dinosaur Fair	....	....
185	Dinosaur Fall	....	....
186	Dinosaur Fish	....	....
187	Dinosaur Fake	....	....
188	Dinosaur Fife	....	....
189	Dinosaur Fab	....	....
190	Dinosaur Base	....	....
191	Dinosaur Bat	....	....
192	Dinosaur Ban	....	....
193	Dinosaur Bam!	....	....
194	Dinosaur Bar	....	....
195	Dinosaur Ball	....	....
196	Dinosaur Bash	....	....
197	Dinosaur Back	....	....
198	Dinosaur Beef	....	....
199	Dinosaur Baby	....	....
200	Nobility Zoo	....	....
201	Nobility Day	....	....
202	Nobility Noah	....	....
203	Nobility Ma	....	....

NUMBER	SEM[3]	KEY WORD	IMAGE
204	Nobility Rah	....	....
205	Nobility Law	....	....
206	Nobility Jaw	....	....
207	Nobility Key	....	....
208	Nobility Fee	....	....
209	Nobility Bay	....	....
210	Nobility Daze	....	....
211	Nobility Dad	....	....
212	Nobility Dan	....	....
213	Nobility Dam	....	....
214	Nobility Dare	....	....
215	Nobility Dale	....	....
216	Nobility Dash	....	....
217	Nobility Deck	....	....
218	Nobility Daffy	....	....
219	Nobility Dab	....	....
220	Nobility Nasa	....	....
221	Nobility Net	....	....
222	Nobility Nan	....	....
223	Nobility Name	....	....
224	Nobility Nero	....	....
225	Nobility Nail	....	....
226	Nobility Nash	....	....
227	Nobility Nag	....	....
228	Nobility Navy	....	....
229	Nobility Nab	....	....
230	Nobility Mace	....	....
231	Nobility Mat	....	....
232	Nobility Man	....	....
233	Nobility Ma'am	....	....
234	Nobility Mare	....	....
235	Nobility Mail	....	....
236	Nobility Mash	....	....
237	Nobility Mac	....	....
238	Nobility Mafia	....	....
239	Nobility Map	....	....
240	Nobility Race	....	....
241	Nobility Rat	....	....
242	Nobility Rain	....	....
243	Nobility Ram	....	....
244	Nobility Rare	....	....
245	Nobility Rail	....	....
246	Nobility Rash	....	....
247	Nobility Rack	....	....
248	Nobility Rafia	....	....
249	Nobility Rap	....	....
250	Nobility Lace	....	....
251	Nobility Lad	....	....
252	Nobility Lane	....	....
253	Nobility Lamb	....	....
254	Nobility Lair	....	....
255	Nobility Lily	....	....
256	Nobility Lash	....	....
257	Nobility Lake	....	....

NUMBER	SEM³	KEY WORD	IMAGE
258	Nobility Laugh	....	....
259	Nobility Lab	....	....
260	Nobility Chase	....	....
261	Nobility Chat	....	....
262	Nobility Chain	....	....
263	Nobility Chime	....	....
264	Nobility Chair	....	....
265	Nobility Chill	....	....
266	Nobility Chacha	....	....
267	Nobility Check	....	....
268	Nobility Chaff	....	....
269	Nobility Chap	....	....
270	Nobility Case	....	....
271	Nobility Cat	....	....
272	Nobility Can	....	....
273	Nobility Cameo	....	....
274	Nobility Car	....	....
275	Nobility Call	....	....
276	Nobility Cash	....	....
277	Nobility Cake	....	....
278	Nobility Café	....	....
279	Nobility Cab	....	....
280	Nobility Face	....	....
281	Nobility Fat	....	....
282	Nobility Fan	....	....
283	Nobility Fame	....	....
284	Nobility Fair	....	....
285	Nobility Fall	....	....
286	Nobility Fish	....	....
287	Nobility Fake	....	....
288	Nobility Fife	....	....
289	Nobility Fab	....	....
290	Nobility Base	....	....
291	Nobility Bat	....	....
292	Nobility Ban	....	....
293	Nobility Bam!	....	....
294	Nobility Bar	....	....
295	Nobility Ball	....	....
296	Nobility Bash	....	....
297	Nobility Back	....	....
298	Nobility Beef	....	....
299	Nobility Baby	....	....
300	Moonlight Zoo	....	....
301	Moonlight Day	....	....
302	Moonlight Noah	....	....
303	Moonlight Ma	....	....
304	Moonlight Rah	....	....
305	Moonlight Law	....	....
306	Moonlight Jaw	....	....
307	Moonlight Key	....	....
308	Moonlight Fee	....	....
309	Moonlight Bay	....	....
310	Moonlight Daze	....	....
311	Moonlight Dad	....	....

NUMBER	SEM³	KEY WORD	IMAGE
312	Moonlight Dan	....	....
313	Moonlight Dam	....	....
314	Moonlight Dare	....	....
315	Moonlight Dale	....	....
316	Moonlight Dash	....	....
317	Moonlight Deck	....	....
318	Moonlight Daffy	....	....
319	Moonlight Dab	....	....
320	Moonlight Nasa	....	....
321	Moonlight Net	....	....
322	Moonlight Nan	....	....
323	Moonlight Name	....	....
324	Moonlight Nero	....	....
325	Moonlight Nail	....	....
326	Moonlight Nash	....	....
327	Moonlight Nag	....	....
328	Moonlight Navy	....	....
329	Moonlight Nab	....	....
330	Moonlight Mace	....	....
331	Moonlight Mat	....	....
332	Moonlight Man	....	....
333	Moonlight Ma'am	....	....
334	Moonlight Mare	....	....
335	Moonlight Mail	....	....
336	Moonlight Mash	....	....
337	Moonlight Mac	....	....
338	Moonlight Mafia	....	....
339	Moonlight Map	....	....
340	Moonlight Race	....	....
341	Moonlight Rat	....	....
342	Moonlight Rain	....	....
343	Moonlight Ram	....	....
344	Moonlight Rare	....	....
345	Moonlight Rail	....	....
346	Moonlight Rash	....	....
347	Moonlight Rack	....	....
348	Moonlight Rafia	....	....
349	Moonlight Rap	....	....
350	Moonlight Lace	....	....
351	Moonlight Lad	....	....
352	Moonlight Lane	....	....
353	Moonlight Lamb	....	....
354	Moonlight Lair	....	....
355	Moonlight Lily	....	....
356	Moonlight Lash	....	....
357	Moonlight Lake	....	....
358	Moonlight Laugh	....	....
359	Moonlight Lab	....	....
360	Moonlight Chase	....	....
361	Moonlight Chat	....	....
362	Moonlight Chain	....	....
363	Moonlight Chime	....	....
364	Moonlight Chair	....	....
365	Moonlight Chill	....	....

NUMBER	SEM³	KEY WORD	IMAGE
366	Moonlight Chacha	....	....
367	Moonlight Check	....	....
368	Moonlight Chaff	....	....
369	Moonlight Chap	....	....
370	Moonlight Case	....	....
371	Moonlight Cat	....	....
372	Moonlight Can	....	....
373	Moonlight Cameo	....	....
374	Moonlight Car	....	....
375	Moonlight Call	....	....
376	Moonlight Cash	....	....
377	Moonlight Cake	....	....
378	Moonlight Café	....	....
379	Moonlight Cab	....	....
380	Moonlight Face	....	....
381	Moonlight Fat	....	....
382	Moonlight Fan	....	....
383	Moonlight Fame	....	....
384	Moonlight Fair	....	....
385	Moonlight Fall	....	....
386	Moonlight Fish	....	....
387	Moonlight Fake	....	....
388	Moonlight Fife	....	....
389	Moonlight Fab	....	....
390	Moonlight Base	....	....
391	Moonlight Bat	....	....
392	Moonlight Ban	....	....
393	Moonlight Bam!	....	....
394	Moonlight Bar	....	....
395	Moonlight Ball	....	....
396	Moonlight Bash	....	....
397	Moonlight Back	....	....
398	Moonlight Beef	....	....
399	Moonlight Baby	....	....
400	Ravine Zoo	....	....
401	Ravine Day	....	....
402	Ravine Noah	....	....
403	Ravine Ma	....	....
404	Ravine Rah	....	....
405	Ravine Law	....	....
406	Ravine Jaw	....	....
407	Ravine Key	....	....
408	Ravine Fee	....	....
409	Ravine Bay	....	....
410	Ravine Daze	....	....
411	Ravine Dad	....	....
412	Ravine Dan	....	....
413	Ravine Dam	....	....
414	Ravine Dare	....	....
415	Ravine Dale	....	....
416	Ravine Dash	....	....
417	Ravine Deck	....	....
418	Ravine Daffy	....	....
419	Ravine Dab	....	....

NUMBER	SEM[3]	KEY WORD	IMAGE
420	Ravine Nasa	....	....
421	Ravine Net	....	....
422	Ravine Nan	....	....
423	Ravine Name	....	....
424	Ravine Nero	....	....
425	Ravine Nail	....	....
426	Ravine Nash	....	....
427	Ravine Nag	....	....
428	Ravine Navy	....	....
429	Ravine Nab	....	....
430	Ravine Mace	....	....
431	Ravine Mat	....	....
432	Ravine Man	....	....
433	Ravine Ma'am	....	....
434	Ravine Mare	....	....
435	Ravine Mail	....	....
436	Ravine Mash	....	....
437	Ravine Mac	....	....
438	Ravine Mafia	....	....
439	Ravine Map	....	....
440	Ravine Race	....	....
441	Ravine Rat	....	....
442	Ravine Rain	....	....
443	Ravine Ram	....	....
444	Ravine Rare	....	....
445	Ravine Rail	....	....
446	Ravine Rash	....	....
447	Ravine Rack	....	....
448	Ravine Rafia	....	....
449	Ravine Rap	....	....
450	Ravine Lace	....	....
451	Ravine Lad	....	....
452	Ravine Lane	....	....
453	Ravine Lamb	....	....
454	Ravine Lair	....	....
455	Ravine Lily	....	....
456	Ravine Lash	....	....
457	Ravine Lake	....	....
458	Ravine Laugh	....	....
459	Ravine Lab	....	....
460	Ravine Chase	....	....
461	Ravine Chat	....	....
462	Ravine Chain	....	....
463	Ravine Chime	....	....
464	Ravine Chair	....	....
465	Ravine Chill	....	....
466	Ravine Chacha	....	....
467	Ravine Check	....	....
468	Ravine Chaff	....	....
469	Ravine Chap	....	....
470	Ravine Case	....	....
471	Ravine Cat	....	....
472	Ravine Can	....	....
473	Ravine Cameo	....	....

NUMBER	SEM³	KEY WORD	IMAGE
474	Ravine Car	....	....
475	Ravine Call	....	....
476	Ravine Cash	....	....
477	Ravine Cake	....	....
478	Ravine Café	....	....
479	Ravine Cab	....	....
480	Ravine Face	....	....
481	Ravine Fat	....	....
482	Ravine Fan	....	....
483	Ravine Fame	....	....
484	Ravine Fair	....	....
485	Ravine Fall	....	....
486	Ravine Fish	....	....
487	Ravine Fake	....	....
488	Ravine Fife	....	....
489	Ravine Fab	....	....
490	Ravine Base	....	....
491	Ravine Bat	....	....
492	Ravine Ban	....	....
493	Ravine Bam!	....	....
494	Ravine Bar	....	....
495	Ravine Ball	....	....
496	Ravine Bash	....	....
497	Ravine Back	....	....
498	Ravine Beef	....	....
499	Ravine Baby	....	....
500	Lightning Zoo	....	....
501	Lightning Day	....	....
502	Lightning Noah	....	....
503	Lightning Ma	....	....
504	Lightning Rah	....	....
505	Lightning Law	....	....
506	Lightning Jaw	....	....
507	Lightning Key	....	....
508	Lightning Fee	....	....
509	Lightning Bay	....	....
510	Lightning Daze	....	....
511	Lightning Dad	....	....
512	Lightning Dan	....	....
513	Lightning Dam	....	....
514	Lightning Dare	....	....
515	Lightning Dale	....	....
516	Lightning Dash	....	....
517	Lightning Deck	....	....
518	Lightning Daffy	....	....
519	Lightning Dab	....	....
520	Lightning Nasa	....	....
521	Lightning Net	....	....
522	Lightning Nan	....	....
523	Lightning Name	....	....
524	Lightning Nero	....	....
525	Lightning Nail	....	....
526	Lightning Nash	....	....
527	Lightning Nag	....	....

NUMBER	SEM³	KEY WORD	IMAGE
528	Lightning Navy	....	....
529	Lightning Nab	....	....
530	Lightning Mace	....	....
531	Lightning Mat	....	....
532	Lightning Man	....	....
533	Lightning Ma'am	....	....
534	Lightning Mare	....	....
535	Lightning Mail	....	....
536	Lightning Mash	....	....
537	Lightning Mac	....	....
538	Lightning Mafia	....	....
539	Lightning Map	....	....
540	Lightning Race	....	....
541	Lightning Rat	....	....
542	Lightning Rain	....	....
543	Lightning Ram	....	....
544	Lightning Rare	....	....
545	Lightning Rail	....	....
546	Lightning Rash	....	....
547	Lightning Rack	....	....
548	Lightning Rafia	....	....
549	Lightning Rap	....	....
550	Lightning Lace	....	....
551	Lightning Lad	....	....
552	Lightning Lane	....	....
553	Lightning Lamb	....	....
554	Lightning Lair	....	....
555	Lightning Lily	....	....
556	Lightning Lash	....	....
557	Lightning Lake	....	....
558	Lightning Laugh	....	....
559	Lightning Lab	....	....
560	Lightning Chase	....	....
561	Lightning Chat	....	....
562	Lightning Chain	....	....
563	Lightning Chime	....	....
564	Lightning Chair	....	....
565	Lightning Chill	....	....
566	Lightning Chacha	....	....
567	Lightning Check	....	....
568	Lightning Chaff	....	....
569	Lightning Chap	....	....
570	Lightning Case	....	....
571	Lightning Cat	....	....
572	Lightning Can	....	....
573	Lightning Cameo	....	....
574	Lightning Car	....	....
575	Lightning Call	....	....
576	Lightning Cash	....	....
577	Lightning Cake	....	....
578	Lightning Café	....	....
579	Lightning Cab	....	....
580	Lightning Face	....	....
581	Lightning Fat	....	....

NUMBER	SEM³	KEY WORD	IMAGE
582	Lightning Fan	....	....
583	Lightning Fame	....	....
584	Lightning Fair	....	....
585	Lightning Fall	....	....
586	Lightning Fish	....	....
587	Lightning Fake	....	....
588	Lightning Fife	....	....
589	Lightning Fab	....	....
590	Lightning Base	....	....
591	Lightning Bat	....	....
592	Lightning Ban	....	....
593	Lightning Bam!	....	....
594	Lightning Bar	....	....
595	Lightning Ball	....	....
596	Lightning Bash	....	....
597	Lightning Back	....	....
598	Lightning Beef	....	....
599	Lightning Baby	....	....
600	Ocean Zoo	....	....
601	Ocean Day	....	....
602	Ocean Noah	....	....
603	Ocean Ma	....	....
604	Ocean Rah	....	....
605	Ocean Law	....	....
606	Ocean Jaw	....	....
607	Ocean Key	....	....
608	Ocean Fee	....	....
609	Ocean Bay	....	....
610	Ocean Daze	....	....
611	Ocean Dad	....	....
612	Ocean Dan	....	....
613	Ocean Dam	....	....
614	Ocean Dare	....	....
615	Ocean Dale	....	....
616	Ocean Dash	....	....
617	Ocean Deck	....	....
618	Ocean Daffy	....	....
619	Ocean Dab	....	....
620	Ocean Nasa	....	....
621	Ocean Net	....	....
622	Ocean Nan	....	....
623	Ocean Name	....	....
624	Ocean Nero	....	....
625	Ocean Nail	....	....
626	Ocean Nash	....	....
627	Ocean Nag	....	....
628	Ocean Navy	....	....
629	Ocean Nab	....	....
630	Ocean Mace	....	....
631	Ocean Mat	....	....
632	Ocean Man	....	....
633	Ocean Ma'am	....	....
634	Ocean Mare	....	....
635	Ocean Mail	....	....

NUMBER	SEM[3]	KEY WORD	IMAGE
636	Ocean Mash		
637	Ocean Mac		
638	Ocean Mafia		
639	Ocean Map		
640	Ocean Race		
641	Ocean Rat		
642	Ocean Rain		
643	Ocean Ram		
644	Ocean Rare		
645	Ocean Rail		
646	Ocean Rash		
647	Ocean Rack		
648	Ocean Rafia		
649	Ocean Rap		
650	Ocean Lace		
651	Ocean Lad		
652	Ocean Lane		
653	Ocean Lamb		
654	Ocean Lair		
655	Ocean Lily		
656	Ocean Lash		
657	Ocean Lake		
658	Ocean Laugh		
659	Ocean Lab		
660	Ocean Chase		
661	Ocean Chat		
662	Ocean Chain		
663	Ocean Chime		
664	Ocean Chair		
665	Ocean Chill		
666	Ocean Chacha		
667	Ocean Check		
668	Ocean Chaff		
669	Ocean Chap		
670	Ocean Case		
671	Ocean Cat		
672	Ocean Can		
673	Ocean Cameo		
674	Ocean Car		
675	Ocean Call		
676	Ocean Cash		
677	Ocean Cake		
678	Ocean Café		
679	Ocean Cab		
680	Ocean Face		
681	Ocean Fat		
682	Ocean Fan		
683	Ocean Fame		
684	Ocean Fair		
685	Ocean Fall		
686	Ocean Fish		
687	Ocean Fake		
688	Ocean Fife		
689	Ocean Fab		

NUMBER	SEM^3	KEY WORD	IMAGE
690	Ocean Base	....	....
691	Ocean Bat	....	....
692	Ocean Ban	....	....
693	Ocean Bam!	....	....
694	Ocean Bar	....	....
695	Ocean Ball	....	....
696	Ocean Bash	....	....
697	Ocean Back	....	....
698	Ocean Beef	....	....
699	Ocean Baby	....	....
700	Concorde Zoo	....	....
701	Concorde Day	....	....
702	Concorde Noah	....	....
703	Concorde Ma	....	....
704	Concorde Rah	....	....
705	Concorde Law	....	....
706	Concorde Jaw	....	....
707	Concorde Key	....	....
708	Concorde Fee	....	....
709	Concorde Bay	....	....
710	Concorde Daze	....	....
711	Concorde Dad	....	....
712	Concorde Dan	....	....
713	Concorde Dam	....	....
714	Concorde Dare	....	....
715	Concorde Dale	....	....
716	Concorde Dash	....	....
717	Concorde Deck	....	....
718	Concorde Daffy	....	....
719	Concorde Dab	....	....
720	Concorde Nasa	....	....
721	Concorde Net	....	....
722	Concorde Nan	....	....
723	Concorde Name	....	....
724	Concorde Nero	....	....
725	Concorde Nail	....	....
726	Concorde Nash	....	....
727	Concorde Nag	....	....
728	Concorde Navy	....	....
729	Concorde Nab	....	....
730	Concorde Mace	....	....
731	Concorde Mat	....	....
732	Concorde Man	....	....
733	Concorde Ma'am	....	....
734	Concorde Mare	....	....
735	Concorde Mail	....	....
736	Concorde Mash	....	....
737	Concorde Mac	....	....
738	Concorde Mafia	....	....
739	Concorde Map	....	....
740	Concorde Race	....	....
741	Concorde Rat	....	....
742	Concorde Rain	....	....
743	Concorde Ram	....	....

NUMBER	SEM³	KEY WORD	IMAGE
744	Concorde Rare	....	....
745	Concorde Rail	....	....
746	Concorde Rash	....	....
747	Concorde Rack	....	....
748	Concorde Rafia	....	....
749	Concorde Rap	....	....
750	Concorde Lace	....	....
751	Concorde Lad	....	....
752	Concorde Lane	....	....
753	Concorde Lamb	....	....
754	Concorde Lair	....	....
755	Concorde Lily	....	....
756	Concorde Lash	....	....
757	Concorde Lake	....	....
758	Concorde Laugh	....	....
759	Concorde Lab	....	....
760	Concorde Chase	....	....
761	Concorde Chat	....	....
762	Concorde Chain	....	....
763	Concorde Chime	....	....
764	Concorde Chair	....	....
765	Concorde Chill	....	....
766	Concorde Chacha	....	....
767	Concorde Check	....	....
768	Concorde Chaff	....	....
769	Concorde Chap	....	....
770	Concorde Case	....	....
771	Concorde Cat	....	....
772	Concorde Can	....	....
773	Concorde Cameo	....	....
774	Concorde Car	....	....
775	Concorde Call	....	....
776	Concorde Cash	....	....
777	Concorde Cake	....	....
778	Concorde Café	....	....
779	Concorde Cab	....	....
780	Concorde Face	....	....
781	Concorde Fat	....	....
782	Concorde Fan	....	....
783	Concorde Fame	....	....
784	Concorde Fair	....	....
785	Concorde Fall	....	....
786	Concorde Fish	....	....
787	Concorde Fake	....	....
788	Concorde Fife	....	....
789	Concorde Fab	....	....
790	Concorde Base	....	....
791	Concorde Bat	....	....
792	Concorde Ban	....	....
793	Concorde Bam!	....	....
794	Concorde Bar	....	....
795	Concorde Ball	....	....
796	Concorde Bash	....	....
797	Concorde Back	....	....

NUMBER	SEM³	KEY WORD	IMAGE
798	Concorde Beef	....	....
799	Concorde Baby	....	....
800	Fire Zoo	....	....
801	Fire Day	....	....
802	Fire Noah	....	....
803	Fire Ma	....	....
804	Fire Rah	....	....
805	Fire Law	....	....
806	Fire Jaw	....	....
807	Fire Key	....	....
808	Fire Fee	....	....
809	Fire Bay	....	....
810	Fire Daze	....	....
811	Fire Dad	....	....
812	Fire Dan	....	....
813	Fire Dam	....	....
814	Fire Dare	....	....
815	Fire Dale	....	....
816	Fire Dash	....	....
817	Fire Deck	....	....
818	Fire Daffy	....	....
819	Fire Dab	....	....
820	Fire Nasa	....	....
821	Fire Net	....	....
822	Fire Nan	....	....
823	Fire Name	....	....
824	Fire Nero	....	....
825	Fire Nail	....	....
826	Fire Nash	....	....
827	Fire Nag	....	....
828	Fire Navy	....	....
829	Fire Nab	....	....
830	Fire Mace	....	....
831	Fire Mat	....	....
832	Fire Man	....	....
833	Fire Ma'am	....	....
834	Fire Mare	....	....
835	Fire Mail	....	....
836	Fire Mash	....	....
837	Fire Mac	....	....
838	Fire Mafia	....	....
839	Fire Map	....	....
840	Fire Race	....	....
841	Fire Rat	....	....
842	Fire Rain	....	....
843	Fire Ram	....	....
844	Fire Rare	....	....
845	Fire Rail	....	....
846	Fire Rash	....	....
847	Fire Rack	....	....
848	Fire Rafia	....	....
849	Fire Rap	....	....
850	Fire Lace	....	....
851	Fire Lad	....	....

NUMBER	SEM³	KEY WORD	IMAGE
852	Fire Lane	....	....
853	Fire Lamb	....	....
854	Fire Lair	....	....
855	Fire Lily	....	....
856	Fire Lash	....	....
857	Fire Lake	....	....
858	Fire Laugh	....	....
859	Fire Lab	....	....
860	Fire Chase	....	....
861	Fire Chat	....	....
862	Fire Chain	....	....
863	Fire Chime	....	....
864	Fire Chair	....	....
865	Fire Chill	....	....
866	Fire Chacha	....	....
867	Fire Check	....	....
868	Fire Chaff	....	....
869	Fire Chap	....	....
870	Fire Case	....	....
871	Fire Cat	....	....
872	Fire Can	....	....
873	Fire Cameo	....	....
874	Fire Car	....	....
875	Fire Call	....	....
876	Fire Cash	....	....
877	Fire Cake	....	....
878	Fire Café	....	....
879	Fire Cab	....	....
880	Fire Face	....	....
881	Fire Fat	....	....
882	Fire Fan	....	....
883	Fire Fame	....	....
884	Fire Fair	....	....
885	Fire Fall	....	....
886	Fire Fish	....	....
887	Fire Fake	....	....
888	Fire Fife	....	....
889	Fire Fab	....	....
890	Fire Base	....	....
891	Fire Bat	....	....
892	Fire Ban	....	....
893	Fire Bam!	....	....
894	Fire Bar	....	....
895	Fire Ball	....	....
896	Fire Bash	....	....
897	Fire Back	....	....
898	Fire Beef	....	....
899	Fire Baby	....	....
900	Paintings Zoo	....	....
901	Paintings Day	....	....
902	Paintings Noah	....	....
903	Paintings Ma	....	....
904	Paintings Rah	....	....
905	Paintings Law	....	....

NUMBER	SEM³	KEY WORD	IMAGE
906	Paintings Jaw	....	....
907	Paintings Key	....	....
908	Paintings Fee	....	....
909	Paintings Bay	....	....
910	Paintings Daze	....	....
911	Paintings Dad	....	....
912	Paintings Dan	....	....
913	Paintings Dam	....	....
914	Paintings Dare	....	....
915	Paintings Dale	....	....
916	Paintings Dash	....	....
917	Paintings Deck	....	....
918	Paintings Daffy	....	....
919	Paintings Dab	....	....
920	Paintings Nasa	....	....
921	Paintings Net	....	....
922	Paintings Nan	....	....
923	Paintings Name	....	....
924	Paintings Nero	....	....
925	Paintings Nail	....	....
926	Paintings Nash	....	....
927	Paintings Nag	....	....
928	Paintings Navy	....	....
929	Paintings Nab	....	....
930	Paintings Mace	....	....
931	Paintings Mat	....	....
932	Paintings Man	....	....
933	Paintings Ma'am	....	....
934	Paintings Mare	....	....
935	Paintings Mail	....	....
936	Paintings Mash	....	....
937	Paintings Mac	....	....
938	Paintings Mafia	....	....
939	Paintings Map	....	....
940	Paintings Race	....	....
941	Paintings Rat	....	....
942	Paintings Rain	....	....
943	Paintings Ram	....	....
944	Paintings Rare	....	....
945	Paintings Rail	....	....
946	Paintings Rash	....	....
947	Paintings Rack	....	....
948	Paintings Rafia	....	....
949	Paintings Rap	....	....
950	Paintings Lace	....	....
951	Paintings Lad	....	....
952	Paintings Lane	....	....
953	Paintings Lamb	....	....
954	Paintings Lair	....	....
955	Paintings Lily	....	....
956	Paintings Lash	....	....
957	Paintings Lake	....	....
958	Paintings Laugh	....	....
959	Paintings Lab	....	....

NUMBER	SEM³	KEY WORD	IMAGE
960	Paintings Chase	....	....
961	Paintings Chat	....	....
962	Paintings Chain	....	....
963	Paintings Chime	....	....
964	Paintings Chair	....	....
965	Paintings Chill	....	....
966	Paintings Chacha	....	....
967	Paintings Check	....	....
968	Paintings Chaff	....	....
969	Paintings Chap	....	....
970	Paintings Case	....	....
971	Paintings Cat	....	....
972	Paintings Can	....	....
973	Paintings Cameo	....	....
974	Paintings Car	....	....
975	Paintings Call	....	....
976	Paintings Cash	....	....
977	Paintings Cake	....	....
978	Paintings Café	....	....
979	Paintings Cab	....	....
980	Paintings Face	....	....
981	Paintings Fat	....	....
982	Paintings Fan	....	....
983	Paintings Fame	....	....
984	Paintings Fair	....	....
985	Paintings Fall	....	....
986	Paintings Fish	....	....
987	Paintings Fake	....	....
988	Paintings Fife	....	....
989	Paintings Fab	....	....
990	Paintings Base	....	....
991	Paintings Bat	....	....
992	Paintings Ban	....	....
993	Paintings Bam!	....	....
994	Paintings Bar	....	....
995	Paintings Ball	....	....
996	Paintings Bash	....	....
997	Paintings Back	....	....
998	Paintings Beef	....	....
999	Paintings Baby	....	....

CHAPTER TWO

SOUND

NUMBER	SEM^3	KEY WORD	IMAGE
1000	Sing Zoo	....	....
1001	Sing Day	....	....
1002	Sing Noah	....	....
1003	Sing Ma	....	....
1004	Sing Rah	....	....
1005	Sing Law	....	....
1006	Sing Jaw	....	....
1007	Sing Key	....	....
1008	Sing Fee	....	....
1009	Sing Bay	....	....
1010	Sing Daze	....	....
1011	Sing Dad	....	....
1012	Sing Dan	....	....
1013	Sing Dam	....	....
1014	Sing Dare	....	....
1015	Sing Dale	....	....
1016	Sing Dash	....	....
1017	Sing Deck	....	....
1018	Sing Daffy	....	....
1019	Sing Dab	....	....
1020	Sing Nasa	....	....
1021	Sing Net	....	....
1022	Sing Nan	....	....
1023	Sing Name	....	....
1024	Sing Nero	....	....
1025	Sing Nail	....	....
1026	Sing Nash	....	....
1027	Sing Nag	....	....
1028	Sing Navy	....	....
1029	Sing Nab	....	....
1030	Sing Mace	....	....
1031	Sing Mat	....	....
1032	Sing Man	....	....
1033	Sing Ma'am	....	....
1034	Sing Mare	....	....
1035	Sing Mail	....	....
1036	Sing Mash	....	....
1037	Sing Mac	....	....
1038	Sing Mafia	....	....
1039	Sing Map	....	....
1040	Sing Race	....	....
1041	Sing Rat	....	....

NUMBER	SEM[3]	KEY WORD	IMAGE
1042	Sing Rain	....	....
1043	Sing Ram	....	....
1044	Sing Rare	....	....
1045	Sing Rail	....	....
1046	Sing Rash	....	....
1047	Sing Rack	....	....
1048	Sing Rafia	....	....
1049	Sing Rap	....	....
1050	Sing Lace	....	....
1051	Sing Lad	....	....
1052	Sing Lane	....	....
1053	Sing Lamb	....	....
1054	Sing Lair	....	....
1055	Sing Lily	....	....
1056	Sing Lash	....	....
1057	Sing Lake	....	....
1058	Sing Laugh	....	....
1059	Sing Lab	....	....
1060	Sing Chase	....	....
1061	Sing Chat	....	....
1062	Sing Chain	....	....
1063	Sing Chime	....	....
1064	Sing Chair	....	....
1065	Sing Chill	....	....
1066	Sing Chacha	....	....
1067	Sing Check	....	....
1068	Sing Chaff	....	....
1069	Sing Chap	....	....
1070	Sing Case	....	....
1071	Sing Cat	....	....
1072	Sing Can	....	....
1073	Sing Cameo	....	....
1074	Sing Car	....	....
1075	Sing Call	....	....
1076	Sing Cash	....	....
1077	Sing Cake	....	....
1078	Sing Café	....	....
1079	Sing Cab	....	....
1080	Sing Face	....	....
1081	Sing Fat	....	....
1082	Sing Fan	....	....
1083	Sing Fame	....	....
1084	Sing Fair	....	....
1085	Sing Fall	....	....
1086	Sing Fish	....	....
1087	Sing Fake	....	....
1088	Sing Fife	....	....
1089	Sing Fab	....	....
1090	Sing Base	....	....
1091	Sing Bat	....	....
1092	Sing Ban	....	....
1093	Sing Bam!	....	....
1094	Sing Bar	....	....
1095	Sing Ball	....	....

NUMBER	SEM[3]	KEY WORD	IMAGE
1096	Sing Bash	....	....
1097	Sing Back	....	....
1098	Sing Beef	....	....
1099	Sing Baby	....	....
1100	Drum Zoo	....	....
1101	Drum Day	....	....
1102	Drum Noah	....	....
1103	Drum Ma	....	....
1104	Drum Rah	....	....
1105	Drum Law	....	....
1106	Drum Jaw	....	....
1107	Drum Key	....	....
1108	Drum Fee	....	....
1109	Drum Bay	....	....
1110	Drum Daze	....	....
1111	Drum Dad	....	....
1112	Drum Dan	....	....
1113	Drum Dam	....	....
1114	Drum Dare	....	....
1115	Drum Dale	....	....
1116	Drum Dash	....	....
1117	Drum Deck	....	....
1118	Drum Daffy	....	....
1119	Drum Dab	....	....
1120	Drum Nasa	....	....
1121	Drum Net	....	....
1122	Drum Nan	....	....
1123	Drum Name	....	....
1124	Drum Nero	....	....
1125	Drum Nail	....	....
1126	Drum Nash	....	....
1127	Drum Nag	....	....
1128	Drum Navy	....	....
1129	Drum Nab	....	....
1130	Drum Mace	....	....
1131	Drum Mat	....	....
1132	Drum Man	....	....
1133	Drum Ma'am	....	....
1134	Drum Mare	....	....
1135	Drum Mail	....	....
1136	Drum Mash	....	....
1137	Drum Mac	....	....
1138	Drum Mafia	....	....
1139	Drum Map	....	....
1140	Drum Race	....	....
1141	Drum Rat	....	....
1142	Drum Rain	....	....
1143	Drum Ram	....	....
1144	Drum Rare	....	....
1145	Drum Rail	....	....
1146	Drum Rash	....	....
1147	Drum Rack	....	....
1148	Drum Rafia	....	....
1149	Drum Rap	....	....

NUMBER	SEM³	KEY WORD	IMAGE
1150	Drum Lace	....	....
1151	Drum Lad	....	....
1152	Drum Lane	....	....
1153	Drum Lamb	....	....
1154	Drum Lair	....	....
1155	Drum Lily	....	....
1156	Drum Lash	....	....
1157	Drum Lake	....	....
1158	Drum Laugh	....	....
1159	Drum Lab	....	....
1160	Drum Chase	....	....
1161	Drum Chat	....	....
1162	Drum Chain	....	....
1163	Drum Chime	....	....
1164	Drum Chair	....	....
1165	Drum Chill	....	....
1166	Drum Chacha	....	....
1167	Drum Check	....	....
1168	Drum Chaff	....	....
1169	Drum Chap	....	....
1170	Drum Case	....	....
1171	Drum Cat	....	....
1172	Drum Can	....	....
1173	Drum Cameo	....	....
1174	Drum Car	....	....
1175	Drum Call	....	....
1176	Drum Cash	....	....
1177	Drum Cake	....	....
1178	Drum Café	....	....
1179	Drum Cab	....	....
1180	Drum Face	....	....
1181	Drum Fat	....	....
1182	Drum Fan	....	....
1183	Drum Fame	....	....
1184	Drum Fair	....	....
1185	Drum Fall	....	....
1186	Drum Fish	....	....
1187	Drum Fake	....	....
1188	Drum Fife	....	....
1189	Drum Fab	....	....
1190	Drum Base	....	....
1191	Drum Bat	....	....
1192	Drum Ban	....	....
1193	Drum Bam!	....	....
1194	Drum Bar	....	....
1195	Drum Ball	....	....
1196	Drum Bash	....	....
1197	Drum Back	....	....
1198	Drum Beef	....	....
1199	Drum Baby	....	....
1200	Wind Zoo	....	....
1201	Wind Day	....	....
1202	Wind Noah	....	....
1203	Wind Ma	....	....

NUMBER	SEM³	KEY WORD	IMAGE
1204	Wind Rah	....	....
1205	Wind Law	....	....
1206	Wind Jaw	....	....
1207	Wind Key	....	....
1208	Wind Fee	....	....
1209	Wind Bay	....	....
1210	Wind Daze	....	....
1211	Wind Dad	....	....
1212	Wind Dan	....	....
1213	Wind Dam	....	....
1214	Wind Dare	....	....
1215	Wind Dale	....	....
1216	Wind Dash	....	....
1217	Wind Deck	....	....
1218	Wind Daffy	....	....
1219	Wind Dab	....	....
1220	Wind Nasa	....	....
1221	Wind Net	....	....
1222	Wind Nan	....	....
1223	Wind Name	....	....
1224	Wind Nero	....	....
1225	Wind Nail	....	....
1226	Wind Nash	....	....
1227	Wind Nag	....	....
1228	Wind Navy	....	....
1229	Wind Nab	....	....
1230	Wind Mace	....	....
1231	Wind Mat	....	....
1232	Wind Man	....	....
1233	Wind Ma'am	....	....
1234	Wind Mare	....	....
1235	Wind Mail	....	....
1236	Wind Mash	....	....
1237	Wind Mac	....	....
1238	Wind Mafia	....	....
1239	Wind Map	....	....
1240	Wind Race	....	....
1241	Wind Rat	....	....
1242	Wind Rain	....	....
1243	Wind Ram	....	....
1244	Wind Rare	....	....
1245	Wind Rail	....	....
1246	Wind Rash	....	....
1247	Wind Rack	....	....
1248	Wind Rafia	....	....
1249	Wind Rap	....	....
1250	Wind Lace	....	....
1251	Wind Lad	....	....
1252	Wind Lane	....	....
1253	Wind Lamb	....	....
1254	Wind Lair	....	....
1255	Wind Lily	....	....
1256	Wind Lash	....	....
1257	Wind Lake	....	....

NUMBER	SEM³	KEY WORD	IMAGE
1258	Wind Laugh	....	....
1259	Wind Lab	....	....
1260	Wind Chase	....	....
1261	Wind Chat	....	....
1262	Wind Chain	....	....
1263	Wind Chime	....	....
1264	Wind Chair	....	....
1265	Wind Chill	....	....
1266	Wind Chacha	....	....
1267	Wind Check	....	....
1268	Wind Chaff	....	....
1269	Wind Chap	....	....
1270	Wind Case	....	....
1271	Wind Cat	....	....
1272	Wind Can	....	....
1273	Wind Cameo	....	....
1274	Wind Car	....	....
1275	Wind Call	....	....
1276	Wind Cash	....	....
1277	Wind Cake	....	....
1278	Wind Café	....	....
1279	Wind Cab	....	....
1280	Wind Face	....	....
1281	Wind Fat	....	....
1282	Wind Fan	....	....
1283	Wind Fame	....	....
1284	Wind Fair	....	....
1285	Wind Fall	....	....
1286	Wind Fish	....	....
1287	Wind Fake	....	....
1288	Wind Fife	....	....
1289	Wind Fab	....	....
1290	Wind Base	....	....
1291	Wind Bat	....	....
1292	Wind Ban	....	....
1293	Wind Bam!	....	....
1294	Wind Bar	....	....
1295	Wind Ball	....	....
1296	Wind Bash	....	....
1297	Wind Back	....	....
1298	Wind Beef	....	....
1299	Wind Baby	....	....
1300	Moan Zoo	....	....
1301	Moan Day	....	....
1302	Moan Noah	....	....
1303	Moan Ma	....	....
1304	Moan Rah	....	....
1305	Moan Law	....	....
1306	Moan Jaw	....	....
1307	Moan Key	....	....
1308	Moan Fee	....	....
1309	Moan Bay	....	....
1310	Moan Daze	....	....
1311	Moan Dad	....	....

NUMBER	SEM³	KEY WORD	IMAGE
1312	Moan Dan	....	....
1313	Moan Dam	....	....
1314	Moan Dare	....	....
1315	Moan Dale	....	....
1316	Moan Dash	....	....
1317	Moan Deck	....	....
1318	Moan Daffy	....	....
1319	Moan Dab	....	....
1320	Moan Nasa	....	....
1321	Moan Net	....	....
1322	Moan Nan	....	....
1323	Moan Name	....	....
1324	Moan Nero	....	....
1325	Moan Nail	....	....
1326	Moan Nash	....	....
1327	Moan Nag	....	....
1328	Moan Navy	....	....
1329	Moan Nab	....	....
1330	Moan Mace	....	....
1331	Moan Mat	....	....
1332	Moan Man	....	....
1333	Moan Ma'am	....	....
1334	Moan Mare	....	....
1335	Moan Mail	....	....
1336	Moan Mash	....	....
1337	Moan Mac	....	....
1338	Moan Mafia	....	....
1339	Moan Map	....	....
1340	Moan Race	....	....
1341	Moan Rat	....	....
1342	Moan Rain	....	....
1343	Moan Ram	....	....
1344	Moan Rare	....	....
1345	Moan Rail	....	....
1346	Moan Rash	....	....
1347	Moan Rack	....	....
1348	Moan Rafia	....	....
1349	Moan Rap	....	....
1350	Moan Lace	....	....
1351	Moan Lad	....	....
1352	Moan Lane	....	....
1353	Moan Lamb	....	....
1354	Moan Lair	....	....
1355	Moan Lily	....	....
1356	Moan Lash	....	....
1357	Moan Lake	....	....
1358	Moan Laugh	....	....
1359	Moan Lab	....	....
1360	Moan Chase	....	....
1361	Moan Chat	....	....
1362	Moan Chain	....	....
1363	Moan Chime	....	....
1364	Moan Chair	....	....
1365	Moan Chill	....	....

NUMBER	SEM³	KEY WORD	IMAGE
1366	Moan Chacha	....	....
1367	Moan Check	....	....
1368	Moan Chaff	....	....
1369	Moan Chap	....	....
1370	Moan Case	....	....
1371	Moan Cat	....	....
1372	Moan Can	....	....
1373	Moan Cameo	....	....
1374	Moan Car	....	....
1375	Moan Call	....	....
1376	Moan Cash	....	....
1377	Moan Cake	....	....
1378	Moan Café	....	....
1379	Moan Cab	....	....
1380	Moan Face	....	....
1381	Moan Fat	....	....
1382	Moan Fan	....	....
1383	Moan Fame	....	....
1384	Moan Fair	....	....
1385	Moan Fall	....	....
1386	Moan Fish	....	....
1387	Moan Fake	....	....
1388	Moan Fife	....	....
1389	Moan Fab	....	....
1390	Moan Base	....	....
1391	Moan Bat	....	....
1392	Moan Ban	....	....
1393	Moan Bam!	....	....
1394	Moan Bar	....	....
1395	Moan Ball	....	....
1396	Moan Bash	....	....
1397	Moan Back	....	....
1398	Moan Beef	....	....
1399	Moan Baby	....	....
1400	Roar Zoo	....	....
1401	Roar Day	....	....
1402	Roar Noah	....	....
1403	Roar Ma	....	....
1404	Roar Rah	....	....
1405	Roar Law	....	....
1406	Roar Jaw	....	....
1407	Roar Key	....	....
1408	Roar Fee	....	....
1409	Roar Bay	....	....
1410	Roar Daze	....	....
1411	Roar Dad	....	....
1412	Roar Dan	....	....
1413	Roar Dam	....	....
1414	Roar Dare	....	....
1415	Roar Dale	....	....
1416	Roar Dash	....	....
1417	Roar Deck	....	....
1418	Roar Daffy	....	....
1419	Roar Dab	....	....

NUMBER	SEM[3]	KEY WORD	IMAGE
1420	Roar Nasa		
1421	Roar Net		
1422	Roar Nan		
1423	Roar Name		
1424	Roar Nero		
1425	Roar Nail		
1426	Roar Nash		
1427	Roar Nag		
1428	Roar Navy		
1429	Roar Nab		
1430	Roar Mace		
1431	Roar Mat		
1432	Roar Man		
1433	Roar Ma'am		
1434	Roar Mare		
1435	Roar Mail		
1436	Roar Mash		
1437	Roar Mac		
1438	Roar Mafia		
1439	Roar Map		
1440	Roar Race		
1441	Roar Rat		
1442	Roar Rain		
1443	Roar Ram		
1444	Roar Rare		
1445	Roar Rail		
1446	Roar Rash		
1447	Roar Rack		
1448	Roar Rafia		
1449	Roar Rap		
1450	Roar Lace		
1451	Roar Lad		
1452	Roar Lane		
1453	Roar Lamb		
1454	Roar Lair		
1455	Roar Lily		
1456	Roar Lash		
1457	Roar Lake		
1458	Roar Laugh		
1459	Roar Lab		
1460	Roar Chase		
1461	Roar Chat		
1462	Roar Chain		
1463	Roar Chime		
1464	Roar Chair		
1465	Roar Chill		
1466	Roar Chacha		
1467	Roar Check		
1468	Roar Chaff		
1469	Roar Chap		
1470	Roar Case		
1471	Roar Cat		
1472	Roar Can		
1473	Roar Cameo		

NUMBER	SEM³	KEY WORD	IMAGE
1474	Roar Car	....	....
1475	Roar Call	....	....
1476	Roar Cash	....	....
1477	Roar Cake	....	....
1478	Roar Café	....	....
1479	Roar Cab	....	....
1480	Roar Face	....	....
1481	Roar Fat	....	....
1482	Roar Fan	....	....
1483	Roar Fame	....	....
1484	Roar Fair	....	....
1485	Roar Fall	....	....
1486	Roar Fish	....	....
1487	Roar Fake	....	....
1488	Roar Fife	....	....
1489	Roar Fab	....	....
1490	Roar Base	....	....
1491	Roar Bat	....	....
1492	Roar Ban	....	....
1493	Roar Bam!	....	....
1494	Roar Bar	....	....
1495	Roar Ball	....	....
1496	Roar Bash	....	....
1497	Roar Back	....	....
1498	Roar Beef	....	....
1499	Roar Baby	....	....
1500	Lap Zoo	....	....
1501	Lap Day	....	....
1502	Lap Noah	....	....
1503	Lap Ma	....	....
1504	Lap Rah	....	....
1505	Lap Law	....	....
1506	Lap Jaw	....	....
1507	Lap Key	....	....
1508	Lap Fee	....	....
1509	Lap Bay	....	....
1510	Lap Daze	....	....
1511	Lap Dad	....	....
1512	Lap Dan	....	....
1513	Lap Dam	....	....
1514	Lap Dare	....	....
1515	Lap Dale	....	....
1516	Lap Dash	....	....
1517	Lap Deck	....	....
1518	Lap Daffy	....	....
1519	Lap Dab	....	....
1520	Lap Nasa	....	....
1521	Lap Net	....	....
1522	Lap Nan	....	....
1523	Lap Name	....	....
1524	Lap Nero	....	....
1525	Lap Nail	....	....
1526	Lap Nash	....	....
1527	Lap Nag	....	....

NUMBER	SEM[3]	KEY WORD	IMAGE
1528	Lap Navy	....	....
1529	Lap Nab	....	....
1530	Lap Mace	....	....
1531	Lap Mat	....	....
1532	Lap Man	....	....
1533	Lap Ma'am	....	....
1534	Lap Mare	....	....
1535	Lap Mail	....	....
1536	Lap Mash	....	....
1537	Lap Mac	....	....
1538	Lap Mafia	....	....
1539	Lap Map	....	....
1540	Lap Race	....	....
1541	Lap Rat	....	....
1542	Lap Rain	....	....
1543	Lap Ram	....	....
1544	Lap Rare	....	....
1545	Lap Rail	....	....
1546	Lap Rash	....	....
1547	Lap Rack	....	....
1548	Lap Rafia	....	....
1549	Lap Rap	....	....
1550	Lap Lace	....	....
1551	Lap Lad	....	....
1552	Lap Lane	....	....
1553	Lap Lamb	....	....
1554	Lap Lair	....	....
1555	Lap Lily	....	....
1556	Lap Lash	....	....
1557	Lap Lake	....	....
1558	Lap Laugh	....	....
1559	Lap Lab	....	....
1560	Lap Chase	....	....
1561	Lap Chat	....	....
1562	Lap Chain	....	....
1563	Lap Chime	....	....
1564	Lap Chair	....	....
1565	Lap Chill	....	....
1566	Lap Chacha	....	....
1567	Lap Check	....	....
1568	Lap Chaff	....	....
1569	Lap Chap	....	....
1570	Lap Case	....	....
1571	Lap Cat	....	....
1572	Lap Can	....	....
1573	Lap Cameo	....	....
1574	Lap Car	....	....
1575	Lap Call	....	....
1576	Lap Cash	....	....
1577	Lap Cake	....	....
1578	Lap Café	....	....
1579	Lap Cab	....	....
1580	Lap Face	....	....
1581	Lap Fat	....	....

NUMBER	SEM³	KEY WORD	IMAGE
1582	Lap Fan	....	....
1583	Lap Fame	....	....
1584	Lap Fair	....	....
1585	Lap Fall	....	....
1586	Lap Fish	....	....
1587	Lap Fake	....	....
1588	Lap Fife	....	....
1589	Lap Fab	....	....
1590	Lap Base	....	....
1591	Lap Bat	....	....
1592	Lap Ban	....	....
1593	Lap Bam!	....	....
1594	Lap Bar	....	....
1595	Lap Ball	....	....
1596	Lap Bash	....	....
1597	Lap Back	....	....
1598	Lap Beef	....	....
1599	Lap Baby	....	....
1600	Shhh Zoo	....	....
1601	Shhh Day	....	....
1602	Shhh Noah	....	....
1603	Shhh Ma	....	....
1604	Shhh Rah	....	....
1605	Shhh Law	....	....
1606	Shhh Jaw	....	....
1607	Shhh Key	....	....
1608	Shhh Fee	....	....
1609	Shhh Bay	....	....
1610	Shhh Daze	....	....
1611	Shhh Dad	....	....
1612	Shhh Dan	....	....
1613	Shhh Dam	....	....
1614	Shhh Dare	....	....
1615	Shhh Dale	....	....
1616	Shhh Dash	....	....
1617	Shhh Deck	....	....
1618	Shhh Daffy	....	....
1619	Shhh Dab	....	....
1620	Shhh Nasa	....	....
1621	Shhh Net	....	....
1622	Shhh Nan	....	....
1623	Shhh Name	....	....
1624	Shhh Nero	....	....
1625	Shhh Nail	....	....
1626	Shhh Nash	....	....
1627	Shhh Nag	....	....
1628	Shhh Navy	....	....
1629	Shhh Nab	....	....
1630	Shhh Mace	....	....
1631	Shhh Mat	....	....
1632	Shhh Man	....	....
1633	Shhh Ma'am	....	....
1634	Shhh Mare	....	....
1635	Shhh Mail	....	....

NUMBER	SEM[3]	KEY WORD	IMAGE
1636	Shhh Mash	....	....
1637	Shhh Mac	....	....
1638	Shhh Mafia	....	....
1639	Shhh Map	....	....
1640	Shhh Race	....	....
1641	Shhh Rat	....	....
1642	Shhh Rain	....	....
1643	Shhh Ram	....	....
1644	Shhh Rare	....	....
1645	Shhh Rail	....	....
1646	Shhh Rash	....	....
1647	Shhh Rack	....	....
1648	Shhh Rafia	....	....
1649	Shhh Rap	....	....
1650	Shhh Lace	....	....
1651	Shhh Lad	....	....
1652	Shhh Lane	....	....
1653	Shhh Lamb	....	....
1654	Shhh Lair	....	....
1655	Shhh Lily	....	....
1656	Shhh Lash	....	....
1657	Shhh Lake	....	....
1658	Shhh Laugh	....	....
1659	Shhh Lab	....	....
1660	Shhh Chase	....	....
1661	Shhh Chat	....	....
1662	Shhh Chain	....	....
1663	Shhh Chime	....	....
1664	Shhh Chair	....	....
1665	Shhh Chill	....	....
1666	Shhh Chacha	....	....
1667	Shhh Check	....	....
1668	Shhh Chaff	....	....
1669	Shhh Chap	....	....
1670	Shhh Case	....	....
1671	Shhh Cat	....	....
1672	Shhh Can	....	....
1673	Shhh Cameo	....	....
1674	Shhh Car	....	....
1675	Shhh Call	....	....
1676	Shhh Cash	....	....
1677	Shhh Cake	....	....
1678	Shhh Café	....	....
1679	Shhh Cab	....	....
1680	Shhh Face	....	....
1681	Shhh Fat	....	....
1682	Shhh Fan	....	....
1683	Shhh Fame	....	....
1684	Shhh Fair	....	....
1685	Shhh Fall	....	....
1686	Shhh Fish	....	....
1687	Shhh Fake	....	....
1688	Shhh Fife	....	....
1689	Shhh Fab	....	....

NUMBER	SEM[3]	KEY WORD	IMAGE
1690	Shhh Base	....	....
1691	Shhh Bat	....	....
1692	Shhh Ban	....	....
1693	Shhh Bam!	....	....
1694	Shhh Bar	....	....
1695	Shhh Ball	....	....
1696	Shhh Bash	....	....
1697	Shhh Back	....	....
1698	Shhh Beef	....	....
1699	Shhh Baby	....	....
1700	Gong Zoo	....	....
1701	Gong Day	....	....
1702	Gong Noah	....	....
1703	Gong Ma	....	....
1704	Gong Rah	....	....
1705	Gong Law	....	....
1706	Gong Jaw	....	....
1707	Gong Key	....	....
1708	Gong Fee	....	....
1709	Gong Bay	....	....
1710	Gong Daze	....	....
1711	Gong Dad	....	....
1712	Gong Dan	....	....
1713	Gong Dam	....	....
1714	Gong Dare	....	....
1715	Gong Dale	....	....
1716	Gong Dash	....	....
1717	Gong Deck	....	....
1718	Gong Daffy	....	....
1719	Gong Dab	....	....
1720	Gong Nasa	....	....
1721	Gong Net	....	....
1722	Gong Nan	....	....
1723	Gong Name	....	....
1724	Gong Nero	....	....
1725	Gong Nail	....	....
1726	Gong Nash	....	....
1727	Gong Nag	....	....
1728	Gong Navy	....	....
1729	Gong Nab	....	....
1730	Gong Mace	....	....
1731	Gong Mat	....	....
1732	Gong Man	....	....
1733	Gong Ma'am	....	....
1734	Gong Mare	....	....
1735	Gong Mail	....	....
1736	Gong Mash	....	....
1737	Gong Mac	....	....
1738	Gong Mafia	....	....
1739	Gong Map	....	....
1740	Gong Race	....	....
1741	Gong Rat	....	....
1742	Gong Rain	....	....
1743	Gong Ram	....	....

NUMBER	SEM³	KEY WORD	IMAGE
1744	Gong Rare	....	....
1745	Gong Rail	....	....
1746	Gong Rash	....	....
1747	Gong Rack	....	....
1748	Gong Rafia	....	....
1749	Gong Rap	....	....
1750	Gong Lace	....	....
1751	Gong Lad	....	....
1752	Gong Lane	....	....
1753	Gong Lamb	....	....
1754	Gong Lair	....	....
1755	Gong Lily	....	....
1756	Gong Lash	....	....
1757	Gong Lake	....	....
1758	Gong Laugh	....	....
1759	Gong Lab	....	....
1760	Gong Chase	....	....
1761	Gong Chat	....	....
1762	Gong Chain	....	....
1763	Gong Chime	....	....
1764	Gong Chair	....	....
1765	Gong Chill	....	....
1766	Gong Chacha	....	....
1767	Gong Check	....	....
1768	Gong Chaff	....	....
1769	Gong Chap	....	....
1770	Gong Case	....	....
1771	Gong Cat	....	....
1772	Gong Can	....	....
1773	Gong Cameo	....	....
1774	Gong Car	....	....
1775	Gong Call	....	....
1776	Gong Cash	....	....
1777	Gong Cake	....	....
1778	Gong Café	....	....
1779	Gong Cab	....	....
1780	Gong Face	....	....
1781	Gong Fat	....	....
1782	Gong Fan	....	....
1783	Gong Fame	....	....
1784	Gong Fair	....	....
1785	Gong Fall	....	....
1786	Gong Fish	....	....
1787	Gong Fake	....	....
1788	Gong Fife	....	....
1789	Gong Fab	....	....
1790	Gong Base	....	....
1791	Gong Bat	....	....
1792	Gong Ban	....	....
1793	Gong Bam!	....	....
1794	Gong Bar	....	....
1795	Gong Ball	....	....
1796	Gong Bash	....	....
1797	Gong Back	....	....

NUMBER	SEM[3]	KEY WORD	IMAGE
1798	Gong Beef	....	....
1799	Gong Baby	....	....
1800	Violin Zoo	....	....
1801	Violin Day	....	....
1802	Violin Noah	....	....
1803	Violin Ma	....	....
1804	Violin Rah	....	....
1805	Violin Law	....	....
1806	Violin Jaw	....	....
1807	Violin Key	....	....
1808	Violin Fee	....	....
1809	Violin Bay	....	....
1810	Violin Daze	....	....
1811	Violin Dad	....	....
1812	Violin Dan	....	....
1813	Violin Dam	....	....
1814	Violin Dare	....	....
1815	Violin Dale	....	....
1816	Violin Dash	....	....
1817	Violin Deck	....	....
1818	Violin Daffy	....	....
1819	Violin Dab	....	....
1820	Violin Nasa	....	....
1821	Violin Net	....	....
1822	Violin Nan	....	....
1823	Violin Name	....	....
1824	Violin Nero	....	....
1825	Violin Nail	....	....
1826	Violin Nash	....	....
1827	Violin Nag	....	....
1828	Violin Navy	....	....
1829	Violin Nab	....	....
1830	Violin Mace	....	....
1831	Violin Mat	....	....
1832	Violin Man	....	....
1833	Violin Ma'am	....	....
1834	Violin Mare	....	....
1835	Violin Mail	....	....
1836	Violin Mash	....	....
1837	Violin Mac	....	....
1838	Violin Mafia	....	....
1839	Violin Map	....	....
1840	Violin Race	....	....
1841	Violin Rat	....	....
1842	Violin Rain	....	....
1843	Violin Ram	....	....
1844	Violin Rare	....	....
1845	Violin Rail	....	....
1846	Violin Rash	....	....
1847	Violin Rack	....	....
1848	Violin Rafia	....	....
1849	Violin Rap	....	....
1850	Violin Lace	....	....
1851	Violin Lad	....	....

NUMBER	SEM[3]	KEY WORD	IMAGE
1852	Violin Lane	....	....
1853	Violin Lamb	....	....
1854	Violin Lair	....	....
1855	Violin Lily	....	....
1856	Violin Lash	....	....
1857	Violin Lake	....	....
1858	Violin Laugh	....	....
1859	Violin Lab	....	....
1860	Violin Chase	....	....
1861	Violin Chat	....	....
1862	Violin Chain	....	....
1863	Violin Chime	....	....
1864	Violin Chair	....	....
1865	Violin Chill	....	....
1866	Violin Chacha	....	....
1867	Violin Check	....	....
1868	Violin Chaff	....	....
1869	Violin Chap	....	....
1870	Violin Case	....	....
1871	Violin Cat	....	....
1872	Violin Can	....	....
1873	Violin Cameo	....	....
1874	Violin Car	....	....
1875	Violin Call	....	....
1876	Violin Cash	....	....
1877	Violin Cake	....	....
1878	Violin Cafe	....	....
1879	Violin Cab	....	....
1880	Violin Face	....	....
1881	Violin Fat	....	....
1882	Violin Fan	....	....
1883	Violin Fame	....	....
1884	Violin Fair	....	....
1885	Violin Fall	....	....
1886	Violin Fish	....	....
1887	Violin Fake	....	....
1888	Violin Fife	....	....
1889	Violin Fab	....	....
1890	Violin Base	....	....
1891	Violin Bat	....	....
1892	Violin Ban	....	....
1893	Violin Bam!	....	....
1894	Violin Bar	....	....
1895	Violin Ball	....	....
1896	Violin Bash	....	....
1897	Violin Back	....	....
1898	Violin Beef	....	....
1899	Violin Baby	....	....
1900	Brook Zoo	....	....
1901	Brook Day	....	....
1902	Brook Noah	....	....
1903	Brook Ma	....	....
1904	Brook Rah	....	....
1905	Brook Law	....	....

NUMBER	SEM³	KEY WORD	IMAGE
1906	Brook Jaw	....	....
1907	Brook Key	....	....
1908	Brook Fee	....	....
1909	Brook Bay	....	....
1910	Brook Daze	....	....
1911	Brook Dad	....	....
1912	Brook Dan	....	....
1913	Brook Dam	....	....
1914	Brook Dare	....	....
1915	Brook Dale	....	....
1916	Brook Dash	....	....
1917	Brook Deck	....	....
1918	Brook Daffy	....	....
1919	Brook Dab	....	....
1920	Brook Nasa	....	....
1921	Brook Net	....	....
1922	Brook Nan	....	....
1923	Brook Name	....	....
1924	Brook Nero	....	....
1925	Brook Nail	....	....
1926	Brook Nash	....	....
1927	Brook Nag	....	....
1928	Brook Navy	....	....
1929	Brook Nab	....	....
1930	Brook Mace	....	....
1931	Brook Mat	....	....
1932	Brook Man	....	....
1933	Brook Ma'am	....	....
1934	Brook Mare	....	....
1935	Brook Mail	....	....
1936	Brook Mash	....	....
1937	Brook Mac	....	....
1938	Brook Mafia	....	....
1939	Brook Map	....	....
1940	Brook Race	....	....
1941	Brook Rat	....	....
1942	Brook Rain	....	....
1943	Brook Ram	....	....
1944	Brook Rare	....	....
1945	Brook Rail	....	....
1946	Brook Rash	....	....
1947	Brook Rack	....	....
1948	Brook Rafia	....	....
1949	Brook Rap	....	....
1950	Brook Lace	....	....
1951	Brook Lad	....	....
1952	Brook Lane	....	....
1953	Brook Lamb	....	....
1954	Brook Lair	....	....
1955	Brook Lily	....	....
1956	Brook Lash	....	....
1957	Brook Lake	....	....
1958	Brook Laugh	....	....
1959	Brook Lab	....	....

NUMBER	SEM[3]	KEY WORD	IMAGE
1960	Brook Chase	....	....
1961	Brook Chat	....	....
1962	Brook Chain	....	....
1963	Brook Chime	....	....
1964	Brook Chair	....	....
1965	Brook Chill	....	....
1966	Brook Chacha	....	....
1967	Brook Check	....	....
1968	Brook Chaff	....	....
1969	Brook Chap	....	....
1970	Brook Case	....	....
1971	Brook Cat	....	....
1972	Brook Can	....	....
1973	Brook Cameo	....	....
1974	Brook Car	....	....
1975	Brook Call	....	....
1976	Brook Cash	....	....
1977	Brook Cake	....	....
1978	Brook Café	....	....
1979	Brook Cab	....	....
1980	Brook Face	....	....
1981	Brook Fat	....	....
1982	Brook Fan	....	....
1983	Brook Fame	....	....
1984	Brook Fair	....	....
1985	Brook Fall	....	....
1986	Brook Fish	....	....
1987	Brook Fake	....	....
1988	Brook Fife	....	....
1989	Brook Fab	....	....
1990	Brook Base	....	....
1991	Brook Bat	....	....
1992	Brook Ban	....	....
1993	Brook Bam!	....	....
1994	Brook Bar	....	....
1995	Brook Ball	....	....
1996	Brook Bash	....	....
1997	Brook Back	....	....
1998	Brook Beef	....	....
1999	Brook Baby	....	....

CHAPTER THREE

SMELL

NUMBER	SEM[3]	KEY WORD	IMAGE
2000	Sea-Weed Zoo	....	....
2001	Sea-Weed Day	....	....
2002	Sea-Weed Noah	....	....
2003	Sea-Weed Ma	....	....
2004	Sea-Weed Rah	....	....
2005	Sea-Weed Law	....	....
2006	Sea-Weed Jaw	....	....
2007	Sea-Weed Key	....	....
2008	Sea-Weed Fee	....	....
2009	Sea-Weed Bay	....	....
2010	Sea-Weed Daze	....	....
2011	Sea-Weed Dad	....	....
2012	Sea-Weed Dan	....	....
2013	Sea-Weed Dam	....	....
2014	Sea-Weed Dare	....	....
2015	Sea-Weed Dale	....	....
2016	Sea-Weed Dash	....	....
2017	Sea-Weed Deck	....	....
2018	Sea-Weed Daffy	....	....
2019	Sea-Weed Dab	....	....
2020	Sea-Weed Nasa	....	....
2021	Sea-Weed Net	....	....
2022	Sea-Weed Nan	....	....
2023	Sea-Weed Name	....	....
2024	Sea-Weed Nero	....	....
2025	Sea-Weed Nail	....	....
2026	Sea-Weed Nash	....	....
2027	Sea-Weed Nag	....	....
2028	Sea-Weed Navy	....	....
2029	Sea-Weed Nab	....	....
2030	Sea-Weed Mace	....	....
2031	Sea-Weed Mat	....	....
2032	Sea-Weed Man	....	....
2033	Sea-Weed Ma'am	....	....
2034	Sea-Weed Mare	....	....
2035	Sea-Weed Mail	....	....
2036	Sea-Weed Mash	....	....
2037	Sea-Weed Mac	....	....
2038	Sea-Weed Mafia	....	....
2039	Sea-Weed Map	....	....
2040	Sea-Weed Race	....	....
2041	Sea-Weed Rat	....	....

NUMBER	SEM[3]	KEY WORD	IMAGE
2042	Sea-Weed Rain	....	....
2043	Sea-Weed Ram	....	....
2044	Sea-Weed Rare	....	....
2045	Sea-Weed Rail	....	....
2046	Sea-Weed Rash	....	....
2047	Sea-Weed Rack	....	....
2048	Sea-Weed Rafia	....	....
2049	Sea-Weed Rap	....	....
2050	Sea-Weed Lace	....	....
2051	Sea-Weed Lad	....	....
2052	Sea-Weed Lane	....	....
2053	Sea-Weed Lamb	....	....
2054	Sea-Weed Lair	....	....
2055	Sea-Weed Lily	....	....
2056	Sea-Weed Lash	....	....
2057	Sea-Weed Lake	....	....
2058	Sea-Weed Laugh	....	....
2059	Sea-Weed Lab	....	....
2060	Sea-Weed Chase	....	....
2061	Sea-Weed Chat	....	....
2062	Sea-Weed Chain	....	....
2063	Sea-Weed Chime	....	....
2064	Sea-Weed Chair	....	....
2065	Sea-Weed Chill	....	....
2066	Sea-Weed Chacha	....	....
2067	Sea-Weed Check	....	....
2068	Sea-Weed Chaff	....	....
2069	Sea-Weed Chap	....	....
2070	Sea-Weed Case	....	....
2071	Sea-Weed Cat	....	....
2072	Sea-Weed Can	....	....
2073	Sea-Weed Cameo	....	....
2074	Sea-Weed Car	....	....
2075	Sea-Weed Call	....	....
2076	Sea-Weed Cash	....	....
2077	Sea-Weed Cake	....	....
2078	Sea-Weed Café	....	....
2079	Sea-Weed Cab	....	....
2080	Sea-Weed Face	....	....
2081	Sea-Weed Fat	....	....
2082	Sea-Weed Fan	....	....
2083	Sea-Weed Fame	....	....
2084	Sea-Weed Fair	....	....
2085	Sea-Weed Fall	....	....
2086	Sea-Weed Fish	....	....
2087	Sea-Weed Fake	....	....
2088	Sea-Weed Fife	....	....
2089	Sea-Weed Fab	....	....
2090	Sea-Weed Base	....	....
2091	Sea-Weed Bat	....	....
2092	Sea-Weed Ban	....	....
2093	Sea-Weed Bam!	....	....
2094	Sea-Weed Bar	....	....
2095	Sea-Weed Ball	....	....

NUMBER	SEM³	KEY WORD	IMAGE
2096	Sea-Weed Bash	....	....
2097	Sea-Weed Back	....	....
2098	Sea-Weed Beef	....	....
2099	Sea-Weed Baby	....	....
2100	Tar Zoo	....	....
2101	Tar Day	....	....
2102	Tar Noah	....	....
2103	Tar Ma	....	....
2104	Tar Rah	....	....
2105	Tar Law	....	....
2106	Tar Jaw	....	....
2107	Tar Key	....	....
2108	Tar Fee	....	....
2109	Tar Bay	....	....
2110	Tar Daze	....	....
2111	Tar Dad	....	....
2112	Tar Dan	....	....
2113	Tar Dam	....	....
2114	Tar Dare	....	....
2115	Tar Dale	....	....
2116	Tar Dash	....	....
2117	Tar Deck	....	....
2118	Tar Daffy	....	....
2119	Tar Dab	....	....
2120	Tar Nasa	....	....
2121	Tar Net	....	....
2122	Tar Nan	....	....
2123	Tar Name	....	....
2124	Tar Nero	....	....
2125	Tar Nail	....	....
2126	Tar Nash	....	....
2127	Tar Nag	....	....
2128	Tar Navy	....	....
2129	Tar Nab	....	....
2130	Tar Mace	....	....
2131	Tar Mat	....	....
2132	Tar Man	....	....
2133	Tar Ma'am	....	....
2134	Tar Mare	....	....
2135	Tar Mail	....	....
2136	Tar Mash	....	....
2137	Tar Mac	....	....
2138	Tar Mafia	....	....
2139	Tar Map	....	....
2140	Tar Race	....	....
2141	Tar Rat	....	....
2142	Tar Rain	....	....
2143	Tar Ram	....	....
2144	Tar Rare	....	....
2145	Tar Rail	....	....
2146	Tar Rash	....	....
2147	Tar Rack	....	....
2148	Tar Rafia	....	....
2149	Tar Rap	....	....

NUMBER	SEM³	KEY WORD	IMAGE
2150	Tar Lace	....	....
2151	Tar Lad	....	....
2152	Tar Lane	....	....
2153	Tar Lamb	....	....
2154	Tar Lair	....	....
2155	Tar Lily	....	....
2156	Tar Lash	....	....
2157	Tar Lake	....	....
2158	Tar Laugh	....	....
2159	Tar Lab	....	....
2160	Tar Chase	....	....
2161	Tar Chat	....	....
2162	Tar Chain	....	....
2163	Tar Chime	....	....
2164	Tar Chair	....	....
2165	Tar Chill	....	....
2166	Tar Chacha	....	....
2167	Tar Check	....	....
2168	Tar Chaff	....	....
2169	Tar Chap	....	....
2170	Tar Case	....	....
2171	Tar Cat	....	....
2172	Tar Can	....	....
2173	Tar Cameo	....	....
2174	Tar Car	....	....
2175	Tar Call	....	....
2176	Tar Cash	....	....
2177	Tar Cake	....	....
2178	Tar Café	....	....
2179	Tar Cab	....	....
2180	Tar Face	....	....
2181	Tar Fat	....	....
2182	Tar Fan	....	....
2183	Tar Fame	....	....
2184	Tar Fair	....	....
2185	Tar Fall	....	....
2186	Tar Fish	....	....
2187	Tar Fake	....	....
2188	Tar Fife	....	....
2189	Tar Fab	....	....
2190	Tar Base	....	....
2191	Tar Bat	....	....
2192	Tar Ban	....	....
2193	Tar Bam!	....	....
2194	Tar Bar	....	....
2195	Tar Ball	....	....
2196	Tar Bash	....	....
2197	Tar Back	....	....
2198	Tar Beef	....	....
2199	Tar Baby	....	....
2200	Nutmeg Zoo	....	....
2201	Nutmeg Day	....	....
2202	Nutmeg Noah	....	....
2203	Nutmeg Ma	....	....

NUMBER	SEM^3	KEY WORD	IMAGE
2204	Nutmeg Rah	....	....
2205	Nutmeg Law	....	....
2206	Nutmeg Jaw	....	....
2207	Nutmeg Key	....	....
2208	Nutmeg Fee	....	....
2209	Nutmeg Bay	....	....
2210	Nutmeg Daze	....	....
2211	Nutmeg Dad	....	....
2212	Nutmeg Dan	....	....
2213	Nutmeg Dam	....	....
2214	Nutmeg Dare	....	....
2215	Nutmeg Dale	....	....
2216	Nutmeg Dash	....	....
2217	Nutmeg Deck	....	....
2218	Nutmeg Daffy	....	....
2219	Nutmeg Dab	....	....
2220	Nutmeg Nasa	....	....
2221	Nutmeg Net	....	....
2222	Nutmeg Nan	....	....
2223	Nutmeg Name	....	....
2224	Nutmeg Nero	....	....
2225	Nutmeg Nail	....	....
2226	Nutmeg Nash	....	....
2227	Nutmeg Nag	....	....
2228	Nutmeg Navy	....	....
2229	Nutmeg Nab	....	....
2230	Nutmeg Mace	....	....
2231	Nutmeg Mat	....	....
2232	Nutmeg Man	....	....
2233	Nutmeg Ma'am	....	....
2234	Nutmeg Mare	....	....
2235	Nutmeg Mail	....	....
2236	Nutmeg Mash	....	....
2237	Nutmeg Mac	....	....
2238	Nutmeg Mafia	....	....
2239	Nutmeg Map	....	....
2240	Nutmeg Race	....	....
2241	Nutmeg Rat	....	....
2242	Nutmeg Rain	....	....
2243	Nutmeg Ram	....	....
2244	Nutmeg Rare	....	....
2245	Nutmeg Rail	....	....
2246	Nutmeg Rash	....	....
2247	Nutmeg Rack	....	....
2248	Nutmeg Rafia	....	....
2249	Nutmeg Rap	....	....
2250	Nutmeg Lace	....	....
2251	Nutmeg Lad	....	....
2252	Nutmeg Lane	....	....
2253	Nutmeg Lamb	....	....
2254	Nutmeg Lair	....	....
2255	Nutmeg Lily	....	....
2256	Nutmeg Lash	....	....
2257	Nutmeg Lake	....	....

NUMBER	SEM[3]	KEY WORD	IMAGE
2258	Nutmeg Laugh	....	....
2259	Nutmeg Lab	....	....
2260	Nutmeg Chase	....	....
2261	Nutmeg Chat	....	....
2262	Nutmeg Chain	....	....
2263	Nutmeg Chime	....	....
2264	Nutmeg Chair	....	....
2265	Nutmeg Chill	....	....
2266	Nutmeg Chacha	....	....
2267	Nutmeg Check	....	....
2268	Nutmeg Chaff	....	....
2269	Nutmeg Chap	....	....
2270	Nutmeg Case	....	....
2271	Nutmeg Cat	....	....
2272	Nutmeg Can	....	....
2273	Nutmeg Cameo	....	....
2274	Nutmeg Car	....	....
2275	Nutmeg Call	....	....
2276	Nutmeg Cash	....	....
2277	Nutmeg Cake	....	....
2278	Nutmeg Café	....	....
2279	Nutmeg Cab	....	....
2280	Nutmeg Face	....	....
2281	Nutmeg Fat	....	....
2282	Nutmeg Fan	....	....
2283	Nutmeg Fame	....	....
2284	Nutmeg Fair	....	....
2285	Nutmeg Fall	....	....
2286	Nutmeg Fish	....	....
2287	Nutmeg Fake	....	....
2288	Nutmeg Fife	....	....
2289	Nutmeg Fab	....	....
2290	Nutmeg Base	....	....
2291	Nutmeg Bat	....	....
2292	Nutmeg Ban	....	....
2293	Nutmeg Bam!	....	....
2294	Nutmeg Bar	....	....
2295	Nutmeg Ball	....	....
2296	Nutmeg Bash	....	....
2297	Nutmeg Back	....	....
2298	Nutmeg Beef	....	....
2299	Nutmeg Baby	....	....
2300	Mint Zoo	....	....
2301	Mint Day	....	....
2302	Mint Noah	....	....
2303	Mint Ma	....	....
2304	Mint Rah	....	....
2305	Mint Law	....	....
2306	Mint Jaw	....	....
2307	Mint Key	....	....
2308	Mint Fee	....	....
2309	Mint Bay	....	....
2310	Mint Daze	....	....
2311	Mint Dad	....	....

NUMBER	SEM³	KEY WORD	IMAGE
2312	Mint Dan	....	....
2313	Mint Dam	....	....
2314	Mint Dare	....	....
2315	Mint Dale	....	....
2316	Mint Dash	....	....
2317	Mint Deck	....	....
2318	Mint Daffy	....	....
2319	Mint Dab	....	....
2320	Mint Nasa	....	....
2321	Mint Net	....	....
2322	Mint Nan	....	....
2323	Mint Name	....	....
2324	Mint Nero	....	....
2325	Mint Nail	....	....
2326	Mint Nash	....	....
2327	Mint Nag	....	....
2328	Mint Navy	....	....
2329	Mint Nab	....	....
2330	Mint Mace	....	....
2331	Mint Mat	....	....
2332	Mint Man	....	....
2333	Mint Ma'am	....	....
2334	Mint Mare	....	....
2335	Mint Mail	....	....
2336	Mint Mash	....	....
2337	Mint Mac	....	....
2338	Mint Mafia	....	....
2339	Mint Map	....	....
2340	Mint Race	....	....
2341	Mint Rat	....	....
2342	Mint Rain	....	....
2343	Mint Ram	....	....
2344	Mint Rare	....	....
2345	Mint Rail	....	....
2346	Mint Rash	....	....
2347	Mint Rack	....	....
2348	Mint Rafia	....	....
2349	Mint Rap	....	....
2350	Mint Lace	....	....
2351	Mint Lad	....	....
2352	Mint Lane	....	....
2353	Mint Lamb	....	....
2354	Mint Lair	....	....
2355	Mint Lily	....	....
2356	Mint Lash	....	....
2357	Mint Lake	....	....
2358	Mint Laugh	....	....
2359	Mint Lab	....	....
2360	Mint Chase	....	....
2361	Mint Chat	....	....
2362	Mint Chain	....	....
2363	Mint Chime	....	....
2364	Mint Chair	....	....
2365	Mint Chill	....	....

NUMBER	SEM³	KEY WORD	IMAGE
2366	Mint Chacha	....	....
2367	Mint Check	....	....
2368	Mint Chaff	....	....
2369	Mint Chap	....	....
2370	Mint Case	....	....
2371	Mint Cat	....	....
2372	Mint Can	....	....
2373	Mint Cameo	....	....
2374	Mint Car	....	....
2375	Mint Call	....	....
2376	Mint Cash	....	....
2377	Mint Cake	....	....
2378	Mint Café	....	....
2379	Mint Cab	....	....
2380	Mint Face	....	....
2381	Mint Fat	....	....
2382	Mint Fan	....	....
2383	Mint Fame	....	....
2384	Mint Fair	....	....
2385	Mint Fall	....	....
2386	Mint Fish	....	....
2387	Mint Fake	....	....
2388	Mint Fife	....	....
2389	Mint Fab	....	....
2390	Mint Base	....	....
2391	Mint Bat	....	....
2392	Mint Ban	....	....
2393	Mint Bam!	....	....
2394	Mint Bar	....	....
2395	Mint Ball	....	....
2396	Mint Bash	....	....
2397	Mint Back	....	....
2398	Mint Beef	....	....
2399	Mint Baby	....	....
2400	Rose Zoo	....	....
2401	Rose Day	....	....
2402	Rose Noah	....	....
2403	Rose Ma	....	....
2404	Rose Rah	....	....
2405	Rose Law	....	....
2406	Rose Jaw	....	....
2407	Rose Key	....	....
2408	Rose Fee	....	....
2409	Rose Bay	....	....
2410	Rose Daze	....	....
2411	Rose Dad	....	....
2412	Rose Dan	....	....
2413	Rose Dam	....	....
2414	Rose Dare	....	....
2415	Rose Dale	....	....
2416	Rose Dash	....	....
2417	Rose Deck	....	....
2418	Rose Daffy	....	....
2419	Rose Dab	....	....

58

NUMBER	SEM³	KEY WORD	IMAGE
2420	Rose Nasa	....	....
2421	Rose Net	....	....
2422	Rose Nan	....	....
2423	Rose Name	....	....
2424	Rose Nero	....	....
2425	Rose Nail	....	....
2426	Rose Nash	....	....
2427	Rose Nag	....	....
2428	Rose Navy	....	....
2429	Rose Nab	....	....
2430	Rose Mace	....	....
2431	Rose Mat	....	....
2432	Rose Man	....	....
2433	Rose Ma'am	....	....
2434	Rose Mare	....	....
2435	Rose Mail	....	....
2436	Rose Mash	....	....
2437	Rose Mac	....	....
2438	Rose Mafia	....	....
2439	Rose Map	....	....
2440	Rose Race	....	....
2441	Rose Rat	....	....
2442	Rose Rain	....	....
2443	Rose Ram	....	....
2444	Rose Rare	....	....
2445	Rose Rail	....	....
2446	Rose Rash	....	....
2447	Rose Rack	....	....
2448	Rose Rafia	....	....
2449	Rose Rap	....	....
2450	Rose Lace	....	....
2451	Rose Lad	....	....
2452	Rose Lane	....	....
2453	Rose Lamb	....	....
2454	Rose Lair	....	....
2455	Rose Lily	....	....
2456	Rose Lash	....	....
2457	Rose Lake	....	....
2458	Rose Laugh	....	....
2459	Rose Lab	....	....
2460	Rose Chase	....	....
2461	Rose Chat	....	....
2462	Rose Chain	....	....
2463	Rose Chime	....	....
2464	Rose Chair	....	....
2465	Rose Chill	....	....
2466	Rose Chacha	....	....
2467	Rose Check	....	....
2468	Rose Chaff	....	....
2469	Rose Chap	....	....
2470	Rose Case	....	....
2471	Rose Cat	....	....
2472	Rose Can	....	....
2473	* Rose Cameo	....	....

NUMBER	SEM³	KEY WORD	IMAGE
2474	Rose Car	....	....
2475	Rose Call	....	....
2476	Rose Cash	....	....
2477	Rose Cake	....	....
2478	Rose Café	....	....
2479	Rose Cab	....	....
2480	Rose Face	....	....
2481	Rose Fat	....	....
2482	Rose Fan	....	....
2483	Rose Fame	....	....
2484	Rose Fair	....	....
2485	Rose Fall	....	....
2486	Rose Fish	....	....
2487	Rose Fake	....	....
2488	Rose Fife	....	....
2489	Rose Fab	....	....
2490	Rose Base	....	....
2491	Rose Bat	....	....
2492	Rose Ban	....	....
2493	Rose Bam!	....	....
2494	Rose Bar	....	....
2495	Rose Ball	....	....
2496	Rose Bash	....	....
2497	Rose Back	....	....
2498	Rose Beef	....	....
2499	Rose Baby	....	....
2500	Leather Zoo	....	....
2501	Leather Day	....	....
2502	Leather Noah	....	....
2503	Leather Ma	....	....
2504	Leather Rah	....	....
2505	Leather Law	....	....
2506	Leather Jaw	....	....
2507	Leather Key	....	....
2508	Leather Fee	....	....
2509	Leather Bay	....	....
2510	Leather Daze	....	....
2511	Leather Dad	....	....
2512	Leather Dan	....	....
2513	Leather Dam	....	....
2514	Leather Dare	....	....
2515	Leather Dale	....	....
2516	Leather Dash	....	....
2517	Leather Deck	....	....
2518	Leather Daffy	....	....
2519	Leather Dab	....	....
2520	Leather Nasa	....	....
2521	Leather Net	....	....
2522	Leather Nan	....	....
2523	Leather Name	....	....
2524	Leather Nero	....	....
2525	Leather Nail	....	....
2526	Leather Nash	....	....
2527	Leather Nag	....	....

NUMBER	SEM[3]	KEY WORD	IMAGE
2528	Leather Navy	....	....
2529	Leather Nab	....	....
2530	Leather Mace	....	....
2531	Leather Mat	....	....
2532	Leather Man	....	....
2533	Leather Ma'am	....	....
2534	Leather Mare	....	....
2535	Leather Mail	....	....
2536	Leather Mash	....	....
2537	Leather Mac	....	....
2538	Leather Mafia	....	....
2539	Leather Map	....	....
2540	Leather Race	....	....
2541	Leather Rat	....	....
2542	Leather Rain	....	....
2543	Leather Ram	....	....
2544	Leather Rare	....	....
2545	Leather Rail	....	....
2546	Leather Rash	....	....
2547	Leather Rack	....	....
2548	Leather Rafia	....	....
2549	Leather Rap	....	....
2550	Leather Lace	....	....
2551	Leather Lad	....	....
2552	Leather Lane	....	....
2553	Leather Lamb	....	....
2554	Leather Lair	....	....
2555	Leather Lily	....	....
2556	Leather Lash	....	....
2557	Leather Lake	....	....
2558	Leather Laugh	....	....
2559	Leather Lab	....	....
2560	Leather Chase	....	....
2561	Leather Chat	....	....
2562	Leather Chain	....	....
2563	Leather Chime	....	....
2564	Leather Chair	....	....
2565	Leather Chill	....	....
2566	Leather Chacha	....	....
2567	Leather Check	....	....
2568	Leather Chaff	....	....
2569	Leather Chap	....	....
2570	Leather Case	....	....
2571	Leather Cat	....	....
2572	Leather Can	....	....
2573	Leather Cameo	....	....
2574	Leather Car	....	....
2575	Leather Call	....	....
2576	Leather Cash	....	....
2577	Leather Cake	....	....
2578	Leather Café	....	....
2579	Leather Cab	....	....
2580	Leather Face	....	....
2581	Leather Fat	....	....

NUMBER	SEM³	KEY WORD	IMAGE
2582	Leather Fan	....	....
2583	Leather Fame	....	....
2584	Leather Fair	....	....
2585	Leather Fall	....	....
2586	Leather Fish	....	....
2587	Leather Fake	....	....
2588	Leather Fife	....	....
2589	Leather Fab	....	....
2590	Leather Base	....	....
2591	Leather Bat	....	....
2592	Leather Ban	....	....
2593	Leather Bam!	....	....
2594	Leather Bar	....	....
2595	Leather Ball	....	....
2596	Leather Bash	....	....
2597	Leather Back	....	....
2598	Leather Beef	....	....
2599	Leather Baby	....	....
2600	Cheese Zoo	....	....
2601	Cheese Day	....	....
2602	Cheese Noah	....	....
2603	Cheese Ma	....	....
2604	Cheese Rah	....	....
2605	Cheese Law	....	....
2606	Cheese Jaw	....	....
2607	Cheese Key	....	....
2608	Cheese Fee	....	....
2609	Cheese Bay	....	....
2610	Cheese Daze	....	....
2611	Cheese Dad	....	....
2612	Cheese Dan	....	....
2613	Cheese Dam	....	....
2614	Cheese Dare	....	....
2615	Cheese Dale	....	....
2616	Cheese Dash	....	....
2617	Cheese Deck	....	....
2618	Cheese Daffy	....	....
2619	Cheese Dab	....	....
2620	Cheese Nasa	....	....
2621	Cheese Net	....	....
2622	Cheese Nan	....	....
2623	Cheese Name	....	....
2624	Cheese Nero	....	....
2625	Cheese Nail	....	....
2626	Cheese Nash	....	....
2627	Cheese Nag	....	....
2628	Cheese Navy	....	....
2629	Cheese Nab	....	....
2630	Cheese Mace	....	....
2631	Cheese Mat	....	....
2632	Cheese Man	....	....
2633	Cheese Ma'am	....	....
2634	Cheese Mare	....	....
2635	Cheese Mail	....	....

NUMBER	SEM³	KEY WORD	IMAGE
2636	Cheese Mash	....	....
2637	Cheese Mac	....	....
2638	Cheese Mafia	....	....
2639	Cheese Map	....	....
2640	Cheese Race	....	....
2641	Cheese Rat	....	....
2642	Cheese Rain	....	....
2643	Cheese Ram	....	....
2644	Cheese Rare	....	....
2645	Cheese Rail	....	....
2646	Cheese Rash	....	....
2647	Cheese Rack	....	....
2648	Cheese Rafia	....	....
2649	Cheese Rap	....	....
2650	Cheese Lace	....	....
2651	Cheese Lad	....	....
2652	Cheese Lane	....	....
2653	Cheese Lamb	....	....
2654	Cheese Lair	....	....
2655	Cheese Lily	....	....
2656	Cheese Lash	....	....
2657	Cheese Lake	....	....
2658	Cheese Laugh	....	....
2659	Cheese Lab	....	....
2660	Cheese Chase	....	....
2661	Cheese Chat	....	....
2662	Cheese Chain	....	....
2663	Cheese Chime	....	....
2664	Cheese Chair	....	....
2665	Cheese Chill	....	....
2666	Cheese Chacha	....	....
2667	Cheese Check	....	....
2668	Cheese Chaff	....	....
2669	Cheese Chap	....	....
2670	Cheese Case	....	....
2671	Cheese Cat	....	....
2672	Cheese Can	....	....
2673	Cheese Cameo	....	....
2674	Cheese Car	....	....
2675	Cheese Call	....	....
2676	Cheese Cash	....	....
2677	Cheese Cake	....	....
2678	Cheese Café	....	....
2679	Cheese Cab	....	....
2680	Cheese Face	....	....
2681	Cheese Fat	....	....
2682	Cheese Fan	....	....
2683	Cheese Fame	....	....
2684	Cheese Fair	....	....
2685	Cheese Fall	....	....
2686	Cheese Fish	....	....
2687	Cheese Fake	....	....
2688	Cheese Fife	....	....
2689	Cheese Fab	....	....

NUMBER	SEM³	KEY WORD	IMAGE
2690	Cheese Base	....	....
2691	Cheese Bat	....	....
2692	Cheese Ban	....	....
2693	Cheese Bam!	....	....
2694	Cheese Bar	....	....
2695	Cheese Ball	....	....
2696	Cheese Bash	....	....
2697	Cheese Back	....	....
2698	Cheese Beef	....	....
2699	Cheese Baby	....	....
2700	Garlic Zoo	....	....
2701	Garlic Day	....	....
2702	Garlic Noah	....	....
2703	Garlic Ma	....	....
2704	Garlic Rah	....	....
2705	Garlic Law	....	....
2706	Garlic Jaw	....	....
2707	Garlic Key	....	....
2708	Garlic Fee	....	....
2709	Garlic Bay	....	....
2710	Garlic Daze	....	....
2711	Garlic Dad	....	....
2712	Garlic Dan	....	....
2713	Garlic Dam	....	....
2714	Garlic Dare	....	....
2715	Garlic Dale	....	....
2716	Garlic Dash	....	....
2717	Garlic Deck	....	....
2718	Garlic Daffy	....	....
2719	Garlic Dab	....	....
2720	Garlic Nasa	....	....
2721	Garlic Net	....	....
2722	Garlic Nan	....	....
2723	Garlic Name	....	....
2724	Garlic Nero	....	....
2725	Garlic Nail	....	....
2726	Garlic Nash	....	....
2727	Garlic Nag	....	....
2728	Garlic Navy	....	....
2729	Garlic Nab	....	....
2730	Garlic Mace	....	....
2731	Garlic Mat	....	....
2732	Garlic Man	....	....
2733	Garlic Ma'am	....	....
2734	Garlic Mare	....	....
2735	Garlic Mail	....	....
2736	Garlic Mash	....	....
2737	Garlic Mac	....	....
2738	Garlic Mafia	....	....
2739	Garlic Map	....	....
2740	Garlic Race	....	....
2741	Garlic Rat	....	....
2742	Garlic Rain	....	....
2743	Garlic Ram	....	....

NUMBER	SEM³	KEY WORD	IMAGE
2744	Garlic Rare	....	....
2745	Garlic Rail	....	....
2746	Garlic Rash	....	....
2747	Garlic Rack	....	....
2748	Garlic Rafia	....	....
2749	Garlic Rap	....	....
2750	Garlic Lace	....	....
2751	Garlic Lad	....	....
2752	Garlic Lane	....	....
2753	Garlic Lamb	....	....
2754	Garlic Lair	....	....
2755	Garlic Lily	....	....
2756	Garlic Lash	....	....
2757	Garlic Lake	....	....
2758	Garlic Laugh	....	....
2759	Garlic Lab	....	....
2760	Garlic Chase	....	....
2761	Garlic Chat	....	....
2762	Garlic Chain	....	....
2763	Garlic Chime	....	....
2764	Garlic Chair	....	....
2765	Garlic Chill	....	....
2766	Garlic Chacha	....	....
2767	Garlic Check	....	....
2768	Garlic Chaff	....	....
2769	Garlic Chap	....	....
2770	Garlic Case	....	....
2771	Garlic Cat	....	....
2772	Garlic Can	....	....
2773	Garlic Cameo	....	....
2774	Garlic Car	....	....
2775	Garlic Call	....	....
2776	Garlic Cash	....	....
2777	Garlic Cake	....	....
2778	Garlic Café	....	....
2779	Garlic Cab	....	....
2780	Garlic Face	....	....
2781	Garlic Fat	....	....
2782	Garlic Fan	....	....
2783	Garlic Fame	....	....
2784	Garlic Fair	....	....
2785	Garlic Fall	....	....
2786	Garlic Fish	....	....
2787	Garlic Fake	....	....
2788	Garlic Fife	....	....
2789	Garlic Fab	....	....
2790	Garlic Base	....	....
2791	Garlic Bat	....	....
2792	Garlic Ban	....	....
2793	Garlic Bam!	....	....
2794	Garlic Bar	....	....
2795	Garlic Ball	....	....
2796	Garlic Bash	....	....
2797	Garlic Back	....	....

NUMBER	SEM³	KEY WORD	IMAGE
2798	Garlic Beef	....	....
2799	Garlic Baby	....	....
2800	Flowers Zoo	....	....
2801	Flowers Day	....	....
2802	Flowers Noah	....	....
2803	Flowers Ma	....	....
2804	Flowers Rah	....	....
2805	Flowers Law	....	....
2806	Flowers Jaw	....	....
2807	Flowers Key	....	....
2808	Flowers Fee	....	....
2809	Flowers Bay	....	....
2810	Flowers Daze	....	....
2811	Flowers Dad	....	....
2812	Flowers Dan	....	....
2813	Flowers Dam	....	....
2814	Flowers Dare	....	....
2815	Flowers Dale	....	....
2816	Flowers Dash	....	....
2817	Flowers Deck	....	....
2818	Flowers Daffy	....	....
2819	Flowers Dab	....	....
2820	Flowers Nasa	....	....
2821	Flowers Net	....	....
2822	Flowers Nan	....	....
2823	Flowers Name	....	....
2824	Flowers Nero	....	....
2825	Flowers Nail	....	....
2826	Flowers Nash	....	....
2827	Flowers Nag	....	....
2828	Flowers Navy	....	....
2829	Flowers Nab	....	....
2830	Flowers Mace	....	....
2831	Flowers Mat	....	....
2832	Flowers Man	....	....
2833	Flowers Ma'am	....	....
2834	Flowers Mare	....	....
2835	Flowers Mail	....	....
2836	Flowers Mash	....	....
2837	Flowers Mac	....	....
2838	Flowers Mafia	....	....
2839	Flowers Map	....	....
2840	Flowers Race	....	....
2841	Flowers Rat	....	....
2842	Flowers Rain	....	....
2843	Flowers Ram	....	....
2844	Flowers Rare	....	....
2845	Flowers Rail	....	....
2846	Flowers Rash	....	....
2847	Flowers Rack	....	....
2848	Flowers Rafia	....	....
2849	Flowers Rap	....	....
2850	Flowers Lace	....	....
2851	Flowers Lad	....	....

NUMBER	SEM³	KEY WORD	IMAGE
2852	Flowers Lane	....	....
2853	Flowers Lamb	....	....
2854	Flowers Lair	....	....
2855	Flowers Lily	....	....
2856	Flowers Lash	....	....
2857	Flowers Lake	....	....
2858	Flowers Laugh	....	....
2859	Flowers Lab	....	....
2860	Flowers Chase	....	....
2861	Flowers Chat	....	....
2862	Flowers Chain	....	....
2863	Flowers Chime	....	....
2864	Flowers Chair	....	....
2865	Flowers Chill	....	....
2866	Flowers Chacha	....	....
2867	Flowers Check	....	....
2868	Flowers Chaff	....	....
2869	Flowers Chap	....	....
2870	Flowers Case	....	....
2871	Flowers Cat	....	....
2872	Flowers Can	....	....
2873	Flowers Cameo	....	....
2874	Flowers Car	....	....
2875	Flowers Call	....	....
2876	Flowers Cash	....	....
2877	Flowers Cake	....	....
2878	Flowers Café	....	....
2879	Flowers Cab	....	....
2880	Flowers Face	....	....
2881	Flowers Fat	....	....
2882	Flowers Fan	....	....
2883	Flowers Fame	....	....
2884	Flowers Fair	....	....
2885	Flowers Fall	....	....
2886	Flowers Fish	....	....
2887	Flowers Fake	....	....
2888	Flowers Fife	....	....
2889	Flowers Fab	....	....
2890	Flowers Base	....	....
2891	Flowers Bat	....	....
2892	Flowers Ban	....	....
2893	Flowers Bam!	....	....
2894	Flowers Bar	....	....
2895	Flowers Ball	....	....
2896	Flowers Bash	....	....
2897	Flowers Back	....	....
2898	Flowers Beef	....	....
2899	Flowers Baby	....	....
2900	Pine Zoo	....	....
2901	Pine Day	....	....
2902	Pine Noah	....	....
2903	Pine Ma	....	....
2904	Pine Rah	....	....
2905	Pine Law	....	....

NUMBER	SEM³	KEY WORD	IMAGE
2906	Pine Jaw	....	....
2907	Pine Key	....	....
2908	Pine Fee	....	....
2909	Pine Bay	....	....
2910	Pine Daze	....	....
2911	Pine Dad	....	....
2912	Pine Dan	....	....
2913	Pine Dam	....	....
2914	Pine Dare	....	....
2915	Pine Dale	....	....
2916	Pine Dash	....	....
2917	Pine Deck	....	....
2918	Pine Daffy	....	....
2919	Pine Dab	....	....
2920	Pine Nasa	....	....
2921	Pine Net	....	....
2922	Pine Nan	....	....
2923	Pine Name	....	....
2924	Pine Nero	....	....
2925	Pine Nail	....	....
2926	Pine Nash	....	....
2927	Pine Nag	....	....
2928	Pine Navy	....	....
2929	Pine Nab	....	....
2930	Pine Mace	....	....
2931	Pine Mat	....	....
2932	Pine Man	....	....
2933	Pine Ma'am	....	....
2934	Pine Mare	....	....
2935	Pine Mail	....	....
2936	Pine Mash	....	....
2937	Pine Mac	....	....
2938	Pine Mafia	....	....
2939	Pine Map	....	....
2940	Pine Race	....	....
2941	Pine Rat	....	....
2942	Pine Rain	....	....
2943	Pine Ram	....	....
2944	Pine Rare	....	....
2945	Pine Rail	....	....
2946	Pine Rash	....	....
2947	Pine Rack	....	....
2948	Pine Rafia	....	....
2949	Pine Rap	....	....
2950	Pine Lace	....	....
2951	Pine Lad	....	....
2952	Pine Lane	....	....
2953	Pine Lamb	....	....
2954	Pine Lair	....	....
2955	Pine Lily	....	....
2956	Pine Lash	....	....
2957	Pine Lake	....	....
2958	Pine Laugh	....	....
2959	Pine Lab	....	....

NUMBER	SEM[3]	KEY WORD	IMAGE
2960	Pine Chase	....	....
2961	Pine Chat	....	....
2962	Pine Chain	....	....
2963	Pine Chime	....	....
2964	Pine Chair	....	....
2965	Pine Chill	....	....
2966	Pine Chacha	....	....
2967	Pine Check	....	....
2968	Pine Chaff	....	....
2969	Pine Chap	....	....
2970	Pine Case	....	....
2971	Pine Cat	....	....
2972	Pine Can	....	....
2973	Pine Cameo	....	....
2974	Pine Car	....	....
2975	Pine Call	....	....
2976	Pine Cash	....	....
2977	Pine Cake	....	....
2978	Pine Café	....	....
2979	Pine Cab	....	....
2980	Pine Face	....	....
2981	Pine Fat	....	....
2982	Pine Fan	....	....
2983	Pine Fame	....	....
2984	Pine Fair	....	....
2985	Pine Fall	....	....
2986	Pine Fish	....	....
2987	Pine Fake	....	....
2988	Pine Fife	....	....
2989	Pine Fab	....	....
2990	Pine Base	....	....
2991	Pine Bat	....	....
2992	Pine Ban	....	....
2993	Pine Bam!	....	....
2994	Pine Bar	....	....
2995	Pine Ball	....	....
2996	Pine Bash	....	....
2997	Pine Back	....	....
2998	Pine Beef	....	....
2999	Pine Baby	....	....

CHAPTER FOUR

TASTE

NUMBER	SEM³	KEY WORD	IMAGE
3000	Spaghetti Zoo	....	....
3001	Spaghetti Day	....	....
3002	Spaghetti Noah	....	....
3003	Spaghetti Ma	....	....
3004	Spaghetti Rah	....	....
3005	Spaghetti Law	....	....
3006	Spaghetti Jaw	....	....
3007	Spaghetti Key	....	....
3008	Spaghetti Fee	....	....
3009	Spaghetti Bay	....	....
3010	Spaghetti Daze	....	....
3011	Spaghetti Dad	....	....
3012	Spaghetti Dan	....	....
3013	Spaghetti Dam	....	....
3014	Spaghetti Dare	....	....
3015	Spaghetti Dale	....	....
3016	Spaghetti Dash	....	....
3017	Spaghetti Deck	....	....
3018	Spaghetti Daffy	....	....
3019	Spaghetti Dab	....	....
3020	Spaghetti Nasa	....	....
3021	Spaghetti Net	....	....
3022	Spaghetti Nan	....	....
3023	Spaghetti Name	....	....
3024	Spaghetti Nero	....	....
3025	Spaghetti Nail	....	....
3026	Spaghetti Nash	....	....
3027	Spaghetti Nag	....	....
3028	Spaghetti Navy	....	....
3029	Spaghetti Nab	....	....
3030	Spaghetti Mace	....	....
3031	Spaghetti Mat	....	....
3032	Spaghetti Man	....	....
3033	Spaghetti Ma'am	....	....
3034	Spaghetti Mare	....	....
3035	Spaghetti Mail	....	....
3036	Spaghetti Mash	....	....
3037	Spaghetti Mac	....	....
3038	Spaghetti Mafia	....	....
3039	Spaghetti Map	....	....
3040	Spaghetti Race	....	....
3041	Spaghetti Rat	....	....

NUMBER	SEM[3]	KEY WORD	IMAGE
3042	Spaghetti Rain	....	....
3043	Spaghetti Ram	....	....
3044	Spaghetti Rare	....	....
3045	Spaghetti Rail	....	....
3046	Spaghetti Rash	....	....
3047	Spaghetti Rack	....	....
3048	Spaghetti Rafia	....	....
3049	Spaghetti Rap	....	....
3050	Spaghetti Lace	....	....
3051	Spaghetti Lad	....	....
3052	Spaghetti Lane	....	....
3053	Spaghetti Lamb	....	....
3054	Spaghetti Lair	....	....
3055	Spaghetti Lily	....	....
3056	Spaghetti Lash	....	....
3057	Spaghetti Lake	....	....
3058	Spaghetti Laugh	....	....
3059	Spaghetti Lab	....	....
3060	Spaghetti Chase	....	....
3061	Spaghetti Chat	....	....
3062	Spaghetti Chain	....	....
3063	Spaghetti Chime	....	....
3064	Spaghetti Chair	....	....
3065	Spaghetti Chill	....	....
3066	Spaghetti Chacha	....	....
3067	Spaghetti Check	....	....
3068	Spaghetti Chaff	....	....
3069	Spaghetti Chap	....	....
3070	Spaghetti Case	....	....
3071	Spaghetti Cat	....	....
3072	Spaghetti Can	....	....
3073	Spaghetti Cameo	....	....
3074	Spaghetti Car	....	....
3075	Spaghetti Call	....	....
3076	Spaghetti Cash	....	....
3077	Spaghetti Cake	....	....
3078	Spaghetti Café	....	....
3079	Spaghetti Cab	....	....
3080	Spaghetti Face	....	....
3081	Spaghetti Fat	....	....
3082	Spaghetti Fan	....	....
3083	Spaghetti Fame	....	....
3084	Spaghetti Fair	....	....
3085	Spaghetti Fall	....	....
3086	Spaghetti Fish	....	....
3087	Spaghetti Fake	....	....
3088	Spaghetti Fife	....	....
3089	Spaghetti Fab	....	....
3090	Spaghetti Base	....	....
3091	Spaghetti Bat	....	....
3092	Spaghetti Ban	....	....
3093	Spaghetti Bam!	....	....
3094	Spaghetti Bar	....	....
3095	Spaghetti Ball	....	....

NUMBER	SEM³	KEY WORD	IMAGE
3096	Spaghetti Bash	....	....
3097	Spaghetti Back	....	....
3098	Spaghetti Beef	....	....
3099	Spaghetti Baby	....	....
3100	Tea Zoo	....	....
3101	Tea Day	....	....
3102	Tea Noah	....	....
3103	Tea Ma	....	....
3104	Tea Rah	....	....
3105	Tea Law	....	....
3106	Tea Jaw	....	....
3107	Tea Key	....	....
3108	Tea Fee	....	....
3109	Tea Bay	....	....
3110	Tea Daze	....	....
3111	Tea Dad	....	....
3112	Tea Dan	....	....
3113	Tea Dam	....	....
3114	Tea Dare	....	....
3115	Tea Dale	....	....
3116	Tea Dash	....	....
3117	Tea Deck	....	....
3118	Tea Daffy	....	....
3119	Tea Dab	....	....
3120	Tea Nasa	....	....
3121	Tea Net	....	....
3122	Tea Nan	....	....
3123	Tea Name	....	....
3124	Tea Nero	....	....
3125	Tea Nail	....	....
3126	Tea Nash	....	....
3127	Tea Nag	....	....
3128	Tea Navy	....	....
3129	Tea Nab	....	....
3130	Tea Mace	....	....
3131	Tea Mat	....	....
3132	Tea Man	....	....
3133	Tea Ma'am	....	....
3134	Tea Mare	....	....
3135	Tea Mail	....	....
3136	Tea Mash	....	....
3137	Tea Mac	....	....
3138	Tea Mafia	....	....
3139	Tea Map	....	....
3140	Tea Race	....	....
3141	Tea Rat	....	....
3142	Tea Rain	....	....
3143	Tea Ram	....	....
3144	Tea Rare	....	....
3145	Tea Rail	....	....
3146	Tea Rash	....	....
3147	Tea Rack	....	....
3148	Tea Rafia	....	....
3149	Tea Rap	....	....

NUMBER	SEM³	KEY WORD	IMAGE
3150	Tea Lace	....	....
3151	Tea Lad	....	....
3152	Tea Lane	....	....
3153	Tea Lamb	....	....
3154	Tea Lair	....	....
3155	Tea Lily	....	....
3156	Tea Lash	....	....
3157	Tea Lake	....	....
3158	Tea Laugh	....	....
3159	Tea Lab	....	....
3160	Tea Chase	....	....
3161	Tea Chat	....	....
3162	Tea Chain	....	....
3163	Tea Chime	....	....
3164	Tea Chair	....	....
3165	Tea Chill	....	....
3166	Tea Chacha	....	....
3167	Tea Check	....	....
3168	Tea Chaff	....	....
3169	Tea Chap	....	....
3170	Tea Case	....	....
3171	Tea Cat	....	....
3172	Tea Can	....	....
3173	Tea Cameo	....	....
3174	Tea Car	....	....
3175	Tea Call	....	....
3176	Tea Cash	....	....
3177	Tea Cake	....	....
3178	Tea Café	....	....
3179	Tea Cab	....	....
3180	Tea Face	....	....
3181	Tea Fat	....	....
3182	Tea Fan	....	....
3183	Tea Fame	....	....
3184	Tea Fair	....	....
3185	Tea Fall	....	....
3186	Tea Fish	....	....
3187	Tea Fake	....	....
3188	Tea Fife	....	....
3189	Tea Fab	....	....
3190	Tea Base	....	....
3191	Tea Bat	....	....
3192	Tea Ban	....	....
3193	Tea Bam!	....	....
3194	Tea Bar	....	....
3195	Tea Ball	....	....
3196	Tea Bash	....	....
3197	Tea Back	....	....
3198	Tea Beef	....	....
3199	Tea Baby	....	....
3200	Nuts Zoo	....	....
3201	Nuts Day	....	....
3202	Nuts Noah	....	....
3203	Nuts Ma	....	....

NUMBER	SEM³	KEY WORD	IMAGE
3204	Nuts Rah	....	....
3205	Nuts Law	....	....
3206	Nuts Jaw	....	....
3207	Nuts Key	....	....
3208	Nuts Fee	....	....
3209	Nuts Bay	....	....
3210	Nuts Daze	....	....
3211	Nuts Dad	....	....
3212	Nuts Dan	....	....
3213	Nuts Dam	....	....
3214	Nuts Dare	....	....
3215	Nuts Dale	....	....
3216	Nuts Dash	....	....
3217	Nuts Deck	....	....
3218	Nuts Daffy	....	....
3219	Nuts Dab	....	....
3220	Nuts Nasa	....	....
3221	Nuts Net	....	....
3222	Nuts Nan	....	....
3223	Nuts Name	....	....
3224	Nuts Nero	....	....
3225	Nuts Nail	....	....
3226	Nuts Nash	....	....
3227	Nuts Nag	....	....
3228	Nuts Navy	....	....
3229	Nuts Nab	....	....
3230	Nuts Mace	....	....
3231	Nuts Mat	....	....
3232	Nuts Man	....	....
3233	Nuts Ma'am	....	....
3234	Nuts Mare	....	....
3235	Nuts Mail	....	....
3236	Nuts Mash	....	....
3237	Nuts Mac	....	....
3238	Nuts Mafia	....	....
3239	Nuts Map	....	....
3240	Nuts Race	....	....
3241	Nuts Rat	....	....
3242	Nuts Rain	....	....
3243	Nuts Ram	....	....
3244	Nuts Rare	....	....
3245	Nuts Rail	....	....
3246	Nuts Rash	....	....
3247	Nuts Rack	....	....
3248	Nuts Rafia	....	....
3249	Nuts Rap	....	....
3250	Nuts Lace	....	....
3251	Nuts Lad	....	....
3252	Nuts Lane	....	....
3253	Nuts Lamb	....	....
3254	Nuts Lair	....	....
3255	Nuts Lily	....	....
3256	Nuts Lash	....	....
3257	Nuts Lake	....	....

NUMBER	SEM³	KEY WORD	IMAGE
3258	Nuts Laugh	....	....
3259	Nuts Lab	....	....
3260	Nuts Chase	....	....
3261	Nuts Chat	....	....
3262	Nuts Chain	....	....
3263	Nuts Chime	....	....
3264	Nuts Chair	....	....
3265	Nuts Chill	....	....
3266	Nuts Chacha	....	....
3267	Nuts Check	....	....
3268	Nuts Chaff	....	....
3269	Nuts Chap	....	....
3270	Nuts Case	....	....
3271	Nuts Cat	....	....
3272	Nuts Can	....	....
3273	Nuts Cameo	....	....
3274	Nuts Car	....	....
3275	Nuts Call	....	....
3276	Nuts Cash	....	....
3277	Nuts Cake	....	....
3278	Nuts Café	....	....
3279	Nuts Cab	....	....
3280	Nuts Face	....	....
3281	Nuts Fat	....	....
3282	Nuts Fan	....	....
3283	Nuts Fame	....	....
3284	Nuts Fair	....	....
3285	Nuts Fall	....	....
3286	Nuts Fish	....	....
3287	Nuts Fake	....	....
3288	Nuts Fife	....	....
3289	Nuts Fab	....	....
3290	Nuts Base	....	....
3291	Nuts Bat	....	....
3292	Nuts Ban	....	....
3293	Nuts Bam!	....	....
3294	Nuts Bar	....	....
3295	Nuts Ball	....	....
3296	Nuts Bash	....	....
3297	Nuts Back	....	....
3298	Nuts Beef	....	....
3299	Nuts Baby	....	....
3300	Mango Zoo	....	....
3301	Mango Day	....	....
3302	Mango Noah	....	....
3303	Mango Ma	....	....
3304	Mango Rah	....	....
3305	Mango Law	....	....
3306	Mango Jaw	....	....
3307	Mango Key	....	....
3308	Mango Fee	....	....
3309	Mango Bay	....	....
3310	Mango Daze	....	....
3311	Mango Dad	....	....

NUMBER	SEM[3]	KEY WORD	IMAGE
3312	Mango Dan	....	....
3313	Mango Dam	....	....
3314	Mango Dare	....	....
3315	Mango Dale	....	....
3316	Mango Dash	....	....
3317	Mango Deck	....	....
3318	Mango Daffy	....	....
3319	Mango Dab	....	....
3320	Mango Nasa	....	....
3321	Mango Net	....	....
3322	Mango Nan	....	....
3323	Mango Name	....	....
3324	Mango Nero	....	....
3325	Mango Nail	....	....
3326	Mango Nash	....	....
3327	Mango Nag	....	....
3328	Mango Navy	....	....
3329	Mango Nab	....	....
3330	Mango Mace	....	....
3331	Mango Mat	....	....
3332	Mango Man	....	....
3333	Mango Ma'am	....	....
3334	Mango Mare	....	....
3335	Mango Mail	....	....
3336	Mango Mash	....	....
3337	Mango Mac	....	....
3338	Mango Mafia	....	....
3339	Mango Map	....	....
3340	Mango Race	....	....
3341	Mango Rat	....	....
3342	Mango Rain	....	....
3343	Mango Ram	....	....
3344	Mango Rare	....	....
3345	Mango Rail	....	....
3346	Mango Rash	....	....
3347	Mango Rack	....	....
3348	Mango Rafia	....	....
3349	Mango Rap	....	....
3350	Mango Lace	....	....
3351	Mango Lad	....	....
3352	Mango Lane	....	....
3353	Mango Lamb	....	....
3354	Mango Lair	....	....
3355	Mango Lily	....	....
3356	Mango Lash	....	....
3357	Mango Lake	....	....
3358	Mango Laugh	....	....
3359	Mango Lab	....	....
3360	Mango Chase	....	....
3361	Mango Chat	....	....
3362	Mango Chain	....	....
3363	Mango Chime	....	....
3364	Mango Chair	....	....
3365	Mango Chill	....	....

NUMBER	SEM³	KEY WORD	IMAGE
3366	Mango Chacha	....	....
3367	Mango Check	....	....
3368	Mango Chaff	....	....
3369	Mango Chap	....	....
3370	Mango Case	....	....
3371	Mango Cat	....	....
3372	Mango Can	....	....
3373	Mango Cameo	....	....
3374	Mango Car	....	....
3375	Mango Call	....	....
3376	Mango Cash	....	....
3377	Mango Cake	....	....
3378	Mango Café	....	....
3379	Mango Cab	....	....
3380	Mango Face	....	....
3381	Mango Fat	....	....
3382	Mango Fan	....	....
3383	Mango Fame	....	....
3384	Mango Fair	....	....
3385	Mango Fall	....	....
3386	Mango Fish	....	....
3387	Mango Fake	....	....
3388	Mango Fife	....	....
3389	Mango Fab	....	....
3390	Mango Base	....	....
3391	Mango Bat	....	....
3392	Mango Ban	....	....
3393	Mango Bam!	....	....
3394	Mango Bar	....	....
3395	Mango Ball	....	....
3396	Mango Bash	....	....
3397	Mango Back	....	....
3398	Mango Beef	....	....
3399	Mango Baby	....	....
3400	Rhubarb Zoo	....	....
3401	Rhubarb Day	....	....
3402	Rhubarb Noah	....	....
3403	Rhubarb Ma	....	....
3404	Rhubarb Rah	....	....
3405	Rhubarb Law	....	....
3406	Rhubarb Jaw	....	....
3407	Rhubarb Key	....	....
3408	Rhubarb Fee	....	....
3409	Rhubarb Bay	....	....
3410	Rhubarb Daze	....	....
3411	Rhubarb Dad	....	....
3412	Rhubarb Dan	....	....
3413	Rhubarb Dam	....	....
3414	Rhubarb Dare	....	....
3415	Rhubarb Dale	....	....
3416	Rhubarb Dash	....	....
3417	Rhubarb Deck	....	....
3418	Rhubarb Daffy	....	....
3419	Rhubarb Dab	....	....

NUMBER	SEM³	KEY WORD	IMAGE
3420	Rhubarb Nasa	....	....
3421	Rhubarb Net	....	....
3422	Rhubarb Nan	....	....
3423	Rhubarb Name	....	....
3424	Rhubarb Nero	....	....
3425	Rhubarb Nail	....	....
3426	Rhubarb Nash	....	....
3427	Rhubarb Nag	....	....
3428	Rhubarb Navy	....	....
3429	Rhubarb Nab	....	....
3430	Rhubarb Mace	....	....
3431	Rhubarb Mat	....	....
3432	Rhubarb Man	....	....
3433	Rhubarb Ma'am	....	....
3434	Rhubarb Mare	....	....
3435	Rhubarb Mail	....	....
3436	Rhubarb Mash	....	....
3437	Rhubarb Mac	....	....
3438	Rhubarb Mafia	....	....
3439	Rhubarb Map	....	....
3440	Rhubarb Race	....	....
3441	Rhubarb Rat	....	....
3442	Rhubarb Rain	....	....
3443	Rhubarb Ram	....	....
3444	Rhubarb Rare	....	....
3445	Rhubarb Rail	....	....
3446	Rhubarb Rash	....	....
3447	Rhubarb Rack	....	....
3448	Rhubarb Rafia	....	....
3449	Rhubarb Rap	....	....
3450	Rhubarb Lace	....	....
3451	Rhubarb Lad	....	....
3452	Rhubarb Lane	....	....
3453	Rhubarb Lamb	....	....
3454	Rhubarb Lair	....	....
3455	Rhubarb Lily	....	....
3456	Rhubarb Lash	....	....
3457	Rhubarb Lake	....	....
3458	Rhubarb Laugh	....	....
3459	Rhubarb Lab	....	....
3460	Rhubarb Chase	....	....
3461	Rhubarb Chat	....	....
3462	Rhubarb Chain	....	....
3463	Rhubarb Chime	....	....
3464	Rhubarb Chair	....	....
3465	Rhubarb Chill	....	....
3466	Rhubarb Chacha	....	....
3467	Rhubarb Check	....	....
3468	Rhubarb Chaff	....	....
3469	Rhubarb Chap	....	....
3470	Rhubarb Case	....	....
3471	Rhubarb Cat	....	....
3472	Rhubarb Can	....	....
3473	Rhubarb Cameo	....	....

NUMBER	SEM^3	KEY WORD	IMAGE
3474	Rhubarb Car	....	....
3475	Rhubarb Call	....	....
3476	Rhubarb Cash	....	....
3477	Rhubarb Cake	....	....
3478	Rhubarb Café	....	....
3479	Rhubarb Cab	....	....
3480	Rhubarb Face	....	....
3481	Rhubarb Fat	....	....
3482	Rhubarb Fan	....	....
3483	Rhubarb Fame	....	....
3484	Rhubarb Fair	....	....
3485	Rhubarb Fall	....	....
3486	Rhubarb Fish	....	....
3487	Rhubarb Fake	....	....
3488	Rhubarb Fife	....	....
3489	Rhubarb Fab	....	....
3490	Rhubarb Base	....	....
3491	Rhubarb Bat	....	....
3492	Rhubarb Ban	....	....
3493	Rhubarb Bam!	....	....
3494	Rhubarb Bar	....	....
3495	Rhubarb Ball	....	....
3496	Rhubarb Bash	....	....
3497	Rhubarb Back	....	....
3498	Rhubarb Beef	....	....
3499	Rhubarb Baby	....	....
3500	Liver Zoo	....	....
3501	Liver Day	....	....
3502	Liver Noah	....	....
3503	Liver Ma	....	....
3504	Liver Rah	....	....
3505	Liver Law	....	....
3506	Liver Jaw	....	....
3507	Liver Key	....	....
3508	Liver Fee	....	....
3509	Liver Bay	....	....
3510	Liver Daze	....	....
3511	Liver Dad	....	....
3512	Liver Dan	....	....
3513	Liver Dam	....	....
3514	Liver Dare	....	....
3515	Liver Dale	....	....
3516	Liver Dash	....	....
3517	Liver Deck	....	....
3518	Liver Daffy	....	....
3519	Liver Dab	....	....
3520	Liver Nasa	....	....
3521	Liver Net	....	....
3522	Liver Nan	....	....
3523	Liver Name	....	....
3524	Liver Nero	....	....
3525	Liver Nail	....	....
3526	Liver Nash	....	....
3527	Liver Nag	....	....

NUMBER	SEM³	KEY WORD	IMAGE
3528	Liver Navy	....	....
3529	Liver Nab	....	....
3530	Liver Mace	....	....
3531	Liver Mat	....	....
3532	Liver Man	....	....
3533	Liver Ma'am	....	....
3534	Liver Mare	....	....
3535	Liver Mail	....	....
3536	Liver Mash	....	....
3537	Liver Mac	....	....
3538	Liver Mafia	....	....
3539	Liver Map	....	....
3540	Liver Race	....	....
3541	Liver Rat	....	....
3542	Liver Rain	....	....
3543	Liver Ram	....	....
3544	Liver Rare	....	....
3545	Liver Rail	....	....
3546	Liver Rash	....	....
3547	Liver Rack	....	....
3548	Liver Rafia	....	....
3549	Liver Rap	....	....
3550	Liver Lace	....	....
3551	Liver Lad	....	....
3552	Liver Lane	....	....
3553	Liver Lamb	....	....
3554	Liver Lair	....	....
3555	Liver Lily	....	....
3556	Liver Lash	....	....
3557	Liver Lake	....	....
3558	Liver Laugh	....	....
3559	Liver Lab	....	....
3560	Liver Chase	....	....
3561	Liver Chat	....	....
3562	Liver Chain	....	....
3563	Liver Chime	....	....
3564	Liver Chair	....	....
3565	Liver Chill	....	....
3566	Liver Chacha	....	....
3567	Liver Check	....	....
3568	Liver Chaff	....	....
3569	Liver Chap	....	....
3570	Liver Case	....	....
3571	Liver Cat	....	....
3572	Liver Can	....	....
3573	Liver Cameo	....	....
3574	Liver Car	....	....
3575	Liver Call	....	....
3576	Liver Cash	....	....
3577	Liver Cake	....	....
3578	Liver Café	....	....
3579	Liver Cab	....	....
3580	Liver Face	....	....
3581	Liver Fat	....	....

NUMBER	SEM[3]	KEY WORD	IMAGE
3582	Liver Fan		
3583	Liver Fame		
3584	Liver Fair		
3585	Liver Fall		
3586	Liver Fish		
3587	Liver Fake		
3588	Liver Fife		
3589	Liver Fab		
3590	Liver Base		
3591	Liver Bat		
3592	Liver Ban		
3593	Liver Bam!		
3594	Liver Bar		
3595	Liver Ball		
3596	Liver Bash		
3597	Liver Back		
3598	Liver Beef		
3599	Liver Baby		
3600	Jam Zoo		
3601	Jam Day		
3602	Jam Noah		
3603	Jam Ma		
3604	Jam Rah		
3605	Jam Law		
3606	Jam Jaw		
3607	Jam Key		
3608	Jam Fee		
3609	Jam Bay		
3610	Jam Daze		
3611	Jam Dad		
3612	Jam Dan		
3613	Jam Dam		
3614	Jam Dare		
3615	Jam Dale		
3616	Jam Dash		
3617	Jam Deck		
3618	Jam Daffy		
3619	Jam Dab		
3620	Jam Nasa		
3621	Jam Net		
3622	Jam Nan		
3623	Jam Name		
3624	Jam Nero		
3625	Jam Nail		
3626	Jam Nash		
3627	Jam Nag		
3628	Jam Navy		
3629	Jam Nab		
3630	Jam Mace		
3631	Jam Mat		
3632	Jam Man		
3633	Jam Ma'am		
3634	Jam Mare		
3635	Jam Mail		

NUMBER	SEM³	KEY WORD	IMAGE
3636	Jam Mash	....	....
3637	Jam Mac	....	....
3638	Jam Mafia	....	....
3639	Jam Map	....	....
3640	Jam Race	....	....
3641	Jam Rat	....	....
3642	Jam Rain	....	....
3643	Jam Ram	....	....
3644	Jam Rare	....	....
3645	Jam Rail	....	....
3646	Jam Rash	....	....
3647	Jam Rack	....	....
3648	Jam Rafia	....	....
3649	Jam Rap	....	....
3650	Jam Lace	....	....
3651	Jam Lad	....	....
3652	Jam Lane	....	....
3653	Jam Lamb	....	....
3654	Jam Lair	....	....
3655	Jam Lily	....	....
3656	Jam Lash	....	....
3657	Jam Lake	....	....
3658	Jam Laugh	....	....
3659	Jam Lab	....	....
3660	Jam Chase	....	....
3661	Jam Chat	....	....
3662	Jam Chain	....	....
3663	Jam Chime	....	....
3664	Jam Chair	....	....
3665	Jam Chill	....	....
3666	Jam Chacha	....	....
3667	Jam Check	....	....
3668	Jam Chaff	....	....
3669	Jam Chap	....	....
3670	Jam Case	....	....
3671	Jam Cat	....	....
3672	Jam Can	....	....
3673	Jam Cameo	....	....
3674	Jam Car	....	....
3675	Jam Call	....	....
3676	Jam Cash	....	....
3677	Jam Cake	....	....
3678	Jam Café	....	....
3679	Jam Cab	....	....
3680	Jam Face	....	....
3681	Jam Fat	....	....
3682	Jam Fan	....	....
3683	Jam Fame	....	....
3684	Jam Fair	....	....
3685	Jam Fall	....	....
3686	Jam Fish	....	....
3687	Jam Fake	....	....
3688	Jam Fife	....	....
3689	Jam Fab	....	....

NUMBER	SEM³	KEY WORD	IMAGE
3690	Jam Base	....	....
3691	Jam Bat	....	....
3692	Jam Ban	....	....
3693	Jam Bam!	....	....
3694	Jam Bar	....	....
3695	Jam Ball	....	....
3696	Jam Bash	....	....
3697	Jam Back	....	....
3698	Jam Beef	....	....
3699	Jam Baby	....	....
3700	Clove Zoo	....	....
3701	Clove Day	....	....
3702	Clove Noah	....	....
3703	Clove Ma	....	....
3704	Clove Rah	....	....
3705	Clove Law	....	....
3706	Clove Jaw	....	....
3707	Clove Key	....	....
3708	Clove Fee	....	....
3709	Clove Bay	....	....
3710	Clove Daze	....	....
3711	Clove Dad	....	....
3712	Clove Dan	....	....
3713	Clove Dam	....	....
3714	Clove Dare	....	....
3715	Clove Dale	....	....
3716	Clove Dash	....	....
3717	Clove Deck	....	....
3718	Clove Daffy	....	....
3719	Clove Dab	....	....
3720	Clove Nasa	....	....
3721	Clove Net	....	....
3722	Clove Nan	....	....
3723	Clove Name	....	....
3724	Clove Nero	....	....
3725	Clove Nail	....	....
3726	Clove Nash	....	....
3727	Clove Nag	....	....
3728	Clove Navy	....	....
3729	Clove Nab	....	....
3730	Clove Mace	....	....
3731	Clove Mat	....	....
3732	Clove Man	....	....
3733	Clove Ma'am	....	....
3734	Clove Mare	....	....
3735	Clove Mail	....	....
3736	Clove Mash	....	....
3737	Clove Mac	....	....
3738	Clove Mafia	....	....
3739	Clove Map	....	....
3740	Clove Race	....	....
3741	Clove Rat	....	....
3742	Clove Rain	....	....
3743	Clove Ram	....	....

NUMBER	SEM³	KEY WORD	IMAGE
3744	Clove Rare	....	....
3745	Clove Rail	....	....
3746	Clove Rash	....	....
3747	Clove Rack	....	....
3748	Clove Rafia	....	....
3749	Clove Rap	....	....
3750	Clove Lace	....	....
3751	Clove Lad	....	....
3752	Clove Lane	....	....
3753	Clove Lamb	....	....
3754	Clove Lair	....	....
3755	Clove Lily	....	....
3756	Clove Lash	....	....
3757	Clove Lake	....	....
3758	Clove Laugh	....	....
3759	Clove Lab	....	....
3760	Clove Chase	....	....
3761	Clove Chat	....	....
3762	Clove Chain	....	....
3763	Clove Chime	....	....
3764	Clove Chair	....	....
3765	Clove Chill	....	....
3766	Clove Chacha	....	....
3767	Clove Check	....	....
3768	Clove Chaff	....	....
3769	Clove Chap	....	....
3770	Clove Case	....	....
3771	Clove Cat	....	....
3772	Clove Can	....	....
3773	Clove Cameo	....	....
3774	Clove Car	....	....
3775	Clove Call	....	....
3776	Clove Cash	....	....
3777	Clove Cake	....	....
3778	Clove Café	....	....
3779	Clove Cab	....	....
3780	Clove Face	....	....
3781	Clove Fat	....	....
3782	Clove Fan	....	....
3783	Clove Fame	....	....
3784	Clove Fair	....	....
3785	Clove Fall	....	....
3786	Clove Fish	....	....
3787	Clove Fake	....	....
3788	Clove Fife	....	....
3789	Clove Fab	....	....
3790	Clove Base	....	....
3791	Clove Bat	....	....
3792	Clove Ban	....	....
3793	Clove Bam!	....	....
3794	Clove Bar	....	....
3795	Clove Ball	....	....
3796	Clove Bash	....	....
3797	Clove Back	....	....

NUMBER	SEM³	KEY WORD	IMAGE
3798	Clove Beef	....	....
3799	Clove Baby	....	....
3800	Fudge Zoo	....	....
3801	Fudge Day	....	....
3802	Fudge Noah	....	....
3803	Fudge Ma	....	....
3804	Fudge Rah	....	....
3805	Fudge Law	....	....
3806	Fudge Jaw	....	....
3807	Fudge Key	....	....
3808	Fudge Fee	....	....
3809	Fudge Bay	....	....
3810	Fudge Daze	....	....
3811	Fudge Dad	....	....
3812	Fudge Dan	....	....
3813	Fudge Dam	....	....
3814	Fudge Dare	....	....
3815	Fudge Dale	....	....
3816	Fudge Dash	....	....
3817	Fudge Deck	....	....
3818	Fudge Daffy	....	....
3819	Fudge Dab	....	....
3820	Fudge Nasa	....	....
3821	Fudge Net	....	....
3822	Fudge Nan	....	....
3823	Fudge Name	....	....
3824	Fudge Nero	....	....
3825	Fudge Nail	....	....
3826	Fudge Nash	....	....
3827	Fudge Nag	....	....
3828	Fudge Navy	....	....
3829	Fudge Nab	....	....
3830	Fudge Mace	....	....
3831	Fudge Mat	....	....
3832	Fudge Man	....	....
3833	Fudge Ma'am	....	....
3834	Fudge Mare	....	....
3835	Fudge Mail	....	....
3836	Fudge Mash	....	....
3837	Fudge Mac	....	....
3838	Fudge Mafia	....	....
3839	Fudge Map	....	....
3840	Fudge Race	....	....
3841	Fudge Rat	....	....
3842	Fudge Rain	....	....
3843	Fudge Ram	....	....
3844	Fudge Rare	....	....
3845	Fudge Rail	....	....
3846	Fudge Rash	....	....
3847	Fudge Rack	....	....
3848	Fudge Rafia	....	....
3849	Fudge Rap	....	....
3850	Fudge Lace	....	....
3851	Fudge Lad	....	....

NUMBER	SEM³	KEY WORD	IMAGE
3852	Fudge Lane	....	....
3853	Fudge Lamb	....	....
3854	Fudge Lair	....	....
3855	Fudge Lily	....	....
3856	Fudge Lash	....	....
3857	Fudge Lake	....	....
3858	Fudge Laugh	....	....
3859	Fudge Lab	....	....
3860	Fudge Chase	....	....
3861	Fudge Chat	....	....
3862	Fudge Chain	....	....
3863	Fudge Chime	....	....
3864	Fudge Chair	....	....
3865	Fudge Chill	....	....
3866	Fudge Chacha	....	....
3867	Fudge Check	....	....
3868	Fudge Chaff	....	....
3869	Fudge Chap	....	....
3870	Fudge Case	....	....
3871	Fudge Cat	....	....
3872	Fudge Can	....	....
3873	Fudge Cameo	....	....
3874	Fudge Car	....	....
3875	Fudge Call	....	....
3876	Fudge Cash	....	....
3877	Fudge Cake	....	....
3878	Fudge Cafe	....	....
3879	Fudge Cab	....	....
3880	Fudge Face	....	....
3881	Fudge Fat	....	....
3882	Fudge Fan	....	....
3883	Fudge Fame	....	....
3884	Fudge Fair	....	....
3885	Fudge Fall	....	....
3886	Fudge Fish	....	....
3887	Fudge Fake	....	....
3888	Fudge Fife	....	....
3889	Fudge Fab	....	....
3890	Fudge Base	....	....
3891	Fudge Bat	....	....
3892	Fudge Ban	....	....
3893	Fudge Bam!	....	....
3894	Fudge Bar	....	....
3895	Fudge Ball	....	....
3896	Fudge Bash	....	....
3897	Fudge Back	....	....
3898	Fudge Beef	....	....
3899	Fudge Baby	....	....
3900	Banana Zoo	....	....
3901	Banana Day	....	....
3902	Banana Noah	....	....
3903	Banana Ma	....	....
3904	Banana Rah	....	....
3905	Banana Law	....	....

NUMBER	SEM³	KEY WORD	IMAGE
3906	Banana Jaw	....	....
3907	Banana Key	....	....
3908	Banana Fee	....	....
3909	Banana Bay	....	....
3910	Banana Daze	....	....
3911	Banana Dad	....	....
3912	Banana Dan	....	....
3913	Banana Dam	....	....
3914	Banana Dare	....	....
3915	Banana Dale	....	....
3916	Banana Dash	....	....
3917	Banana Deck	....	....
3918	Banana Daffy	....	....
3919	Banana Dab	....	....
3920	Banana Nasa	....	....
3921	Banana Net	....	....
3922	Banana Nan	....	....
3923	Banana Name	....	....
3924	Banana Nero	....	....
3925	Banana Nail	....	....
3926	Banana Nash	....	....
3927	Banana Nag	....	....
3928	Banana Navy	....	....
3929	Banana Nab	....	....
3930	Banana Mace	....	....
3931	Banana Mat	....	....
3932	Banana Man	....	....
3933	Banana Ma'am	....	....
3934	Banana Mare	....	....
3935	Banana Mail	....	....
3936	Banana Mash	....	....
3937	Banana Mac	....	....
3938	Banana Mafia	....	....
3939	Banana Map	....	....
3940	Banana Race	....	....
3941	Banana Rat	....	....
3942	Banana Rain	....	....
3943	Banana Ram	....	....
3944	Banana Rare	....	....
3945	Banana Rail	....	....
3946	Banana Rash	....	....
3947	Banana Rack	....	....
3948	Banana Rafia	....	....
3949	Banana Rap	....	....
3950	Banana Lace	....	....
3951	Banana Lad	....	....
3952	Banana Lane	....	....
3953	Banana Lamb	....	....
3954	Banana Lair	....	....
3955	Banana Lily	....	....
3956	Banana Lash	....	....
3957	Banana Lake	....	....
3958	Banana Laugh	....	....
3959	Banana Lab	....	....

NUMBER	SEM[3]	KEY WORD	IMAGE
3960	Banana Chase	....	....
3961	Banana Chat	....	....
3962	Banana Chain	....	....
3963	Banana Chime	....	....
3964	Banana Chair	....	....
3965	Banana Chill	....	....
3966	Banana Chacha	....	....
3967	Banana Check	....	....
3968	Banana Chaff	....	....
3969	Banana Chap	....	....
3970	Banana Case	....	....
3971	Banana Cat	....	....
3972	Banana Can	....	....
3973	Banana Cameo	....	....
3974	Banana Car	....	....
3975	Banana Call	....	....
3976	Banana Cash	....	....
3977	Banana Cake	....	....
3978	Banana Café	....	....
3979	Banana Cab	....	....
3980	Banana Face	....	....
3981	Banana Fat	....	....
3982	Banana Fan	....	....
3983	Banana Fame	....	....
3984	Banana Fair	....	....
3985	Banana Fall	....	....
3986	Banana Fish	....	....
3987	Banana Fake	....	....
3988	Banana Fife	....	....
3989	Banana Fab	....	....
3990	Banana Base	....	....
3991	Banana Bat	....	....
3992	Banana Ban	....	....
3993	Banana Bam!	....	....
3994	Banana Bar	....	....
3995	Banana Ball	....	....
3996	Banana Bash	....	....
3997	Banana Back	....	....
3998	Banana Beef	....	....
3999	Banana Baby	....	....

CHAPTER FIVE

TOUCH

NUMBER	SEM³	KEY WORD	IMAGE
4000	Sand Zoo	....	....
4001	Sand Day	....	....
4002	Sand Noah	....	....
4003	Sand Ma	....	....
4004	Sand Rah	....	....
4005	Sand Law	....	....
4006	Sand Jaw	....	....
4007	Sand Key	....	....
4008	Sand Fee	....	....
4009	Sand Bay	....	....
4010	Sand Daze	....	....
4011	Sand Dad	....	....
4012	Sand Dan	....	....
4013	Sand Dam	....	....
4014	Sand Dare	....	....
4015	Sand Dale	....	....
4016	Sand Dash	....	....
4017	Sand Deck	....	....
4018	Sand Daffy	....	....
4019	Sand Dab	....	....
4020	Sand Nasa	....	....
4021	Sand Net	....	....
4022	Sand Nan	....	....
4023	Sand Name	....	....
4024	Sand Nero	....	....
4025	Sand Nail	....	....
4026	Sand Nash	....	....
4027	Sand Nag	....	....
4028	Sand Navy	....	....
4029	Sand Nab	....	....
4030	Sand Mace	....	....
4031	Sand Mat	....	....
4032	Sand Man	....	....
4033	Sand Ma'am	....	....
4034	Sand Mare	....	....
4035	Sand Mail	....	....
4036	Sand Mash	....	....
4037	Sand Mac	....	....
4038	Sand Mafia	....	....
4039	Sand Map	....	....
4040	Sand Race	....	....
4041	Sand Rat	....	....

NUMBER	SEM³	KEY WORD	IMAGE
4042	Sand Rain	....	....
4043	Sand Ram	....	....
4044	Sand Rare	....	....
4045	Sand Rail	....	....
4046	Sand Rash	....	....
4047	Sand Rack	....	....
4048	Sand Rafia	....	....
4049	Sand Rap	....	....
4050	Sand Lace	....	....
4051	Sand Lad	....	....
4052	Sand Lane	....	....
4053	Sand Lamb	....	....
4054	Sand Lair	....	....
4055	Sand Lily	....	....
4056	Sand Lash	....	....
4057	Sand Lake	....	....
4058	Sand Laugh	....	....
4059	Sand Lab	....	....
4060	Sand Chase	....	....
4061	Sand Chat	....	....
4062	Sand Chain	....	....
4063	Sand Chime	....	....
4064	Sand Chair	....	....
4065	Sand Chill	....	....
4066	Sand Chacha	....	....
4067	Sand Check	....	....
4068	Sand Chaff	....	....
4069	Sand Chap	....	....
4070	Sand Case	....	....
4071	Sand Cat	....	....
4072	Sand Can	....	....
4073	Sand Cameo	....	....
4074	Sand Car	....	....
4075	Sand Call	....	....
4076	Sand Cash	....	....
4077	Sand Cake	....	....
4078	Sand Café	....	....
4079	Sand Cab	....	....
4080	Sand Face	....	....
4081	Sand Fat	....	....
4082	Sand Fan	....	....
4083	Sand Fame	....	....
4084	Sand Fair	....	....
4085	Sand Fall	....	....
4086	Sand Fish	....	....
4087	Sand Fake	....	....
4088	Sand Fife	....	....
4089	Sand Fab	....	....
4090	Sand Base	....	....
4091	Sand Bat	....	....
4092	Sand Ban	....	....
4093	Sand Bam!	....	....
4094	Sand Bar	....	....
4095	Sand Ball	....	....

NUMBER	SEM³	KEY WORD	IMAGE
4096	Sand Bash	....	....
4097	Sand Back	....	....
4098	Sand Beef	....	....
4099	Sand Baby	....	....
4100	Damp Zoo	....	....
4101	Damp Day	....	....
4102	Damp Noah	....	....
4103	Damp Ma	....	....
4104	Damp Rah	....	....
4105	Damp Law	....	....
4106	Damp Jaw	....	....
4107	Damp Key	....	....
4108	Damp Fee	....	....
4109	Damp Bay	....	....
4110	Damp Daze	....	....
4111	Damp Dad	....	....
4112	Damp Dan	....	....
4113	Damp Dam	....	....
4114	Damp Dare	....	....
4115	Damp Dale	....	....
4116	Damp Dash	....	....
4117	Damp Deck	....	....
4118	Damp Daffy	....	....
4119	Damp Dab	....	....
4120	Damp Nasa	....	....
4121	Damp Net	....	....
4122	Damp Nan	....	....
4123	Damp Name	....	....
4124	Damp Nero	....	....
4125	Damp Nail	....	....
4126	Damp Nash	....	....
4127	Damp Nag	....	....
4128	Damp Navy	....	....
4129	Damp Nab	....	....
4130	Damp Mace	....	....
4131	Damp Mat	....	....
4132	Damp Man	....	....
4133	Damp Ma'am	....	....
4134	Damp Mare	....	....
4135	Damp Mail	....	....
4136	Damp Mash	....	....
4137	Damp Mac	....	....
4138	Damp Mafia	....	....
4139	Damp Map	....	....
4140	Damp Race	....	....
4141	Damp Rat	....	....
4142	Damp Rain	....	....
4143	Damp Ram	....	....
4144	Damp Rare	....	....
4145	Damp Rail	....	....
4146	Damp Rash	....	....
4147	Damp Rack	....	....
4148	Damp Rafia	....	....
4149	Damp Rap	....	....

NUMBER	SEM³	KEY WORD	IMAGE
4150	Damp Lace	....	....
4151	Damp Lad	....	....
4152	Damp Lane	....	....
4153	Damp Lamb	....	....
4154	Damp Lair	....	....
4155	Damp Lily	....	....
4156	Damp Lash	....	....
4157	Damp Lake	....	....
4158	Damp Laugh	....	....
4159	Damp Lab	....	....
4160	Damp Chase	....	....
4161	Damp Chat	....	....
4162	Damp Chain	....	....
4163	Damp Chime	....	....
4164	Damp Chair	....	....
4165	Damp Chill	....	....
4166	Damp Chacha	....	....
4167	Damp Check	....	....
4168	Damp Chaff	....	....
4169	Damp Chap	....	....
4170	Damp Case	....	....
4171	Damp Cat	....	....
4172	Damp Can	....	....
4173	Damp Cameo	....	....
4174	Damp Car	....	....
4175	Damp Call	....	....
4176	Damp Cash	....	....
4177	Damp Cake	....	....
4178	Damp Café	....	....
4179	Damp Cab	....	....
4180	Damp Face	....	....
4181	Damp Fat	....	....
4182	Damp Fan	....	....
4183	Damp Fame	....	....
4184	Damp Fair	....	....
4185	Damp Fall	....	....
4186	Damp Fish	....	....
4187	Damp Fake	....	....
4188	Damp Fife	....	....
4189	Damp Fab	....	....
4190	Damp Base	....	....
4191	Damp Bat	....	....
4192	Damp Ban	....	....
4193	Damp Bam!	....	....
4194	Damp Bar	....	....
4195	Damp Ball	....	....
4196	Damp Bash	....	....
4197	Damp Back	....	....
4198	Damp Beef	....	....
4199	Damp Baby	....	....
4200	Honey Zoo	....	....
4201	Honey Day	....	....
4202	Honey Noah	....	....
4203	Honey Ma	....	....

NUMBER	SEM[3]	KEY WORD	IMAGE
4204	Honey Rah	....	....
4205	Honey Law	....	....
4206	Honey Jaw	....	....
4207	Honey Key	....	....
4208	Honey Fee	....	....
4209	Honey Bay	....	....
4210	Honey Daze	....	....
4211	Honey Dad	....	....
4212	Honey Dan	....	....
4213	Honey Dam	....	....
4214	Honey Dare	....	....
4215	Honey Dale	....	....
4216	Honey Dash	....	....
4217	Honey Deck	....	....
4218	Honey Daffy	....	....
4219	Honey Dab	....	....
4220	Honey Nasa	....	....
4221	Honey Net	....	....
4222	Honey Nan	....	....
4223	Honey Name	....	....
4224	Honey Nero	....	....
4225	Honey Nail	....	....
4226	Honey Nash	....	....
4227	Honey Nag	....	....
4228	Honey Navy	....	....
4229	Honey Nab	....	....
4230	Honey Mace	....	....
4231	Honey Mat	....	....
4232	Honey Man	....	....
4233	Honey Ma'am	....	....
4234	Honey Mare	....	....
4235	Honey Mail	....	....
4236	Honey Mash	....	....
4237	Honey Mac	....	....
4238	Honey Mafia	....	....
4239	Honey Map	....	....
4240	Honey Race	....	....
4241	Honey Rat	....	....
4242	Honey Rain	....	....
4243	Honey Ram	....	....
4244	Honey Rare	....	....
4245	Honey Rail	....	....
4246	Honey Rash	....	....
4247	Honey Rack	....	....
4248	Honey Rafia	....	....
4249	Honey Rap	....	....
4250	Honey Lace	....	....
4251	Honey Lad	....	....
4252	Honey Lane	....	....
4253	Honey Lamb	....	....
4254	Honey Lair	....	....
4255	Honey Lily	....	....
4256	Honey Lash	....	....
4257	Honey Lake	....	....

NUMBER	SEM³	KEY WORD	IMAGE
4258	Honey Laugh	....	....
4259	Honey Lab	....	....
4260	Honey Chase	....	....
4261	Honey Chat	....	....
4262	Honey Chain	....	....
4263	Honey Chime	....	....
4264	Honey Chair	....	....
4265	Honey Chill	....	....
4266	Honey Chacha	....	....
4267	Honey Check	....	....
4268	Honey Chaff	....	....
4269	Honey Chap	....	....
4270	Honey Case	....	....
4271	Honey Cat	....	....
4272	Honey Can	....	....
4273	Honey Cameo	....	....
4274	Honey Car	....	....
4275	Honey Call	....	....
4276	Honey Cash	....	....
4277	Honey Cake	....	....
4278	Honey Café	....	....
4279	Honey Cab	....	....
4280	Honey Face	....	....
4281	Honey Fat	....	....
4282	Honey Fan	....	....
4283	Honey Fame	....	....
4284	Honey Fair	....	....
4285	Honey Fall	....	....
4286	Honey Fish	....	....
4287	Honey Fake	....	....
4288	Honey Fife	....	....
4289	Honey Fab	....	....
4290	Honey Base	....	....
4291	Honey Bat	....	....
4292	Honey Ban	....	....
4293	Honey Bam!	....	....
4294	Honey Bar	....	....
4295	Honey Ball	....	....
4296	Honey Bash	....	....
4297	Honey Back	....	....
4298	Honey Beef	....	....
4299	Honey Baby	....	....
4300	Mud Zoo	....	....
4301	Mud Day	....	....
4302	Mud Noah	....	....
4303	Mud Ma	....	....
4304	Mud Rah	....	....
4305	Mud Law	....	....
4306	Mud Jaw	....	....
4307	Mud Key	....	....
4308	Mud Fee	....	....
4309	Mud Bay	....	....
4310	Mud Daze	....	....
4311	Mud Dad	....	....

NUMBER	SEM³	KEY WORD	IMAGE
4312	Mud Dan	....	....
4313	Mud Dam	....	....
4314	Mud Dare	....	....
4315	Mud Dale	....	....
4316	Mud Dash	....	....
4317	Mud Deck	....	....
4318	Mud Daffy	....	....
4319	Mud Dab	....	....
4320	Mud Nasa	....	....
4321	Mud Net	....	....
4322	Mud Nan	....	....
4323	Mud Name	....	....
4324	Mud Nero	....	....
4325	Mud Nail	....	....
4326	Mud Nash	....	....
4327	Mud Nag	....	....
4328	Mud Navy	....	....
4329	Mud Nab	....	....
4330	Mud Mace	....	....
4331	Mud Mat	....	....
4332	Mud Man	....	....
4333	Mud Ma'am	....	....
4334	Mud Mare	....	....
4335	Mud Mail	....	....
4336	Mud Mash	....	....
4337	Mud Mac	....	....
4338	Mud Mafia	....	....
4339	Mud Map	....	....
4340	Mud Race	....	....
4341	Mud Rat	....	....
4342	Mud Rain	....	....
4343	Mud Ram	....	....
4344	Mud Rare	....	....
4345	Mud Rail	....	....
4346	Mud Rash	....	....
4347	Mud Rack	....	....
4348	Mud Rafia	....	....
4349	Mud Rap	....	....
4350	Mud Lace	....	....
4351	Mud Lad	....	....
4352	Mud Lane	....	....
4353	Mud Lamb	....	....
4354	Mud Lair	....	....
4355	Mud Lily	....	....
4356	Mud Lash	....	....
4357	Mud Lake	....	....
4358	Mud Laugh	....	....
4359	Mud Lab	....	....
4360	Mud Chase	....	....
4361	Mud Chat	....	....
4362	Mud Chain	....	....
4363	Mud Chime	....	....
4364	Mud Chair	....	....
4365	Mud Chill	....	....

NUMBER	SEM³	KEY WORD	IMAGE
4366	Mud Chacha	....	....
4367	Mud Check	....	....
4368	Mud Chaff	....	....
4369	Mud Chap	....	....
4370	Mud Case	....	....
4371	Mud Cat	....	....
4372	Mud Can	....	....
4373	Mud Cameo	....	....
4374	Mud Car	....	....
4375	Mud Call	....	....
4376	Mud Cash	....	....
4377	Mud Cake	....	....
4378	Mud Café	....	....
4379	Mud Cab	....	....
4380	Mud Face	....	....
4381	Mud Fat	....	....
4382	Mud Fan	....	....
4383	Mud Fame	....	....
4384	Mud Fair	....	....
4385	Mud Fall	....	....
4386	Mud Fish	....	....
4387	Mud Fake	....	....
4388	Mud Fife	....	....
4389	Mud Fab	....	....
4390	Mud Base	....	....
4391	Mud Bat	....	....
4392	Mud Ban	....	....
4393	Mud Bam!	....	....
4394	Mud Bar	....	....
4395	Mud Ball	....	....
4396	Mud Bash	....	....
4397	Mud Back	....	....
4398	Mud Beef	....	....
4399	Mud Baby	....	....
4400	Rock Zoo	....	....
4401	Rock Day	....	....
4402	Rock Noah	....	....
4403	Rock Ma	....	....
4404	Rock Rah	....	....
4405	Rock Law	....	....
4406	Rock Jaw	....	....
4407	Rock Key	....	....
4408	Rock Fee	....	....
4409	Rock Bay	....	....
4410	Rock Daze	....	....
4411	Rock Dad	....	....
4412	Rock Dan	....	....
4413	Rock Dam	....	....
4414	Rock Dare	....	....
4415	Rock Dale	....	....
4416	Rock Dash	....	....
4417	Rock Deck	....	....
4418	Rock Daffy	....	....
4419	Rock Dab	....	....

96

NUMBER	SEM³	KEY WORD	IMAGE
4420	Rock Nasa	....	....
4421	Rock Net	....	....
4422	Rock Nan	....	....
4423	Rock Name	....	....
4424	Rock Nero	....	....
4425	Rock Nail	....	....
4426	Rock Nash	....	....
4427	Rock Nag	....	....
4428	Rock Navy	....	....
4429	Rock Nab	....	....
4430	Rock Mace	....	....
4431	Rock Mat	....	....
4432	Rock Man	....	....
4433	Rock Ma'am	....	....
4434	Rock Mare	....	....
4435	Rock Mail	....	....
4436	Rock Mash	....	....
4437	Rock Mac	....	....
4438	Rock Mafia	....	....
4439	Rock Map	....	....
4440	Rock Race	....	....
4441	Rock Rat	....	....
4442	Rock Rain	....	....
4443	Rock Ram	....	....
4444	Rock Rare	....	....
4445	Rock Rail	....	....
4446	Rock Rash	....	....
4447	Rock Rack	....	....
4448	Rock Rafia	....	....
4449	Rock Rap	....	....
4450	Rock Lace	....	....
4451	Rock Lad	....	....
4452	Rock Lane	....	....
4453	Rock Lamb	....	....
4454	Rock Lair	....	....
4455	Rock Lily	....	....
4456	Rock Lash	....	....
4457	Rock Lake	....	....
4458	Rock Laugh	....	....
4459	Rock Lab	....	....
4460	Rock Chase	....	....
4461	Rock Chat	....	....
4462	Rock Chain	....	....
4463	Rock Chime	....	....
4464	Rock Chair	....	....
4465	Rock Chill	....	....
4466	Rock Chacha	....	....
4467	Rock Check	....	....
4468	Rock Chaff	....	....
4469	Rock Chap	....	....
4470	Rock Case	....	....
4471	Rock Cat	....	....
4472	Rock Can	....	....
4473	Rock Cameo	....	....

NUMBER	SEM³	KEY WORD	IMAGE
4474	Rock Car	....	....
4475	Rock Call	....	....
4476	Rock Cash	....	....
4477	Rock Cake	....	....
4478	Rock Café	....	....
4479	Rock Cab	....	....
4480	Rock Face	....	....
4481	Rock Fat	....	....
4482	Rock Fan	....	....
4483	Rock Fame	....	....
4484	Rock Fair	....	....
4485	Rock Fall	....	....
4486	Rock Fish	....	....
4487	Rock Fake	....	....
4488	Rock Fife	....	....
4489	Rock Fab	....	....
4490	Rock Base	....	....
4491	Rock Bat	....	....
4492	Rock Ban	....	....
4493	Rock Bam!	....	....
4494	Rock Bar	....	....
4495	Rock Ball	....	....
4496	Rock Bash	....	....
4497	Rock Back	....	....
4498	Rock Beef	....	....
4499	Rock Baby	....	....
4500	Oil Zoo	....	....
4501	Oil Day	....	....
4502	Oil Noah	....	....
4503	Oil Ma	....	....
4504	Oil Rah	....	....
4505	Oil Law	....	....
4506	Oil Jaw	....	....
4507	Oil Key	....	....
4508	Oil Fee	....	....
4509	Oil Bay	....	....
4510	Oil Daze	....	....
4511	Oil Dad	....	....
4512	Oil Dan	....	....
4513	Oil Dam	....	....
4514	Oil Dare	....	....
4515	Oil Dale	....	....
4516	Oil Dash	....	....
4517	Oil Deck	....	....
4518	Oil Daffy	....	....
4519	Oil Dab	....	....
4520	Oil Nasa	....	....
4521	Oil Net	....	....
4522	Oil Nan	....	....
4523	Oil Name	....	....
4524	Oil Nero	....	....
4525	Oil Nail	....	....
4526	Oil Nash	....	....
4527	Oil Nag	....	....

NUMBER	SEM^3	KEY WORD	IMAGE
4528	Oil Navy	....	....
4529	Oil Nab	....	....
4530	Oil Mace	....	....
4531	Oil Mat	....	....
4532	Oil Man	....	....
4533	Oil Ma'am	....	....
4534	Oil Mare	....	....
4535	Oil Mail	....	....
4536	Oil Mash	....	....
4537	Oil Mac	....	....
4538	Oil Mafia	....	....
4539	Oil Map	....	....
4540	Oil Race	....	....
4541	Oil Rat	....	....
4542	Oil Rain	....	....
4543	Oil Ram	....	....
4544	Oil Rare	....	....
4545	Oil Rail	....	....
4546	Oil Rash	....	....
4547	Oil Rack	....	....
4548	Oil Rafia	....	....
4549	Oil Rap	....	....
4550	Oil Lace	....	....
4551	Oil Lad	....	....
4552	Oil Lane	....	....
4553	Oil Lamb	....	....
4554	Oil Lair	....	....
4555	Oil Lily	....	....
4556	Oil Lash	....	....
4557	Oil Lake	....	....
4558	Oil Laugh	....	....
4559	Oil Lab	....	....
4560	Oil Chase	....	....
4561	Oil Chat	....	....
4562	Oil Chain	....	....
4563	Oil Chime	....	....
4564	Oil Chair	....	....
4565	Oil Chill	....	....
4566	Oil Chacha	....	....
4567	Oil Check	....	....
4568	Oil Chaff	....	....
4569	Oil Chap	....	....
4570	Oil Case	....	....
4571	Oil Cat	....	....
4572	Oil Can	....	....
4573	Oil Cameo	....	....
4574	Oil Car	....	....
4575	Oil Call	....	....
4576	Oil Cash	....	....
4577	Oil Cake	....	....
4578	Oil Café	....	....
4579	Oil Cab	....	....
4580	Oil Face	....	....
4581	Oil Fat	....	....

NUMBER	SEM³	KEY WORD	IMAGE
4582	Oil Fan	....	....
4583	Oil Fame	....	....
4584	Oil Fair	....	....
4585	Oil Fall	....	....
4586	Oil Fish	....	....
4587	Oil Fake	....	....
4588	Oil Fife	....	....
4589	Oil Fab	....	....
4590	Oil Base	....	....
4591	Oil Bat	....	....
4592	Oil Ban	....	....
4593	Oil Bam!	....	....
4594	Oil Bar	....	....
4595	Oil Ball	....	....
4596	Oil Bash	....	....
4597	Oil Back	....	....
4598	Oil Beef	....	....
4599	Oil Baby	....	....
4600	Jelly Zoo	....	....
4601	Jelly Day	....	....
4602	Jelly Noah	....	....
4603	Jelly Ma	....	....
4604	Jelly Rah	....	....
4605	Jelly Law	....	....
4606	Jelly Jaw	....	....
4607	Jelly Key	....	....
4608	Jelly Fee	....	....
4609	Jelly Bay	....	....
4610	Jelly Daze	....	....
4611	Jelly Dad	....	....
4612	Jelly Dan	....	....
4613	Jelly Dam	....	....
4614	Jelly Dare	....	....
4615	Jelly Dale	....	....
4616	Jelly Dash	....	....
4617	Jelly Deck	....	....
4618	Jelly Daffy	....	....
4619	Jelly Dab	....	....
4620	Jelly Nasa	....	....
4621	Jelly Net	....	....
4622	Jelly Nan	....	....
4623	Jelly Name	....	....
4624	Jelly Nero	....	....
4625	Jelly Nail	....	....
4626	Jelly Nash	....	....
4627	Jelly Nag	....	....
4628	Jelly Navy	....	....
4629	Jelly Nab	....	....
4630	Jelly Mace	....	....
4631	Jelly Mat	....	....
4632	Jelly Man	....	....
4633	Jelly Ma'am	....	....
4634	Jelly Mare	....	....
4635	Jelly Mail	....	....

NUMBER	SEM[3]	KEY WORD	IMAGE
4636	Jelly Mash	....	....
4637	Jelly Mac	....	....
4638	Jelly Mafia	....	....
4639	Jelly Map	....	....
4640	Jelly Race	....	....
4641	Jelly Rat	....	....
4642	Jelly Rain	....	....
4643	Jelly Ram	....	....
4644	Jelly Rare	....	....
4645	Jelly Rail	....	....
4646	Jelly Rash	....	....
4647	Jelly Rack	....	....
4648	Jelly Rafia	....	....
4649	Jelly Rap	....	....
4650	Jelly Lace	....	....
4651	Jelly Lad	....	....
4652	Jelly Lane	....	....
4653	Jelly Lamb	....	....
4654	Jelly Lair	....	....
4655	Jelly Lily	....	....
4656	Jelly Lash	....	....
4657	Jelly Lake	....	....
4658	Jelly Laugh	....	....
4659	Jelly Lab	....	....
4660	Jelly Chase	....	....
4661	Jelly Chat	....	....
4662	Jelly Chain	....	....
4663	Jelly Chime	....	....
4664	Jelly Chair	....	....
4665	Jelly Chill	....	....
4666	Jelly Chacha	....	....
4667	Jelly Check	....	....
4668	Jelly Chaff	....	....
4669	Jelly Chap	....	....
4670	Jelly Case	....	....
4671	Jelly Cat	....	....
4672	Jelly Can	....	....
4673	Jelly Cameo	....	....
4674	Jelly Car	....	....
4675	Jelly Call	....	....
4676	Jelly Cash	....	....
4677	Jelly Cake	....	....
4678	Jelly Café	....	....
4679	Jelly Cab	....	....
4680	Jelly Face	....	....
4681	Jelly Fat	....	....
4682	Jelly Fan	....	....
4683	Jelly Fame	....	....
4684	Jelly Fair	....	....
4685	Jelly Fall	....	....
4686	Jelly Fish	....	....
4687	Jelly Fake	....	....
4688	Jelly Fife	....	....
4689	Jelly Fab	....	....

NUMBER	SEM[3]	KEY WORD	IMAGE
4690	Jelly Base	....	....
4691	Jelly Bat	....	....
4692	Jelly Ban	....	....
4693	Jelly Bam!	....	....
4694	Jelly Bar	....	....
4695	Jelly Ball	....	....
4696	Jelly Bash	....	....
4697	Jelly Back	....	....
4698	Jelly Beef	....	....
4699	Jelly Baby	....	....
4700	Grass Zoo	....	....
4701	Grass Day	....	....
4702	Grass Noah	....	....
4703	Grass Ma	....	....
4704	Grass Rah	....	....
4705	Grass Law	....	....
4706	Grass Jaw	....	....
4707	Grass Key	....	....
4708	Grass Fee	....	....
4709	Grass Bay	....	....
4710	Grass Daze	....	....
4711	Grass Dad	....	....
4712	Grass Dan	....	....
4713	Grass Dam	....	....
4714	Grass Dare	....	....
4715	Grass Dale	....	....
4716	Grass Dash	....	....
4717	Grass Deck	....	....
4718	Grass Daffy	....	....
4719	Grass Dab	....	....
4720	Grass Nasa	....	....
4721	Grass Net	....	....
4722	Grass Nan	....	....
4723	Grass Name	....	....
4724	Grass Nero	....	....
4725	Grass Nail	....	....
4726	Grass Nash	....	....
4727	Grass Nag	....	....
4728	Grass Navy	....	....
4729	Grass Nab	....	....
4730	Grass Mace	....	....
4731	Grass Mat	....	....
4732	Grass Man	....	....
4733	Grass Ma'am	....	....
4734	Grass Mare	....	....
4735	Grass Mail	....	....
4736	Grass Mash	....	....
4737	Grass Mac	....	....
4738	Grass Mafia	....	....
4739	Grass Map	....	....
4740	Grass Race	....	....
4741	Grass Rat	....	....
4742	Grass Rain	....	....
4743	Grass Ram	....	....

NUMBER	SEM³	KEY WORD	IMAGE
4744	Grass Rare	....	....
4745	Grass Rail	....	....
4746	Grass Rash	....	....
4747	Grass Rack	....	....
4748	Grass Rafia	....	....
4749	Grass Rap	....	....
4750	Grass Lace	....	....
4751	Grass Lad	....	....
4752	Grass Lane	....	....
4753	Grass Lamb	....	....
4754	Grass Lair	....	....
4755	Grass Lily	....	....
4756	Grass Lash	....	....
4757	Grass Lake	....	....
4758	Grass Laugh	....	....
4759	Grass Lab	....	....
4760	Grass Chase	....	....
4761	Grass Chat	....	....
4762	Grass Chain	....	....
4763	Grass Chime	....	....
4764	Grass Chair	....	....
4765	Grass Chill	....	....
4766	Grass Chacha	....	....
4767	Grass Check	....	....
4768	Grass Chaff	....	....
4769	Grass Chap	....	....
4770	Grass Case	....	....
4771	Grass Cat	....	....
4772	Grass Can	....	....
4773	Grass Cameo	....	....
4774	Grass Car	....	....
4775	Grass Call	....	....
4776	Grass Cash	....	....
4777	Grass Cake	....	....
4778	Grass Café	....	....
4779	Grass Cab	....	....
4780	Grass Face	....	....
4781	Grass Fat	....	....
4782	Grass Fan	....	....
4783	Grass Fame	....	....
4784	Grass Fair	....	....
4785	Grass Fall	....	....
4786	Grass Fish	....	....
4787	Grass Fake	....	....
4788	Grass Fife	....	....
4789	Grass Fab	....	....
4790	Grass Base	....	....
4791	Grass Bat	....	....
4792	Grass Ban	....	....
4793	Grass Bam!	....	....
4794	Grass Bar	....	....
4795	Grass Ball	....	....
4796	Grass Bash	....	....
4797	Grass Back	....	....

NUMBER	SEM[3]	KEY WORD	IMAGE
4798	Grass Beef	....	....
4799	Grass Baby	....	....
4800	Velvet Zoo	....	....
4801	Velvet Day	....	....
4802	Velvet Noah	....	....
4803	Velvet Ma	....	....
4804	Velvet Rah	....	....
4805	Velvet Law	....	....
4806	Velvet Jaw	....	....
4807	Velvet Key	....	....
4808	Velvet Fee	....	....
4809	Velvet Bay	....	....
4810	Velvet Daze	....	....
4811	Velvet Dad	....	....
4812	Velvet Dan	....	....
4813	Velvet Dam	....	....
4814	Velvet Dare	....	....
4815	Velvet Dale	....	....
4816	Velvet Dash	....	....
4817	Velvet Deck	....	....
4818	Velvet Daffy	....	....
4819	Velvet Dab	....	....
4820	Velvet Nasa	....	....
4821	Velvet Net	....	....
4822	Velvet Nan	....	....
4823	Velvet Name	....	....
4824	Velvet Nero	....	....
4825	Velvet Nail	....	....
4826	Velvet Nash	....	....
4827	Velvet Nag	....	....
4828	Velvet Navy	....	....
4829	Velvet Nab	....	....
4830	Velvet Mace	....	....
4831	Velvet Mat	....	....
4832	Velvet Man	....	....
4833	Velvet Ma'am	....	....
4834	Velvet Mare	....	....
4835	Velvet Mail	....	....
4836	Velvet Mash	....	....
4837	Velvet Mac	....	....
4838	Velvet Mafia	....	....
4839	Velvet Map	....	....
4840	Velvet Race	....	....
4841	Velvet Rat	....	....
4842	Velvet Rain	....	....
4843	Velvet Ram	....	....
4844	Velvet Rare	....	....
4845	Velvet Rail	....	....
4846	Velvet Rash	....	....
4847	Velvet Rack	....	....
4848	Velvet Rafia	....	....
4849	Velvet Rap	....	....
4850	Velvet Lace	....	....
4851	Velvet Lad	....	....

NUMBER	SEM³	KEY WORD	IMAGE
4852	Velvet Lane	....	....
4853	Velvet Lamb	....	....
4854	Velvet Lair	....	....
4855	Velvet Lily	....	....
4856	Velvet Lash	....	....
4857	Velvet Lake	....	....
4858	Velvet Laugh	....	....
4859	Velvet Lab	....	....
4860	Velvet Chase	....	....
4861	Velvet Chat	....	....
4862	Velvet Chain	....	....
4863	Velvet Chime	....	....
4864	Velvet Chair	....	....
4865	Velvet Chill	....	....
4866	Velvet Chacha	....	....
4867	Velvet Check	....	....
4868	Velvet Chaff	....	....
4869	Velvet Chap	....	....
4870	Velvet Case	....	....
4871	Velvet Cat	....	....
4872	Velvet Can	....	....
4873	Velvet Cameo	....	....
4874	Velvet Car	....	....
4875	Velvet Call	....	....
4876	Velvet Cash	....	....
4877	Velvet Cake	....	....
4878	Velvet Café	....	....
4879	Velvet Cab	....	....
4880	Velvet Face	....	....
4881	Velvet Fat	....	....
4882	Velvet Fan	....	....
4883	Velvet Fame	....	....
4884	Velvet Fair	....	....
4885	Velvet Fall	....	....
4886	Velvet Fish	....	....
4887	Velvet Fake	....	....
4888	Velvet Fife	....	....
4889	Velvet Fab	....	....
4890	Velvet Base	....	....
4891	Velvet Bat	....	....
4892	Velvet Ban	....	....
4893	Velvet Bam!	....	....
4894	Velvet Bar	....	....
4895	Velvet Ball	....	....
4896	Velvet Bash	....	....
4897	Velvet Back	....	....
4898	Velvet Beef	....	....
4899	Velvet Baby	....	....
4900	Bark Zoo	....	....
4901	Bark Day	....	....
4902	Bark Noah	....	....
4903	Bark Ma	....	....
4904	Bark Rah	....	....
4905	Bark Law	....	....

NUMBER	SEM³	KEY WORD	IMAGE
4906	Bark Jaw	....	....
4907	Bark Key	....	....
4908	Bark Fee	....	....
4909	Bark Bay	....	....
4910	Bark Daze	....	....
4911	Bark Dad	....	....
4912	Bark Dan	....	....
4913	Bark Dam	....	....
4914	Bark Dare	....	....
4915	Bark Dale	....	....
4916	Bark Dash	....	....
4917	Bark Deck	....	....
4918	Bark Daffy	....	....
4919	Bark Dab	....	....
4920	Bark Nasa	....	....
4921	Bark Net	....	....
4922	Bark Nan	....	....
4923	Bark Name	....	....
4924	Bark Nero	....	....
4925	Bark Nail	....	....
4926	Bark Nash	....	....
4927	Bark Nag	....	....
4928	Bark Navy	....	....
4929	Bark Nab	....	....
4930	Bark Mace	....	....
4931	Bark Mat	....	....
4932	Bark Man	....	....
4933	Bark Ma'am	....	....
4934	Bark Mare	....	....
4935	Bark Mail	....	....
4936	Bark Mash	....	....
4937	Bark Mac	....	....
4938	Bark Mafia	....	....
4939	Bark Map	....	....
4940	Bark Race	....	....
4941	Bark Rat	....	....
4942	Bark Rain	....	....
4943	Bark Ram	....	....
4944	Bark Rare	....	....
4945	Bark Rail	....	....
4946	Bark Rash	....	....
4947	Bark Rack	....	....
4948	Bark Rafia	....	....
4949	Bark Rap	....	....
4950	Bark Lace	....	....
4951	Bark Lad	....	....
4952	Bark Lane	....	....
4953	Bark Lamb	....	....
4954	Bark Lair	....	....
4955	Bark Lily	....	....
4956	Bark Lash	....	....
4957	Bark Lake	....	....
4958	Bark Laugh	....	....
4959	Bark Lab	....	....

NUMBER	SEM³	KEY WORD	IMAGE
4960	Bark Chase	....	....
4961	Bark Chat	....	....
4962	Bark Chain	....	....
4963	Bark Chime	....	....
4964	Bark Chair	....	....
4965	Bark Chill	....	....
4966	Bark Chacha	....	....
4967	Bark Check	....	....
4968	Bark Chaff	....	....
4969	Bark Chap	....	....
4970	Bark Case	....	....
4971	Bark Cat	....	....
4972	Bark Can	....	....
4973	Bark Cameo	....	....
4974	Bark Car	....	....
4975	Bark Call	....	....
4976	Bark Cash	....	....
4977	Bark Cake	....	....
4978	Bark Café	....	....
4979	Bark Cab	....	....
4980	Bark Face	....	....
4981	Bark Fat	....	....
4982	Bark Fan	....	....
4983	Bark Fame	....	....
4984	Bark Fair	....	....
4985	Bark Fall	....	....
4986	Bark Fish	....	....
4987	Bark Fake	....	....
4988	Bark Fife	....	....
4989	Bark Fab	....	....
4990	Bark Base	....	....
4991	Bark Bat	....	....
4992	Bark Ban	....	....
4993	Bark Bam!	....	....
4994	Bark Bar	....	....
4995	Bark Ball	....	....
4996	Bark Bash	....	....
4997	Bark Back	....	....
4998	Bark Beef	....	....
4999	Bark Baby	....	....

CHAPTER SIX

SENSATION

NUMBER	SEM^3	KEY WORD	IMAGE
5000	Swimming Zoo	....	....
5001	Swimming Day	....	....
5002	Swimming Noah	....	....
5003	Swimming Ma	....	....
5004	Swimming Rah	....	....
5005	Swimming Law	....	....
5006	Swimming Jaw	....	....
5007	Swimming Key	....	....
5008	Swimming Fee	....	....
5009	Swimming Bay	....	....
5010	Swimming Daze	....	....
5011	Swimming Dad	....	....
5012	Swimming Dan	....	....
5013	Swimming Dam	....	....
5014	Swimming Dare	....	....
5015	Swimming Dale	....	....
5016	Swimming Dash	....	....
5017	Swimming Deck	....	....
5018	Swimming Daffy	....	....
5019	Swimming Dab	....	....
5020	Swimming Nasa	....	....
5021	Swimming Net	....	....
5022	Swimming Nan	....	....
5023	Swimming Name	....	....
5024	Swimming Nero	....	....
5025	Swimming Nail	....	....
5026	Swimming Nash	....	....
5027	Swimming Nag	....	....
5028	Swimming Navy	....	....
5029	Swimming Nab	....	....
5030	Swimming Mace	....	....
5031	Swimming Mat	....	....
5032	Swimming Man	....	....
5033	Swimming Ma'am	....	....
5034	Swimming Mare	....	....
5035	Swimming Mail	....	....
5036	Swimming Mash	....	....
5037	Swimming Mac	....	....
5038	Swimming Mafia	....	....
5039	Swimming Map	....	....
5040	Swimming Race	....	....
5041	Swimming Rat	....	....

NUMBER	SEM³	KEY WORD	IMAGE
5042	Swimming Rain	....	....
5043	Swimming Ram	....	....
5044	Swimming Rare	....	....
5045	Swimming Rail	....	....
5046	Swimming Rash	....	....
5047	Swimming Rack	....	....
5048	Swimming Rafia	....	....
5049	Swimming Rap	....	....
5050	Swimming Lace	....	....
5051	Swimming Lad	....	....
5052	Swimming Lane	....	....
5053	Swimming Lamb	....	....
5054	Swimming Lair	....	....
5055	Swimming Lily	....	....
5056	Swimming Lash	....	....
5057	Swimming Lake	....	....
5058	Swimming Laugh	....	....
5059	Swimming Lab	....	....
5060	Swimming Chase	....	....
5061	Swimming Chat	....	....
5062	Swimming Chain	....	....
5063	Swimming Chime	....	....
5064	Swimming Chair	....	....
5065	Swimming Chill	....	....
5066	Swimming Chacha	....	....
5067	Swimming Check	....	....
5068	Swimming Chaff	....	....
5069	Swimming Chap	....	....
5070	Swimming Case	....	....
5071	Swimming Cat	....	....
5072	Swimming Can	....	....
5073	Swimming Cameo	....	....
5074	Swimming Car	....	....
5075	Swimming Call	....	....
5076	Swimming Cash	....	....
5077	Swimming Cake	....	....
5078	Swimming Café	....	....
5079	Swimming Cab	....	....
5080	Swimming Face	....	....
5081	Swimming Fat	....	....
5082	Swimming Fan	....	....
5083	Swimming Fame	....	....
5084	Swimming Fair	....	....
5085	Swimming Fall	....	....
5086	Swimming Fish	....	....
5087	Swimming Fake	....	....
5088	Swimming Fife	....	....
5089	Swimming Fab	....	....
5090	Swimming Base	....	....
5091	Swimming Bat	....	....
5092	Swimming Ban	....	....
5093	Swimming Bam!	....	....
5094	Swimming Bar	....	....
5095	Swimming Ball	....	....

NUMBER	SEM[3]	KEY WORD	IMAGE
5096	Swimming Bash		
5097	Swimming Back		
5098	Swimming Beef		
5099	Swimming Baby		
5100	Dancing Zoo		
5101	Dancing Day		
5102	Dancing Noah		
5103	Dancing Ma		
5104	Dancing Rah		
5105	Dancing Law		
5106	Dancing Jaw		
5107	Dancing Key		
5108	Dancing Fee		
5109	Dancing Bay		
5110	Dancing Daze		
5111	Dancing Dad		
5112	Dancing Dan		
5113	Dancing Dam		
5114	Dancing Dare		
5115	Dancing Dale		
5116	Dancing Dash		
5117	Dancing Deck		
5118	Dancing Daffy		
5119	Dancing Dab		
5120	Dancing Nasa		
5121	Dancing Net		
5122	Dancing Nan		
5123	Dancing Name		
5124	Dancing Nero		
5125	Dancing Nail		
5126	Dancing Nash		
5127	Dancing Nag		
5128	Dancing Navy		
5129	Dancing Nab		
5130	Dancing Mace		
5131	Dancing Mat		
5132	Dancing Man		
5133	Dancing Ma'am		
5134	Dancing Mare		
5135	Dancing Mail		
5136	Dancing Mash		
5137	Dancing Mac		
5138	Dancing Mafia		
5139	Dancing Map		
5140	Dancing Race		
5141	Dancing Rat		
5142	Dancing Rain		
5143	Dancing Ram		
5144	Dancing Rare		
5145	Dancing Rail		
5146	Dancing Rash		
5147	Dancing Rack		
5148	Dancing Rafia		
5149	Dancing Rap		

NUMBER	SEM³	KEY WORD	IMAGE
5150	Dancing Lace	....	....
5151	Dancing Lad	....	....
5152	Dancing Lane	....	....
5153	Dancing Lamb	....	....
5154	Dancing Lair	....	....
5155	Dancing Lily	....	....
5156	Dancing Lash	....	....
5157	Dancing Lake	....	....
5158	Dancing Laugh	....	....
5159	Dancing Lab	....	....
5160	Dancing Chase	....	....
5161	Dancing Chat	....	....
5162	Dancing Chain	....	....
5163	Dancing Chime	....	....
5164	Dancing Chair	....	....
5165	Dancing Chill	....	....
5166	Dancing Chacha	....	....
5167	Dancing Check	....	....
5168	Dancing Chaff	....	....
5169	Dancing Chap	....	....
5170	Dancing Case	....	....
5171	Dancing Cat	....	....
5172	Dancing Can	....	....
5173	Dancing Cameo	....	....
5174	Dancing Car	....	....
5175	Dancing Call	....	....
5176	Dancing Cash	....	....
5177	Dancing Cake	....	....
5178	Dancing Café	....	....
5179	Dancing Cab	....	....
5180	Dancing Face	....	....
5181	Dancing Fat	....	....
5182	Dancing Fan	....	....
5183	Dancing Fame	....	....
5184	Dancing Fair	....	....
5185	Dancing Fall	....	....
5186	Dancing Fish	....	....
5187	Dancing Fake	....	....
5188	Dancing Fife	....	....
5189	Dancing Fab	....	....
5190	Dancing Base	....	....
5191	Dancing Bat	....	....
5192	Dancing Ban	....	....
5193	Dancing Bam!	....	....
5194	Dancing Bar	....	....
5195	Dancing Ball	....	....
5196	Dancing Bash	....	....
5197	Dancing Back	....	....
5198	Dancing Beef	....	....
5199	Dancing Baby	....	....
5200	Energy Zoo	....	....
5201	Energy Day	....	....
5202	Energy Noah	....	....
5203	Energy Ma	....	....

NUMBER	SEM³	KEY WORD	IMAGE
5204	Energy Rah	....	....
5205	Energy Law	....	....
5206	Energy Jaw	....	....
5207	Energy Key	....	....
5208	Energy Fee	....	....
5209	Energy Bay	....	....
5210	Energy Daze	....	....
5211	Energy Dad	....	....
5212	Energy Dan	....	....
5213	Energy Dam	....	....
5214	Energy Dare	....	....
5215	Energy Dale	....	....
5216	Energy Dash	....	....
5217	Energy Deck	....	....
5218	Energy Daffy	....	....
5219	Energy Dab	....	....
5220	Energy Nasa	....	....
5221	Energy Net	....	....
5222	Energy Nan	....	....
5223	Energy Name	....	....
5224	Energy Nero	....	....
5225	Energy Nail	....	....
5226	Energy Nash	....	....
5227	Energy Nag	....	....
5228	Energy Navy	....	....
5229	Energy Nab	....	....
5230	Energy Mace	....	....
5231	Energy Mat	....	....
5232	Energy Man	....	....
5233	Energy Ma'am	....	....
5234	Energy Mare	....	....
5235	Energy Mail	....	....
5236	Energy Mash	....	....
5237	Energy Mac	....	....
5238	Energy Mafia	....	....
5239	Energy Map	....	....
5240	Energy Race	....	....
5241	Energy Rat	....	....
5242	Energy Rain	....	....
5243	Energy Ram	....	....
5244	Energy Rare	....	....
5245	Energy Rail	....	....
5246	Energy Rash	....	....
5247	Energy Rack	....	....
5248	Energy Rafia	....	....
5249	Energy Rap	....	....
5250	Energy Lace	....	....
5251	Energy Lad	....	....
5252	Energy Lane	....	....
5253	Energy Lamb	....	....
5254	Energy Lair	....	....
5255	Energy Lily	....	....
5256	Energy Lash	....	....
5257	Energy Lake	....	....

112

NUMBER	SEM³	KEY WORD	IMAGE
5258	Energy Laugh	....	....
5259	Energy Lab	....	....
5260	Energy Chase	....	....
5261	Energy Chat	....	....
5262	Energy Chain	....	....
5263	Energy Chime	....	....
5264	Energy Chair	....	....
5265	Energy Chill	....	....
5266	Energy Chacha	....	....
5267	Energy Check	....	....
5268	Energy Chaff	....	....
5269	Energy Chap	....	....
5270	Energy Case	....	....
5271	Energy Cat	....	....
5272	Energy Can	....	....
5273	Energy Cameo	....	....
5274	Energy Car	....	....
5275	Energy Call	....	....
5276	Energy Cash	....	....
5277	Energy Cake	....	....
5278	Energy Café	....	....
5279	Energy Cab	....	....
5280	Energy Face	....	....
5281	Energy Fat	....	....
5282	Energy Fan	....	....
5283	Energy Fame	....	....
5284	Energy Fair	....	....
5285	Energy Fall	....	....
5286	Energy Fish	....	....
5287	Energy Fake	....	....
5288	Energy Fife	....	....
5289	Energy Fab	....	....
5290	Energy Base	....	....
5291	Energy Bat	....	....
5292	Energy Ban	....	....
5293	Energy Bam!	....	....
5294	Energy Bar	....	....
5295	Energy Ball	....	....
5296	Energy Bash	....	....
5297	Energy Back	....	....
5298	Energy Beef	....	....
5299	Energy Baby	....	....
5300	Mingling Zoo	....	....
5301	Mingling Day	....	....
5302	Mingling Noah	....	....
5303	Mingling Ma	....	....
5304	Mingling Rah	....	....
5305	Mingling Law	....	....
5306	Mingling Jaw	....	....
5307	Mingling Key	....	....
5308	Mingling Fee	....	....
5309	Mingling Bay	....	....
5310	Mingling Daze	....	....
5311	Mingling Dad	....	....

NUMBER	SEM³	KEY WORD	IMAGE
5312	Mingling Dan	....	....
5313	Mingling Dam	....	....
5314	Mingling Dare	....	....
5315	Mingling Dale	....	....
5316	Mingling Dash	....	....
5317	Mingling Deck	....	....
5318	Mingling Daffy	....	....
5319	Mingling Dab	....	....
5320	Mingling Nasa	....	....
5321	Mingling Net	....	....
5322	Mingling Nan	....	....
5323	Mingling Name	....	....
5324	Mingling Nero	....	....
5325	Mingling Nail	....	....
5326	Mingling Nash	....	....
5327	Mingling Nag	....	....
5328	Mingling Navy	....	....
5329	Mingling Nab	....	....
5330	Mingling Mace	....	....
5331	Mingling Mat	....	....
5332	Mingling Man	....	....
5333	Mingling Ma'am	....	....
5334	Mingling Mare	....	....
5335	Mingling Mail	....	....
5336	Mingling Mash	....	....
5337	Mingling Mac	....	....
5338	Mingling Mafia	....	....
5339	Mingling Map	....	....
5340	Mingling Race	....	....
5341	Mingling Rat	....	....
5342	Mingling Rain	....	....
5343	Mingling Ram	....	....
5344	Mingling Rare	....	....
5345	Mingling Rail	....	....
5346	Mingling Rash	....	....
5347	Mingling Rack	....	....
5348	Mingling Rafia	....	....
5349	Mingling Rap	....	....
5350	Mingling Lace	....	....
5351	Mingling Lad	....	....
5352	Mingling Lane	....	....
5353	Mingling Lamb	....	....
5354	Mingling Lair	....	....
5355	Mingling Lily	....	....
5356	Mingling Lash	....	....
5357	Mingling Lake	....	....
5358	Mingling Laugh	....	....
5359	Mingling Lab	....	....
5360	Mingling Chase	....	....
5361	Mingling Chat	....	....
5362	Mingling Chain	....	....
5363	Mingling Chime	....	....
5364	Mingling Chair	....	....
5365	Mingling Chill	....	....

NUMBER	SEM[3]	KEY WORD	IMAGE
5366	Mingling Chacha		
5367	Mingling Check		
5368	Mingling Chaff		
5369	Mingling Chap		
5370	Mingling Case		
5371	Mingling Cat		
5372	Mingling Can		
5373	Mingling Cameo		
5374	Mingling Car		
5375	Mingling Call		
5376	Mingling Cash		
5377	Mingling Cake		
5378	Mingling Café		
5379	Mingling Cab		
5380	Mingling Face		
5381	Mingling Fat		
5382	Mingling Fan		
5383	Mingling Fame		
5384	Mingling Fair		
5385	Mingling Fall		
5386	Mingling Fish		
5387	Mingling Fake		
5388	Mingling Fife		
5389	Mingling Fab		
5390	Mingling Base		
5391	Mingling Bat		
5392	Mingling Ban		
5393	Mingling Bam!		
5394	Mingling Bar		
5395	Mingling Ball		
5396	Mingling Bash		
5397	Mingling Back		
5398	Mingling Beef		
5399	Mingling Baby		
5400	Warm Zoo		
5401	Warm Day		
5402	Warm Noah		
5403	Warm Ma		
5404	Warm Rah		
5405	Warm Law		
5406	Warm Jaw		
5407	Warm Key		
5408	Warm Fee		
5409	Warm Bay		
5410	Warm Daze		
5411	Warm Dad		
5412	Warm Dan		
5413	Warm Dam		
5414	Warm Dare		
5415	Warm Dale		
5416	Warm Dash		
5417	Warm Deck		
5418	Warm Daffy		
5419	Warm Dab		

NUMBER	SEM³	KEY WORD	IMAGE
5420	Warm Nasa	....	....
5421	Warm Net	....	....
5422	Warm Nan	....	....
5423	Warm Name	....	....
5424	Warm Nero	....	....
5425	Warm Nail	....	....
5426	Warm Nash	....	....
5427	Warm Nag	....	....
5428	Warm Navy	....	....
5429	Warm Nab	....	....
5430	Warm Mace	....	....
5431	Warm Mat	....	....
5432	Warm Man	....	....
5433	Warm Ma'am	....	....
5434	Warm Mare	....	....
5435	Warm Mail	....	....
5436	Warm Mash	....	....
5437	Warm Mac	....	....
5438	Warm Mafia	....	....
5439	Warm Map	....	....
5440	Warm Race	....	....
5441	Warm Rat	....	....
5442	Warm Rain	....	....
5443	Warm Ram	....	....
5444	Warm Rare	....	....
5445	Warm Rail	....	....
5446	Warm Rash	....	....
5447	Warm Rack	....	....
5448	Warm Rafia	....	....
5449	Warm Rap	....	....
5450	Warm Lace	....	....
5451	Warm Lad	....	....
5452	Warm Lane	....	....
5453	Warm Lamb	....	....
5454	Warm Lair	....	....
5455	Warm Lily	....	....
5456	Warm Lash	....	....
5457	Warm Lake	....	....
5458	Warm Laugh	....	....
5459	Warm Lab	....	....
5460	Warm Chase	....	....
5461	Warm Chat	....	....
5462	Warm Chain	....	....
5463	Warm Chime	....	....
5464	Warm Chair	....	....
5465	Warm Chill	....	....
5466	Warm Chacha	....	....
5467	Warm Check	....	....
5468	Warm Chaff	....	....
5469	Warm Chap	....	....
5470	Warm Case	....	....
5471	Warm Cat	....	....
5472	Warm Can	....	....
5473	Warm Cameo	....	....

NUMBER	SEM³	KEY WORD	IMAGE
5474	Warm Car	....	....
5475	Warm Call	....	....
5476	Warm Cash	....	....
5477	Warm Cake	....	....
5478	Warm Café	....	....
5479	Warm Cab	....	....
5480	Warm Face	....	....
5481	Warm Fat	....	....
5482	Warm Fan	....	....
5483	Warm Fame	....	....
5484	Warm Fair	....	....
5485	Warm Fall	....	....
5486	Warm Fish	....	....
5487	Warm Fake	....	....
5488	Warm Fife	....	....
5489	Warm Fab	....	....
5490	Warm Base	....	....
5491	Warm Bat	....	....
5492	Warm Ban	....	....
5493	Warm Bam!	....	....
5494	Warm Bar	....	....
5495	Warm Ball	....	....
5496	Warm Bash	....	....
5497	Warm Back	....	....
5498	Warm Beef	....	....
5499	Warm Baby	....	....
5500	Loving Zoo	....	....
5501	Loving Day	....	....
5502	Loving Noah	....	....
5503	Loving Ma	....	....
5504	Loving Rah	....	....
5505	Loving Law	....	....
5506	Loving Jaw	....	....
5507	Loving Key	....	....
5508	Loving Fee	....	....
5509	Loving Bay	....	....
5510	Loving Daze	....	....
5511	Loving Dad	....	....
5512	Loving Dan	....	....
5513	Loving Dam	....	....
5514	Loving Dare	....	....
5515	Loving Dale	....	....
5516	Loving Dash	....	....
5517	Loving Deck	....	....
5518	Loving Daffy	....	....
5519	Loving Dab	....	....
5520	Loving Nasa	....	....
5521	Loving Net	....	....
5522	Loving Nan	....	....
5523	Loving Name	....	....
5524	Loving Nero	....	....
5525	Loving Nail	....	....
5526	Loving Nash	....	....
5527	Loving Nag	....	....

NUMBER	SEM³	KEY WORD	IMAGE
5528	Loving Navy	....	....
5529	Loving Nab	....	....
5530	Loving Mace	....	....
5531	Loving Mat	....	....
5532	Loving Man	....	....
5533	Loving Ma'am	....	....
5534	Loving Mare	....	....
5535	Loving Mail	....	....
5536	Loving Mash	....	....
5537	Loving Mac	....	....
5538	Loving Mafia	....	....
5539	Loving Map	....	....
5540	Loving Race	....	....
5541	Loving Rat	....	....
5542	Loving Rain	....	....
5543	Loving Ram	....	....
5544	Loving Rare	....	....
5545	Loving Rail	....	....
5546	Loving Rash	....	....
5547	Loving Rack	....	....
5548	Loving Rafia	....	....
5549	Loving Rap	....	....
5550	Loving Lace	....	....
5551	Loving Lad	....	....
5552	Loving Lane	....	....
5553	Loving Lamb	....	....
5554	Loving Lair	....	....
5555	Loving Lily	....	....
5556	Loving Lash	....	....
5557	Loving Lake	....	....
5558	Loving Laugh	....	....
5559	Loving Lab	....	....
5560	Loving Chase	....	....
5561	Loving Chat	....	....
5562	Loving Chain	....	....
5563	Loving Chime	....	....
5564	Loving Chair	....	....
5565	Loving Chill	....	....
5566	Loving Chacha	....	....
5567	Loving Check	....	....
5568	Loving Chaff	....	....
5569	Loving Chap	....	....
5570	Loving Case	....	....
5571	Loving Cat	....	....
5572	Loving Can	....	....
5573	Loving Cameo	....	....
5574	Loving Car	....	....
5575	Loving Call	....	....
5576	Loving Cash	....	....
5577	Loving Cake	....	....
5578	Loving Café	....	....
5579	Loving Cab	....	....
5580	Loving Face	....	....
5581	Loving Fat	....	....

NUMBER	SEM³	KEY WORD	IMAGE
5582	Loving Fan	....	....
5583	Loving Fame	....	....
5584	Loving Fair	....	....
5585	Loving Fall	....	....
5586	Loving Fish	....	....
5587	Loving Fake	....	....
5588	Loving Fife	....	....
5589	Loving Fab	....	....
5590	Loving Base	....	....
5591	Loving Bat	....	....
5592	Loving Ban	....	....
5593	Loving Bam!	....	....
5594	Loving Bar	....	....
5595	Loving Ball	....	....
5596	Loving Bash	....	....
5597	Loving Back	....	....
5598	Loving Beef	....	....
5599	Loving Baby	....	....
5600	Shaking Zoo	....	....
5601	Shaking Day	....	....
5602	Shaking Noah	....	....
5603	Shaking Ma	....	....
5604	Shaking Rah	....	....
5605	Shaking Law	....	....
5606	Shaking Jaw	....	....
5607	Shaking Key	....	....
5608	Shaking Fee	....	....
5609	Shaking Bay	....	....
5610	Shaking Daze	....	....
5611	Shaking Dad	....	....
5612	Shaking Dan	....	....
5613	Shaking Dam	....	....
5614	Shaking Dare	....	....
5615	Shaking Dale	....	....
5616	Shaking Dash	....	....
5617	Shaking Deck	....	....
5618	Shaking Daffy	....	....
5619	Shaking Dab	....	....
5620	Shaking Nasa	....	....
5621	Shaking Net	....	....
5622	Shaking Nan	....	....
5623	Shaking Name	....	....
5624	Shaking Nero	....	....
5625	Shaking Nail	....	....
5626	Shaking Nash	....	....
5627	Shaking Nag	....	....
5628	Shaking Navy	....	....
5629	Shaking Nab	....	....
5630	Shaking Mace	....	....
5631	Shaking Mat	....	....
5632	Shaking Man	....	....
5633	Shaking Ma'am	....	....
5634	Shaking Mare	....	....
5635	Shaking Mail	....	....

NUMBER	SEM[3]	KEY WORD	IMAGE
5636	Shaking Mash	....	....
5637	Shaking Mac	....	....
5638	Shaking Mafia	....	....
5639	Shaking Map	....	....
5640	Shaking Race	....	....
5641	Shaking Rat	....	....
5642	Shaking Rain	....	....
5643	Shaking Ram	....	....
5644	Shaking Rare	....	....
5645	Shaking Rail	....	....
5646	Shaking Rash	....	....
5647	Shaking Rack	....	....
5648	Shaking Rafia	....	....
5649	Shaking Rap	....	....
5650	Shaking Lace	....	....
5651	Shaking Lad	....	....
5652	Shaking Lane	....	....
5653	Shaking Lamb	....	....
5654	Shaking Lair	....	....
5655	Shaking Lily	....	....
5656	Shaking Lash	....	....
5657	Shaking Lake	....	....
5658	Shaking Laugh	....	....
5659	Shaking Lab	....	....
5660	Shaking Chase	....	....
5661	Shaking Chat	....	....
5662	Shaking Chain	....	....
5663	Shaking Chime	....	....
5664	Shaking Chair	....	....
5665	Shaking Chill	....	....
5666	Shaking Chacha	....	....
5667	Shaking Check	....	....
5668	Shaking Chaff	....	....
5669	Shaking Chap	....	....
5670	Shaking Case	....	....
5671	Shaking Cat	....	....
5672	Shaking Can	....	....
5673	Shaking Cameo	....	....
5674	Shaking Car	....	....
5675	Shaking Call	....	....
5676	Shaking Cash	....	....
5677	Shaking Cake	....	....
5678	Shaking Café	....	....
5679	Shaking Cab	....	....
5680	Shaking Face	....	....
5681	Shaking Fat	....	....
5682	Shaking Fan	....	....
5683	Shaking Fame	....	....
5684	Shaking Fair	....	....
5685	Shaking Fall	....	....
5686	Shaking Fish	....	....
5687	Shaking Fake	....	....
5688	Shaking Fife	....	....
5689	Shaking Fab	....	....

NUMBER	SEM³	KEY WORD	IMAGE
5690	Shaking Base	....	....
5691	Shaking Bat	....	....
5692	Shaking Ban	....	....
5693	Shaking Bam!	....	....
5694	Shaking Bar	....	....
5695	Shaking Ball	....	....
5696	Shaking Bash	....	....
5697	Shaking Back	....	....
5698	Shaking Beef	....	....
5699	Shaking Baby	....	....
5700	Climbing Zoo	....	....
5701	Climbing Day	....	....
5702	Climbing Noah	....	....
5703	Climbing Ma	....	....
5704	Climbing Rah	....	....
5705	Climbing Law	....	....
5706	Climbing Jaw	....	....
5707	Climbing Key	....	....
5708	Climbing Fee	....	....
5709	Climbing Bay	....	....
5710	Climbing Daze	....	....
5711	Climbing Dad	....	....
5712	Climbing Dan	....	....
5713	Climbing Dam	....	....
5714	Climbing Dare	....	....
5715	Climbing Dale	....	....
5716	Climbing Dash	....	....
5717	Climbing Deck	....	....
5718	Climbing Daffy	....	....
5719	Climbing Dab	....	....
5720	Climbing Nasa	....	....
5721	Climbing Net	....	....
5722	Climbing Nan	....	....
5723	Climbing Name	....	....
5724	Climbing Nero	....	....
5725	Climbing Nail	....	....
5726	Climbing Nash	....	....
5727	Climbing Nag	....	....
5728	Climbing Navy	....	....
5729	Climbing Nab	....	....
5730	Climbing Mace	....	....
5731	Climbing Mat	....	....
5732	Climbing Man	....	....
5733	Climbing Ma'am	....	....
5734	Climbing Mare	....	....
5735	Climbing Mail	....	....
5736	Climbing Mash	....	....
5737	Climbing Mac	....	....
5738	Climbing Mafia	....	....
5739	Climbing Map	....	....
5740	Climbing Race	....	....
5741	Climbing Rat	....	....
5742	Climbing Rain	....	....
5743	Climbing Ram	....	....

NUMBER	SEM³	KEY WORD	IMAGE
5744	Climbing Rare	....	....
5745	Climbing Rail	....	....
5746	Climbing Rash	....	....
5747	Climbing Rack	....	....
5748	Climbing Rafia	....	....
5749	Climbing Rap	....	....
5750	Climbing Lace	....	....
5751	Climbing Lad	....	....
5752	Climbing Lane	....	....
5753	Climbing Lamb	....	....
5754	Climbing Lair	....	....
5755	Climbing Lily	....	....
5756	Climbing Lash	....	....
5757	Climbing Lake	....	....
5758	Climbing Laugh	....	....
5759	Climbing Lab	....	....
5760	Climbing Chase	....	....
5761	Climbing Chat	....	....
5762	Climbing Chain	....	....
5763	Climbing Chime	....	....
5764	Climbing Chair	....	....
5765	Climbing Chill	....	....
5766	Climbing Chacha	....	....
5767	Climbing Check	....	....
5768	Climbing Chaff	....	....
5769	Climbing Chap	....	....
5770	Climbing Case	....	....
5771	Climbing Cat	....	....
5772	Climbing Can	....	....
5773	Climbing Cameo	....	....
5774	Climbing Car	....	....
5775	Climbing Call	....	....
5776	Climbing Cash	....	....
5777	Climbing Cake	....	....
5778	Climbing Café	....	....
5779	Climbing Cab	....	....
5780	Climbing Face	....	....
5781	Climbing Fat	....	....
5782	Climbing Fan	....	....
5783	Climbing Fame	....	....
5784	Climbing Fair	....	....
5785	Climbing Fall	....	....
5786	Climbing Fish	....	....
5787	Climbing Fake	....	....
5788	Climbing Fife	....	....
5789	Climbing Fab	....	....
5790	Climbing Base	....	....
5791	Climbing Bat	....	....
5792	Climbing Ban	....	....
5793	Climbing Bam!	....	....
5794	Climbing Bar	....	....
5795	Climbing Ball	....	....
5796	Climbing Bash	....	....
5797	Climbing Back	....	....

NUMBER	SEM³	KEY WORD	IMAGE
5798	Climbing Beef	....	....
5799	Climbing Baby	....	....
5800	Flying Zoo	....	....
5801	Flying Day	....	....
5802	Flying Noah	....	....
5803	Flying Ma	....	....
5804	Flying Rah	....	....
5805	Flying Law	....	....
5806	Flying Jaw	....	....
5807	Flying Key	....	....
5808	Flying Fee	....	....
5809	Flying Bay	....	....
5810	Flying Daze	....	....
5811	Flying Dad	....	....
5812	Flying Dan	....	....
5813	Flying Dam	....	....
5814	Flying Dare	....	....
5815	Flying Dale	....	....
5816	Flying Dash	....	....
5817	Flying Deck	....	....
5818	Flying Daffy	....	....
5819	Flying Dab	....	....
5820	Flying Nasa	....	....
5821	Flying Net	....	....
5822	Flying Nan	....	....
5823	Flying Name	....	....
5824	Flying Nero	....	....
5825	Flying Nail	....	....
5826	Flying Nash	....	....
5827	Flying Nag	....	....
5828	Flying Navy	....	....
5829	Flying Nab	....	....
5830	Flying Mace	....	....
5831	Flying Mat	....	....
5832	Flying Man	....	....
5833	Flying Ma'am	....	....
5834	Flying Mare	....	....
5835	Flying Mail	....	....
5836	Flying Mash	....	....
5837	Flying Mac	....	....
5838	Flying Mafia	....	....
5839	Flying Map	....	....
5840	Flying Race	....	....
5841	Flying Rat	....	....
5842	Flying Rain	....	....
5843	Flying Ram	....	....
5844	Flying Rare	....	....
5845	Flying Rail	....	....
5846	Flying Rash	....	....
5847	Flying Rack	....	....
5848	Flying Rafia	....	....
5849	Flying Rap	....	....
5850	Flying Lace	....	....
5851	Flying Lad	....	....

NUMBER	SEM³	KEY WORD	IMAGE
5852	Flying Lane	....	....
5853	Flying Lamb	....	....
5854	Flying Lair	....	....
5855	Flying Lily	....	....
5856	Flying Lash	....	....
5857	Flying Lake	....	....
5858	Flying Laugh	....	....
5859	Flying Lab	....	....
5860	Flying Chase	....	....
5861	Flying Chat	....	....
5862	Flying Chain	....	....
5863	Flying Chime	....	....
5864	Flying Chair	....	....
5865	Flying Chill	....	....
5866	Flying Chacha	....	....
5867	Flying Check	....	....
5868	Flying Chaff	....	....
5869	Flying Chap	....	....
5870	Flying Case	....	....
5871	Flying Cat	....	....
5872	Flying Can	....	....
5873	Flying Cameo	....	....
5874	Flying Car	....	....
5875	Flying Call	....	....
5876	Flying Cash	....	....
5877	Flying Cake	....	....
5878	Flying Cafe	....	....
5879	Flying Cab	....	....
5880	Flying Face	....	....
5881	Flying Fat	....	....
5882	Flying Fan	....	....
5883	Flying Fame	....	....
5884	Flying Fair	....	....
5885	Flying Fall	....	....
5886	Flying Fish	....	....
5887	Flying Fake	....	....
5888	Flying Fife	....	....
5889	Flying Fab	....	....
5890	Flying Base	....	....
5891	Flying Bat	....	....
5892	Flying Ban	....	....
5893	Flying Bam!	....	....
5894	Flying Bar	....	....
5895	Flying Ball	....	....
5896	Flying Bash	....	....
5897	Flying Back	....	....
5898	Flying Beef	....	....
5899	Flying Baby	....	....
5900	Peacefulness Zoo	....	....
5901	Peacefulness Day	....	....
5902	Peacefulness Noah	....	....
5903	Peacefulness Ma	....	....
5904	Peacefulness Rah	....	....
5905	Peacefulness Law	....	....

124

NUMBER	SEM³	KEY WORD	IMAGE
5906	Peacefulness Jaw	....	....
5907	Peacefulness Key	....	....
5908	Peacefulness Fee	....	....
5909	Peacefulness Bay	....	....
5910	Peacefulness Daze	....	....
5911	Peacefulness Dad	....	....
5912	Peacefulness Dan	....	....
5913	Peacefulness Dam	....	....
5914	Peacefulness Dare	....	....
5915	Peacefulness Dale	....	....
5916	Peacefulness Dash	....	....
5917	Peacefulness Deck	....	....
5918	Peacefulness Daffy	....	....
5919	Peacefulness Dab	....	....
5920	Peacefulness Nasa	....	....
5921	Peacefulness Net	....	....
5922	Peacefulness Nan	....	....
5923	Peacefulness Name	....	....
5924	Peacefulness Nero	....	....
5925	Peacefulness Nail	....	....
5926	Peacefulness Nash	....	....
5927	Peacefulness Nag	....	....
5928	Peacefulness Navy	....	....
5929	Peacefulness Nab	....	....
5930	Peacefulness Mace	....	....
5931	Peacefulness Mat	....	....
5932	Peacefulness Man	....	....
5933	Peacefulness Ma'am	....	....
5934	Peacefulness Mare	....	....
5935	Peacefulness Mail	....	....
5936	Peacefulness Mash	....	....
5937	Peacefulness Mac	....	....
5938	Peacefulness Mafia	....	....
5939	Peacefulness Map	....	....
5940	Peacefulness Race	....	....
5941	Peacefulness Rat	....	....
5942	Peacefulness Rain	....	....
5943	Peacefulness Ram	....	....
5944	Peacefulness Rare	....	....
5945	Peacefulness Rail	....	....
5946	Peacefulness Rash	....	....
5947	Peacefulness Rack	....	....
5948	Peacefulness Rafia	....	....
5949	Peacefulness Rap	....	....
5950	Peacefulness Lace	....	....
5951	Peacefulness Lad	....	....
5952	Peacefulness Lane	....	....
5953	Peacefulness Lamb	....	....
5954	Peacefulness Lair	....	....
5955	Peacefulness Lily	....	....
5956	Peacefulness Lash	....	....
5957	Peacefulness Lake	....	....
5958	Peacefulness Laugh	....	....
5959	Peacefulness Lab	....	....

NUMBER	SEM[3]	KEY WORD	IMAGE
5960	Peacefulness Chase	....	....
5961	Peacefulness Chat	....	....
5962	Peacefulness Chain	....	....
5963	PeacefulnessChime	....	....
5964	Peacefulness Chair	....	....
5965	Peacefulness Chill	....	....
5966	PeacefulnessChacha	....	....
5967	PeacefulnessCheck	....	....
5968	Peacefulness Chaff	....	....
5969	Peacefulness Chap	....	....
5970	Peacefulness Case	....	....
5971	Peacefulness Cat	....	....
5972	Peacefulness Can	....	....
5973	PeacefulnessCameo	....	....
5974	Peacefulness Car	....	....
5975	Peacefulness Call	....	....
5976	Peacefulness Cash	....	....
5977	Peacefulness Cake	....	....
5978	Peacefulness Café	....	....
5979	Peacefulness Cab	....	....
5980	Peacefulness Face	....	....
5981	Peacefulness Fat	....	....
5982	Peacefulness Fan	....	....
5983	Peacefulness Fame	....	....
5984	Peacefulness Fair	....	....
5985	Peacefulness Fall	....	....
5986	Peacefulness Fish	....	....
5987	Peacefulness Fake	....	....
5988	Peacefulness Fife	....	....
5989	Peacefulness Fab	....	....
5990	Peacefulness Base	....	....
5991	Peacefulness Bat	....	....
5992	Peacefulness Ban	....	....
5993	Peacefulness Bam!	....	....
5994	Peacefulness Bar	....	....
5995	Peacefulness Ball	....	....
5996	Peacefulness Bash	....	....
5997	Peacefulness Back	....	....
5998	Peacefulness Beef	....	....
5999	Peacefulness Baby	....	....

CHAPTER SEVEN

ANIMALS

NUMBER	SEM[3]	KEY WORD	IMAGE
6000	Zebra Zoo	....	....
6001	Zebra Day	....	....
6002	Zebra Noah	....	....
6003	Zebra Ma	....	....
6004	Zebra Rah	....	....
6005	Zebra Law	....	....
6006	Zebra Jaw	....	....
6007	Zebra Key	....	....
6008	Zebra Fee	....	....
6009	Zebra Bay	....	....
6010	Zebra Daze	....	....
6011	Zebra Dad	....	....
6012	Zebra Dan	....	....
6013	Zebra Dam	....	....
6014	Zebra Dare	....	....
6015	Zebra Dale	....	....
6016	Zebra Dash	....	....
6017	Zebra Deck	....	....
6018	Zebra Daffy	....	....
6019	Zebra Dab	....	....
6020	Zebra Nasa	....	....
6021	Zebra Net	....	....
6022	Zebra Nan	....	....
6023	Zebra Name	....	....
6024	Zebra Nero	....	....
6025	Zebra Nail	....	....
6026	Zebra Nash	....	....
6027	Zebra Nag	....	....
6028	Zebra Navy	....	....
6029	Zebra Nab	....	....
6030	Zebra Mace	....	....
6031	Zebra Mat	....	....
6032	Zebra Man	....	....
6033	Zebra Ma'am	....	....
6034	Zebra Mare	....	....
6035	Zebra Mail	....	....
6036	Zebra Mash	....	....
6037	Zebra Mac	....	....
6038	Zebra Mafia	....	....
6039	Zebra Map	....	....
6040	Zebra Race	....	....
6041	Zebra Rat	....	....

NUMBER	SEM[3]	KEY WORD	IMAGE
6042	Zebra Rain	....	....
6043	Zebra Ram	....	....
6044	Zebra Rare	....	....
6045	Zebra Rail	....	....
6046	Zebra Rash	....	....
6047	Zebra Rack	....	....
6048	Zebra Rafia	....	....
6049	Zebra Rap	....	....
6050	Zebra Lace	....	....
6051	Zebra Lad	....	....
6052	Zebra Lane	....	....
6053	Zebra Lamb	....	....
6054	Zebra Lair	....	....
6055	Zebra Lily	....	....
6056	Zebra Lash	....	....
6057	Zebra Lake	....	....
6058	Zebra Laugh	....	....
6059	Zebra Lab	....	....
6060	Zebra Chase	....	....
6061	Zebra Chat	....	....
6062	Zebra Chain	....	....
6063	Zebra Chime	....	....
6064	Zebra Chair	....	....
6065	Zebra Chill	....	....
6066	Zebra Chacha	....	....
6067	Zebra Check	....	....
6068	Zebra Chaff	....	....
6069	Zebra Chap	....	....
6070	Zebra Case	....	....
6071	Zebra Cat	....	....
6072	Zebra Can	....	....
6073	Zebra Cameo	....	....
6074	Zebra Car	....	....
6075	Zebra Call	....	....
6076	Zebra Cash	....	....
6077	Zebra Cake	....	....
6078	Zebra Café	....	....
6079	Zebra Cab	....	....
6080	Zebra Face	....	....
6081	Zebra Fat	....	....
6082	Zebra Fan	....	....
6083	Zebra Fame	....	....
6084	Zebra Fair	....	....
6085	Zebra Fall	....	....
6086	Zebra Fish	....	....
6087	Zebra Fake	....	....
6088	Zebra Fife	....	....
6089	Zebra Fab	....	....
6090	Zebra Base	....	....
6091	Zebra Bat	....	....
6092	Zebra Ban	....	....
6093	Zebra Bam!	....	....
6094	Zebra Bar	....	....
6095	Zebra Ball	....	....

NUMBER	SEM³	KEY WORD	IMAGE
6096	Zebra Bash	....	....
6097	Zebra Back	....	....
6098	Zebra Beef	....	....
6099	Zebra Baby	....	....
6100	Dog Zoo	....	....
6101	Dog Day	....	....
6102	Dog Noah	....	....
6103	Dog Ma	....	....
6104	Dog Rah	....	....
6105	Dog Law	....	....
6106	Dog Jaw	....	....
6107	Dog Key	....	....
6108	Dog Fee	....	....
6109	Dog Bay	....	....
6110	Dog Daze	....	....
6111	Dog Dad	....	....
6112	Dog Dan	....	....
6113	Dog Dam	....	....
6114	Dog Dare	....	....
6115	Dog Dale	....	....
6116	Dog Dash	....	....
6117	Dog Deck	....	....
6118	Dog Daffy	....	....
6119	Dog Dab	....	....
6120	Dog Nasa	....	....
6121	Dog Net	....	....
6122	Dog Nan	....	....
6123	Dog Name	....	....
6124	Dog Nero	....	....
6125	Dog Nail	....	....
6126	Dog Nash	....	....
6127	Dog Nag	....	....
6128	Dog Navy	....	....
6129	Dog Nab	....	....
6130	Dog Mace	....	....
6131	Dog Mat	....	....
6132	Dog Man	....	....
6133	Dog Ma'am	....	....
6134	Dog Mare	....	....
6135	Dog Mail	....	....
6136	Dog Mash	....	....
6137	Dog Mac	....	....
6138	Dog Mafia	....	....
6139	Dog Map	....	....
6140	Dog Race	....	....
6141	Dog Rat	....	....
6142	Dog Rain	....	....
6143	Dog Ram	....	....
6144	Dog Rare	....	....
6145	Dog Rail	....	....
6146	Dog Rash	....	....
6147	Dog Rack	....	....
6148	Dog Rafia	....	....
6149	Dog Rap	....	....

NUMBER	SEM[3]	KEY WORD	IMAGE
6150	Dog Lace	....	....
6151	Dog Lad	....	....
6152	Dog Lane	....	....
6153	Dog Lamb	....	....
6154	Dog Lair	....	....
6155	Dog Lily	....	....
6156	Dog Lash	....	....
6157	Dog Lake	....	....
6158	Dog Laugh	....	....
6159	Dog Lab	....	....
6160	Dog Chase	....	....
6161	Dog Chat	....	....
6162	Dog Chain	....	....
6163	Dog Chime	....	....
6164	Dog Chair	....	....
6165	Dog Chill	....	....
6166	Dog Chacha	....	....
6167	Dog Check	....	....
6168	Dog Chaff	....	....
6169	Dog Chap	....	....
6170	Dog Case	....	....
6171	Dog Cat	....	....
6172	Dog Can	....	....
6173	Dog Cameo	....	....
6174	Dog Car	....	....
6175	Dog Call	....	....
6176	Dog Cash	....	....
6177	Dog Cake	....	....
6178	Dog Café	....	....
6179	Dog Cab	....	....
6180	Dog Face	....	....
6181	Dog Fat	....	....
6182	Dog Fan	....	....
6183	Dog Fame	....	....
6184	Dog Fair	....	....
6185	Dog Fall	....	....
6186	Dog Fish	....	....
6187	Dog Fake	....	....
6188	Dog Fife	....	....
6189	Dog Fab	....	....
6190	Dog Base	....	....
6191	Dog Bat	....	....
6192	Dog Ban	....	....
6193	Dog Bam!	....	....
6194	Dog Bar	....	....
6195	Dog Ball	....	....
6196	Dog Bash	....	....
6197	Dog Back	....	....
6198	Dog Beef	....	....
6199	Dog Baby	....	....
6200	Newt Zoo	....	....
6201	Newt Day	....	....
6202	Newt Noah	....	....
6203	Newt Ma	....	....

NUMBER	SEM[3]	KEY WORD	IMAGE
6204	Newt Rah	....	....
6205	Newt Law	....	....
6206	Newt Jaw	....	....
6207	Newt Key	....	....
6208	Newt Fee	....	....
6209	Newt Bay	....	....
6210	Newt Daze	....	....
6211	Newt Dad	....	....
6212	Newt Dan	....	....
6213	Newt Dam	....	....
6214	Newt Dare	....	....
6215	Newt Dale	....	....
6216	Newt Dash	....	....
6217	Newt Deck	....	....
6218	Newt Daffy	....	....
6219	Newt Dab	....	....
6220	Newt Nasa	....	....
6221	Newt Net	....	....
6222	Newt Nan	....	....
6223	Newt Name	....	....
6224	Newt Nero	....	....
6225	Newt Nail	....	....
6226	Newt Nash	....	....
6227	Newt Nag	....	....
6228	Newt Navy	....	....
6229	Newt Nab	....	....
6230	Newt Mace	....	....
6231	Newt Mat	....	....
6232	Newt Man	....	....
6233	Newt Ma'am	....	....
6234	Newt Mare	....	....
6235	Newt Mail	....	....
6236	Newt Mash	....	....
6237	Newt Mac	....	....
6238	Newt Mafia	....	....
6239	Newt Map	....	....
6240	Newt Race	....	....
6241	Newt Rat	....	....
6242	Newt Rain	....	....
6243	Newt Ram	....	....
6244	Newt Rare	....	....
6245	Newt Rail	....	....
6246	Newt Rash	....	....
6247	Newt Rack	....	....
6248	Newt Rafia	....	....
6249	Newt Rap	....	....
6250	Newt Lace	....	....
6251	Newt Lad	....	....
6252	Newt Lane	....	....
6253	Newt Lamb	....	....
6254	Newt Lair	....	....
6255	Newt Lily	....	....
6256	Newt Lash	....	....
6257	Newt Lake	....	....

131

NUMBER	SEM³	KEY WORD	IMAGE
6258	Newt Laugh	....	....
6259	Newt Lab	....	....
6260	Newt Chase	....	....
6261	Newt Chat	....	....
6262	Newt Chain	....	....
6263	Newt Chime	....	....
6264	Newt Chair	....	....
6265	Newt Chill	....	....
6266	Newt Chacha	....	....
6267	Newt Check	....	....
6268	Newt Chaff	....	....
6269	Newt Chap	....	....
6270	Newt Case	....	....
6271	Newt Cat	....	....
6272	Newt Can	....	....
6273	Newt Cameo	....	....
6274	Newt Car	....	....
6275	Newt Call	....	....
6276	Newt Cash	....	....
6277	Newt Cake	....	....
6278	Newt Café	....	....
6279	Newt Cab	....	....
6280	Newt Face	....	....
6281	Newt Fat	....	....
6282	Newt Fan	....	....
6283	Newt Fame	....	....
6284	Newt Fair	....	....
6285	Newt Fall	....	....
6286	Newt Fish	....	....
6287	Newt Fake	....	....
6288	Newt Fife	....	....
6289	Newt Fab	....	....
6290	Newt Base	....	....
6291	Newt Bat	....	....
6292	Newt Ban	....	....
6293	Newt Bam!	....	....
6294	Newt Bar	....	....
6295	Newt Ball	....	....
6296	Newt Bash	....	....
6297	Newt Back	....	....
6298	Newt Beef	....	....
6299	Newt Baby	....	....
6300	Moose Zoo	....	....
6301	Moose Day	....	....
6302	Moose Noah	....	....
6303	Moose Ma	....	....
6304	Moose Rah	....	....
6305	Moose Law	....	....
6306	Moose Jaw	....	....
6307	Moose Key	....	....
6308	Moose Fee	....	....
6309	Moose Bay	....	....
6310	Moose Daze	....	....
6311	Moose Dad	....	....

NUMBER	SEM³	KEY WORD	IMAGE
6312	Moose Dan		
6313	Moose Dam		
6314	Moose Dare		
6315	Moose Dale		
6316	Moose Dash		
6317	Moose Deck		
6318	Moose Daffy		
6319	Moose Dab		
6320	Moose Nasa		
6321	Moose Net		
6322	Moose Nan		
6323	Moose Name		
6324	Moose Nero		
6325	Moose Nail		
6326	Moose Nash		
6327	Moose Nag		
6328	Moose Navy		
6329	Moose Nab		
6330	Moose Mace		
6331	Moose Mat		
6332	Moose Man		
6333	Moose Ma'am		
6334	Moose Mare		
6335	Moose Mail		
6336	Moose Mash		
6337	Moose Mac		
6338	Moose Mafia		
6339	Moose Map		
6340	Moose Race		
6341	Moose Rat		
6342	Moose Rain		
6343	Moose Ram		
6344	Moose Rare		
6345	Moose Rail		
6346	Moose Rash		
6347	Moose Rack		
6348	Moose Rafia		
6349	Moose Rap		
6350	Moose Lace		
6351	Moose Lad		
6352	Moose Lane		
6353	Moose Lamb		
6354	Moose Lair		
6355	Moose Lily		
6356	Moose Lash		
6357	Moose Lake		
6358	Moose Laugh		
6359	Moose Lab		
6360	Moose Chase		
6361	Moose Chat		
6362	Moose Chain		
6363	Moose Chime		
6364	Moose Chair		
6365	Moose Chill		

NUMBER	SEM³	KEY WORD	IMAGE
6366	Moose Chacha	....	....
6367	Moose Check	....	....
6368	Moose Chaff	....	....
6369	Moose Chap	....	....
6370	Moose Case	....	....
6371	Moose Cat	....	....
6372	Moose Can	....	....
6373	Moose Cameo	....	....
6374	Moose Car	....	....
6375	Moose Call	....	....
6376	Moose Cash	....	....
6377	Moose Cake	....	....
6378	Moose Café	....	....
6379	Moose Cab	....	....
6380	Moose Face	....	....
6381	Moose Fat	....	....
6382	Moose Fan	....	....
6383	Moose Fame	....	....
6384	Moose Fair	....	....
6385	Moose Fall	....	....
6386	Moose Fish	....	....
6387	Moose Fake	....	....
6388	Moose Fife	....	....
6389	Moose Fab	....	....
6390	Moose Base	....	....
6391	Moose Bat	....	....
6392	Moose Ban	....	....
6393	Moose Bam!	....	....
6394	Moose Bar	....	....
6395	Moose Ball	....	....
6396	Moose Bash	....	....
6397	Moose Back	....	....
6398	Moose Beef	....	....
6399	Moose Baby	....	....
6400	Rhinoceros Zoo	....	....
6401	Rhinoceros Day	....	....
6402	Rhinoceros Noah	....	....
6403	Rhinoceros Ma	....	....
6404	Rhinoceros Rah	....	....
6405	Rhinoceros Law	....	....
6406	Rhinoceros Jaw	....	....
6407	Rhinoceros Key	....	....
6408	Rhinoceros Fee	....	....
6409	Rhinoceros Bay	....	....
6410	Rhinoceros Daze	....	....
6411	Rhinoceros Dad	....	....
6412	Rhinoceros Dan	....	....
6413	Rhinoceros Dam	....	....
6414	Rhinoceros Dare	....	....
6415	Rhinoceros Dale	....	....
6416	Rhinoceros Dash	....	....
6417	Rhinoceros Deck	....	....
6418	Rhinoceros Daffy	....	....
6419	Rhinoceros Dab	....	....

NUMBER	SEM[3]	KEY WORD	IMAGE
6420	Rhinoceros Nasa	....	....
6421	Rhinoceros Net	....	....
6422	Rhinoceros Nan	....	....
6423	Rhinoceros Name	....	....
6424	Rhinoceros Nero	....	....
6425	Rhinoceros Nail	....	....
6426	Rhinoceros Nash	....	....
6427	Rhinoceros Nag	....	....
6428	Rhinoceros Navy	....	....
6429	Rhinoceros Nab	....	....
6430	Rhinoceros Mace	....	....
6431	Rhinoceros Mat	....	....
6432	Rhinoceros Man	....	....
6433	Rhinoceros Ma'am	....	....
6434	Rhinoceros Mare	....	....
6435	Rhinoceros Mail	....	....
6436	Rhinoceros Mash	....	....
6437	Rhinoceros Mac	....	....
6438	Rhinoceros Mafia	....	....
6439	Rhinoceros Map	....	....
6440	Rhinoceros Race	....	....
6441	Rhinoceros Rat	....	....
6442	Rhinoceros Rain	....	....
6443	Rhinoceros Ram	....	....
6444	Rhinoceros Rare	....	....
6445	Rhinoceros Rail	....	....
6446	Rhinoceros Rash	....	....
6447	Rhinoceros Rack	....	....
6448	Rhinoceros Rafia	....	....
6449	Rhinoceros Rap	....	....
6450	Rhinoceros Lace	....	....
6451	Rhinoceros Lad	....	....
6452	Rhinoceros Lane	....	....
6453	Rhinoceros Lamb	....	....
6454	Rhinoceros Lair	....	....
6455	Rhinoceros Lily	....	....
6456	Rhinoceros Lash	....	....
6457	Rhinoceros Lake	....	....
6458	Rhinoceros Laugh	....	....
6459	Rhinoceros Lab	....	....
6460	Rhinoceros Chase	....	....
6461	Rhinoceros Chat	....	....
6462	Rhinoceros Chain	....	....
6463	Rhinoceros Chime	....	....
6464	Rhinoceros Chair	....	....
6465	Rhinoceros Chill	....	....
6466	Rhinoceros Chacha	....	....
6467	Rhinoceros Check	....	....
6468	Rhinoceros Chaff	....	....
6469	Rhinoceros Chap	....	....
6470	Rhinoceros Case	....	....
6471	Rhinoceros Cat	....	....
6472	Rhinoceros Can	....	....
6473	Rhinoceros Cameo	....	....

135

NUMBER	SEM³	KEY WORD	IMAGE
6474	Rhinoceros Car	....	....
6475	Rhinoceros Call	....	....
6476	Rhinoceros Cash	....	....
6477	Rhinoceros Cake	....	....
6478	Rhinoceros Café	....	....
6479	Rhinoceros Cab	....	....
6480	Rhinoceros Face	....	....
6481	Rhinoceros Fat	....	....
6482	Rhinoceros Fan	....	....
6483	Rhinoceros Fame	....	....
6484	Rhinoceros Fair	....	....
6485	Rhinoceros Fall	....	....
6486	Rhinoceros Fish	....	....
6487	Rhinoceros Fake	....	....
6488	Rhinoceros Fife	....	....
6489	Rhinoceros Fab	....	....
6490	Rhinoceros Base	....	....
6491	Rhinoceros Bat	....	....
6492	Rhinoceros Ban	....	....
6493	Rhinoceros Bam!	....	....
6494	Rhinoceros Bar	....	....
6495	Rhinoceros Ball	....	....
6496	Rhinoceros Bash	....	....
6497	Rhinoceros Back	....	....
6498	Rhinoceros Beef	....	....
6499	Rhinoceros Baby	....	....
6500	Elephant Zoo	....	....
6501	Elephant Day	....	....
6502	Elephant Noah	....	....
6503	Elephant Ma	....	....
6504	Elephant Rah	....	....
6505	Elephant Law	....	....
6506	Elephant Jaw	....	....
6507	Elephant Key	....	....
6508	Elephant Fee	....	....
6509	Elephant Bay	....	....
6510	Elephant Daze	....	....
6511	Elephant Dad	....	....
6512	Elephant Dan	....	....
6513	Elephant Dam	....	....
6514	Elephant Dare	....	....
6515	Elephant Dale	....	....
6516	Elephant Dash	....	....
6517	Elephant Deck	....	....
6518	Elephant Daffy	....	....
6519	Elephant Dab	....	....
6520	Elephant Nasa	....	....
6521	Elephant Net	....	....
6522	Elephant Nan	....	....
6523	Elephant Name	....	....
6524	Elephant Nero	....	....
6525	Elephant Nail	....	....
6526	Elephant Nash	....	....
6527	Elephant Nag	....	....

NUMBER	SEM[3]	KEY WORD	IMAGE
6528	Elephant Navy	....	....
6529	Elephant Nab	....	....
6530	Elephant Mace	....	....
6531	Elephant Mat	....	....
6532	Elephant Man	....	....
6533	Elephant Ma'am	....	....
6534	Elephant Mare	....	....
6535	Elephant Mail	....	....
6536	Elephant Mash	....	....
6537	Elephant Mac	....	....
6538	Elephant Mafia	....	....
6539	Elephant Map	....	....
6540	Elephant Race	....	....
6541	Elephant Rat	....	....
6542	Elephant Rain	....	....
6543	Elephant Ram	....	....
6544	Elephant Rare	....	....
6545	Elephant Rail	....	....
6546	Elephant Rash	....	....
6547	Elephant Rack	....	....
6548	Elephant Rafia	....	....
6549	Elephant Rap	....	....
6550	Elephant Lace	....	....
6551	Elephant Lad	....	....
6552	Elephant Lane	....	....
6553	Elephant Lamb	....	....
6554	Elephant Lair	....	....
6555	Elephant Lily	....	....
6556	Elephant Lash	....	....
6557	Elephant Lake	....	....
6558	Elephant Laugh	....	....
6559	Elephant Lab	....	....
6560	Elephant Chase	....	....
6561	Elephant Chat	....	....
6562	Elephant Chain	....	....
6563	Elephant Chime	....	....
6564	Elephant Chair	....	....
6565	Elephant Chill	....	....
6566	Elephant Chacha	....	....
6567	Elephant Check	....	....
6568	Elephant Chaff	....	....
6569	Elephant Chap	....	....
6570	Elephant Case	....	....
6571	Elephant Cat	....	....
6572	Elephant Can	....	....
6573	Elephant Cameo	....	....
6574	Elephant Car	....	....
6575	Elephant Call	....	....
6576	Elephant Cash	....	....
6577	Elephant Cake	....	....
6578	Elephant Café	....	....
6579	Elephant Cab	....	....
6580	Elephant Face	....	....
6581	Elephant Fat	....	....

NUMBER	SEM[3]	KEY WORD	IMAGE
6582	Elephant Fan	....	....
6583	Elephant Fame	....	....
6584	Elephant Fair	....	....
6585	Elephant Fall	....	....
6586	Elephant Fish	....	....
6587	Elephant Fake	....	....
6588	Elephant Fife	....	....
6589	Elephant Fab	....	....
6590	Elephant Base	....	....
6591	Elephant Bat	....	....
6592	Elephant Ban	....	....
6593	Elephant Bam!	....	....
6594	Elephant Bar	....	....
6595	Elephant Ball	....	....
6596	Elephant Bash	....	....
6597	Elephant Back	....	....
6598	Elephant Beef	....	....
6599	Elephant Baby	....	....
6600	Chimpanzee Zoo	....	....
6601	Chimpanzee Day	....	....
6602	Chimpanzee Noah	....	....
6603	Chimpanzee Ma	....	....
6604	Chimpanzee Rah	....	....
6605	Chimpanzee Law	....	....
6606	Chimpanzee Jaw	....	....
6607	Chimpanzee Key	....	....
6608	Chimpanzee Fee	....	....
6609	Chimpanzee Bay	....	....
6610	Chimpanzee Daze	....	....
6611	Chimpanzee Dad	....	....
6612	Chimpanzee Dan	....	....
6613	Chimpanzee Dam	....	....
6614	Chimpanzee Dare	....	....
6615	Chimpanzee Dale	....	....
6616	Chimpanzee Dash	....	....
6617	Chimpanzee Deck	....	....
6618	Chimpanzee Daffy	....	....
6619	Chimpanzee Dab	....	....
6620	Chimpanzee Nasa	....	....
6621	Chimpanzee Net	....	....
6622	Chimpanzee Nan	....	....
6623	Chimpanzee Name	....	....
6624	Chimpanzee Nero	....	....
6625	Chimpanzee Nail	....	....
6626	Chimpanzee Nash	....	....
6627	Chimpanzee Nag	....	....
6628	Chimpanzee Navy	....	....
6629	Chimpanzee Nab	....	....
6630	Chimpanzee Mace	....	....
6631	Chimpanzee Mat	....	....
6632	Chimpanzee Man	....	....
6633	ChimpanzeeMa'am	....	....
6634	Chimpanzee Mare	....	....
6635	Chimpanzee Mail	....	....

NUMBER	SEM³	KEY WORD	IMAGE
6636	Chimpanzee Mash	....	....
6637	Chimpanzee Mac	....	....
6638	Chimpanzee Mafia	....	....
6639	Chimpanzee Map	....	....
6640	Chimpanzee Race	....	....
6641	Chimpanzee Rat	....	....
6642	Chimpanzee Rain	....	....
6643	Chimpanzee Ram	....	....
6644	Chimpanzee Rare	....	....
6645	Chimpanzee Rail	....	....
6646	Chimpanzee Rash	....	....
6647	Chimpanzee Rack	....	....
6648	Chimpanzee Rafia	....	....
6649	Chimpanzee Rap	....	....
6650	Chimpanzee Lace	....	....
6651	Chimpanzee Lad	....	....
6652	Chimpanzee Lane	....	....
6653	Chimpanzee Lamb	....	....
6654	Chimpanzee Lair	....	....
6655	Chimpanzee Lily	....	....
6656	Chimpanzee Lash	....	....
6657	Chimpanzee Lake	....	....
6658	Chimpanzee Laugh	....	....
6659	Chimpanzee Lab	....	....
6660	Chimpanzee Chase	....	....
6661	Chimpanzee Chat	....	....
6662	Chimpanzee Chain	....	....
6663	Chimpanzee Chime	....	....
6664	Chimpanzee Chair	....	....
6665	Chimpanzee Chill	....	....
6666	Chimpanzee Chacha	....	....
6667	Chimpanzee Check	....	....
6668	Chimpanzee Chaff	....	....
6669	Chimpanzee Chap	....	....
6670	Chimpanzee Case	....	....
6671	Chimpanzee Cat	....	....
6672	Chimpanzee Can	....	....
6673	Chimpanzee Cameo	....	....
6674	Chimpanzee Car	....	....
6675	Chimpanzee Call	....	....
6676	Chimpanzee Cash	....	....
6677	Chimpanzee Cake	....	....
6678	Chimpanzee Café	....	....
6679	Chimpanzee Cab	....	....
6680	Chimpanzee Face	....	....
6681	Chimpanzee Fat	....	....
6682	Chimpanzee Fan	....	....
6683	Chimpanzee Fame	....	....
6684	Chimpanzee Fair	....	....
6685	Chimpanzee Fall	....	....
6686	Chimpanzee Fish	....	....
6687	Chimpanzee Fake	....	....
6688	Chimpanzee Fife	....	....
6689	Chimpanzee Fab	....	....

NUMBER	SEM[3]	KEY WORD	IMAGE
6690	Chimpanzee Base		
6691	Chimpanzee Bat		
6692	Chimpanzee Ban		
6693	Chimpanzee Bam!		
6694	Chimpanzee Bar		
6695	Chimpanzee Ball		
6696	Chimpanzee Bash		
6697	Chimpanzee Back		
6698	Chimpanzee Beef		
6699	Chimpanzee Baby		
6700	Kangaroo Zoo		
6701	Kangaroo Day		
6702	Kangaroo Noah		
6703	Kangaroo Ma		
6704	Kangaroo Rah		
6705	Kangaroo Law		
6706	Kangaroo Jaw		
6707	Kangaroo Key		
6708	Kangaroo Fee		
6709	Kangaroo Bay		
6710	Kangaroo Daze		
6711	Kangaroo Dad		
6712	Kangaroo Dan		
6713	Kangaroo Dam		
6714	Kangaroo Dare		
6715	Kangaroo Dale		
6716	Kangaroo Dash		
6717	Kangaroo Deck		
6718	Kangaroo Daffy		
6719	Kangaroo Dab		
6720	Kangaroo Nasa		
6721	Kangaroo Net		
6722	Kangaroo Nan		
6723	Kangaroo Name		
6724	Kangaroo Nero		
6725	Kangaroo Nail		
6726	Kangaroo Nash		
6727	Kangaroo Nag		
6728	Kangaroo Navy		
6729	Kangaroo Nab		
6730	Kangaroo Mace		
6731	Kangaroo Mat		
6732	Kangaroo Man		
6733	Kangaroo Ma'am		
6734	Kangaroo Mare		
6735	Kangaroo Mail		
6736	Kangaroo Mash		
6737	Kangaroo Mac		
6738	Kangaroo Mafia		
6739	Kangaroo Map		
6740	Kangaroo Race		
6741	Kangaroo Rat		
6742	Kangaroo Rain		
6743	Kangaroo Ram		

140

NUMBER	SEM³	KEY WORD	IMAGE
6744	Kangaroo Rare	....	....
6745	Kangaroo Rail	....	....
6746	Kangaroo Rash	....	....
6747	Kangaroo Rack	....	....
6748	Kangaroo Rafia	....	....
6749	Kangaroo Rap	....	....
6750	Kangaroo Lace	....	....
6751	Kangaroo Lad	....	....
6752	Kangaroo Lane	....	....
6753	Kangaroo Lamb	....	....
6754	Kangaroo Lair	....	....
6755	Kangaroo Lily	....	....
6756	Kangaroo Lash	....	....
6757	Kangaroo Lake	....	....
6758	Kangaroo Laugh	....	....
6759	Kangaroo Lab	....	....
6760	Kangaroo Chase	....	....
6761	Kangaroo Chat	....	....
6762	Kangaroo Chain	....	....
6763	Kangaroo Chime	....	....
6764	Kangaroo Chair	....	....
6765	Kangaroo Chill	....	....
6766	Kangaroo Chacha	....	....
6767	Kangaroo Check	....	....
6768	Kangaroo Chaff	....	....
6769	Kangaroo Chap	....	....
6770	Kangaroo Case	....	....
6771	Kangaroo Cat	....	....
6772	Kangaroo Can	....	....
6773	Kangaroo Cameo	....	....
6774	Kangaroo Car	....	....
6775	Kangaroo Call	....	....
6776	Kangaroo Cash	....	....
6777	Kangaroo Cake	....	....
6778	Kangaroo Café	....	....
6779	Kangaroo Cab	....	....
6780	Kangaroo Face	....	....
6781	Kangaroo Fat	....	....
6782	Kangaroo Fan	....	....
6783	Kangaroo Fame	....	....
6784	Kangaroo Fair	....	....
6785	Kangaroo Fall	....	....
6786	Kangaroo Fish	....	....
6787	Kangaroo Fake	....	....
6788	Kangaroo Fife	....	....
6789	Kangaroo Fab	....	....
6790	Kangaroo Base	....	....
6791	Kangaroo Bat	....	....
6792	Kangaroo Ban	....	....
6793	Kangaroo Bam!	....	....
6794	Kangaroo Bar	....	....
6795	Kangaroo Ball	....	....
6796	Kangaroo Bash	....	....
6797	Kangaroo Back	....	....

NUMBER	SEM³	KEY WORD	IMAGE
6798	Kangaroo Beef	....	....
6799	Kangaroo Baby	....	....
6800	Fawn Zoo	....	....
6801	Fawn Day	....	....
6802	Fawn Noah	....	....
6803	Fawn Ma	....	....
6804	Fawn Rah	....	....
6805	Fawn Law	....	....
6806	Fawn Jaw	....	....
6807	Fawn Key	....	....
6808	Fawn Fee	....	....
6809	Fawn Bay	....	....
6810	Fawn Daze	....	....
6811	Fawn Dad	....	....
6812	Fawn Dan	....	....
6813	Fawn Dam	....	....
6814	Fawn Dare	....	....
6815	Fawn Dale	....	....
6816	Fawn Dash	....	....
6817	Fawn Deck	....	....
6818	Fawn Daffy	....	....
6819	Fawn Dab	....	....
6820	Fawn Nasa	....	....
6821	Fawn Net	....	....
6822	Fawn Nan	....	....
6823	Fawn Name	....	....
6824	Fawn Nero	....	....
6825	Fawn Nail	....	....
6826	Fawn Nash	....	....
6827	Fawn Nag	....	....
6828	Fawn Navy	....	....
6829	Fawn Nab	....	....
6830	Fawn Mace	....	....
6831	Fawn Mat	....	....
6832	Fawn Man	....	....
6833	Fawn Ma'am	....	....
6834	Fawn Mare	....	....
6835	Fawn Mail	....	....
6836	Fawn Mash	....	....
6837	Fawn Mac	....	....
6838	Fawn Mafia	....	....
6839	Fawn Map	....	....
6840	Fawn Race	....	....
6841	Fawn Rat	....	....
6842	Fawn Rain	....	....
6843	Fawn Ram	....	....
6844	Fawn Rare	....	....
6845	Fawn Rail	....	....
6846	Fawn Rash	....	....
6847	Fawn Rack	....	....
6848	Fawn Rafia	....	....
6849	Fawn Rap	....	....
6850	Fawn Lace	....	....
6851	Fawn Lad	....	....

NUMBER	SEM³	KEY WORD	IMAGE
6852	Fawn Lane	....	....
6853	Fawn Lamb	....	....
6854	Fawn Lair	....	....
6855	Fawn Lily	....	....
6856	Fawn Lash	....	....
6857	Fawn Lake	....	....
6858	Fawn Laugh	....	....
6859	Fawn Lab	....	....
6860	Fawn Chase	....	....
6861	Fawn Chat	....	....
6862	Fawn Chain	....	....
6863	Fawn Chime	....	....
6864	Fawn Chair	....	....
6865	Fawn Chill	....	....
6866	Fawn Chacha	....	....
6867	Fawn Check	....	....
6868	Fawn Chaff	....	....
6869	Fawn Chap	....	....
6870	Fawn Case	....	....
6871	Fawn Cat	....	....
6872	Fawn Can	....	....
6873	Fawn Cameo	....	....
6874	Fawn Car	....	....
6875	Fawn Call	....	....
6876	Fawn Cash	....	....
6877	Fawn Cake	....	....
6878	Fawn Café	....	....
6879	Fawn Cab	....	....
6880	Fawn Face	....	....
6881	Fawn Fat	....	....
6882	Fawn Fan	....	....
6883	Fawn Fame	....	....
6884	Fawn Fair	....	....
6885	Fawn Fall	....	....
6886	Fawn Fish	....	....
6887	Fawn Fake	....	....
6888	Fawn Fife	....	....
6889	Fawn Fab	....	....
6890	Fawn Base	....	....
6891	Fawn Bat	....	....
6892	Fawn Ban	....	....
6893	Fawn Bam!	....	....
6894	Fawn Bar	....	....
6895	Fawn Ball	....	....
6896	Fawn Bash	....	....
6897	Fawn Back	....	....
6898	Fawn Beef	....	....
6899	Fawn Baby	....	....
6900	Bear Zoo	....	....
6901	Bear Day	....	....
6902	Bear Noah	....	....
6903	Bear Ma	....	....
6904	Bear Rah	....	....
6905	Bear Law	....	....

143

NUMBER	SEM³	KEY WORD	IMAGE
6906	Bear Jaw	....	....
6907	Bear Key	....	....
6908	Bear Fee	....	....
6909	Bear Bay	....	....
6910	Bear Daze	....	....
6911	Bear Dad	....	....
6912	Bear Dan	....	....
6913	Bear Dam	....	....
6914	Bear Dare	....	....
6915	Bear Dale	....	....
6916	Bear Dash	....	....
6917	Bear Deck	....	....
6918	Bear Daffy	....	....
6919	Bear Dab	....	....
6920	Bear Nasa	....	....
6921	Bear Net	....	....
6922	Bear Nan	....	....
6923	Bear Name	....	....
6924	Bear Nero	....	....
6925	Bear Nail	....	....
6926	Bear Nash	....	....
6927	Bear Nag	....	....
6928	Bear Navy	....	....
6929	Bear Nab	....	....
6930	Bear Mace	....	....
6931	Bear Mat	....	....
6932	Bear Man	....	....
6933	Bear Ma'am	....	....
6934	Bear Mare	....	....
6935	Bear Mail	....	....
6936	Bear Mash	....	....
6937	Bear Mac	....	....
6938	Bear Mafia	....	....
6939	Bear Map	....	....
6940	Bear Race	....	....
6941	Bear Rat	....	....
6942	Bear Rain	....	....
6943	Bear Ram	....	....
6944	Bear Rare	....	....
6945	Bear Rail	....	....
6946	Bear Rash	....	....
6947	Bear Rack	....	....
6948	Bear Rafia	....	....
6949	Bear Rap	....	....
6950	Bear Lace	....	....
6951	Bear Lad	....	....
6952	Bear Lane	....	....
6953	Bear Lamb	....	....
6954	Bear Lair	....	....
6955	Bear Lily	....	....
6956	Bear Lash	....	....
6957	Bear Lake	....	....
6958	Bear Laugh	....	....
6959	Bear Lab	....	....

144

NUMBER	SEM[3]	KEY WORD	IMAGE
6960	Bear Chase	....	....
6961	Bear Chat	....	....
6962	Bear Chain	....	....
6963	Bear Chime	....	....
6964	Bear Chair	....	....
6965	Bear Chill	....	....
6966	Bear Chacha	....	....
6967	Bear Check	....	....
6968	Bear Chaff	....	....
6969	Bear Chap	....	....
6970	Bear Case	....	....
6971	Bear Cat	....	....
6972	Bear Can	....	....
6973	Bear Cameo	....	....
6974	Bear Car	....	....
6975	Bear Call	....	....
6976	Bear Cash	....	....
6977	Bear Cake	....	....
6978	Bear Café	....	....
6979	Bear Cab	....	....
6980	Bear Face	....	....
6981	Bear Fat	....	....
6982	Bear Fan	....	....
6983	Bear Fame	....	....
6984	Bear Fair	....	....
6985	Bear Fall	....	....
6986	Bear Fish	....	....
6987	Bear Fake	....	....
6988	Bear Fife	....	....
6989	Bear Fab	....	....
6990	Bear Base	....	....
6991	Bear Bat	....	....
6992	Bear Ban	....	....
6993	Bear Bam!	....	....
6994	Bear Bar	....	....
6995	Bear Ball	....	....
6996	Bear Bash	....	....
6997	Bear Back	....	....
6998	Bear Beef	....	....
6999	Bear Baby	....	....

CHAPTER EIGHT

BIRDS

NUMBER	SEM^3	KEY WORD	IMAGE
7000	Seagull Zoo	....	....
7001	Seagull Day	....	....
7002	Seagull Noah	....	....
7003	Seagull Ma	....	....
7004	Seagull Rah	....	....
7005	Seagull Law	....	....
7006	Seagull Jaw	....	....
7007	Seagull Key	....	....
7008	Seagull Fee	....	....
7009	Seagull Bay	....	....
7010	Seagull Daze	....	....
7011	Seagull Dad	....	....
7012	Seagull Dan	....	....
7013	Seagull Dam	....	....
7014	Seagull Dare	....	....
7015	Seagull Dale	....	....
7016	Seagull Dash	....	....
7017	Seagull Deck	....	....
7018	Seagull Daffy	....	....
7019	Seagull Dab	....	....
7020	Seagull Nasa	....	....
7021	Seagull Net	....	....
7022	Seagull Nan	....	....
7023	Seagull Name	....	....
7024	Seagull Nero	....	....
7025	Seagull Nail	....	....
7026	Seagull Nash	....	....
7027	Seagull Nag	....	....
7028	Seagull Navy	....	....
7029	Seagull Nab	....	....
7030	Seagull Mace	....	....
7031	Seagull Mat	....	....
7032	Seagull Man	....	....
7033	Seagull Ma'am	....	....
7034	Seagull Mare	....	....
7035	Seagull Mail	....	....
7036	Seagull Mash	....	....
7037	Seagull Mac	....	....
7038	Seagull Mafia	....	....
7039	Seagull Map	....	....
7040	Seagull Race	....	....
7041	Seagull Rat	....	....

NUMBER	SEM[3]	KEY WORD	IMAGE
7042	Seagull Rain	....	....
7043	Seagull Ram	....	....
7044	Seagull Rare	....	....
7045	Seagull Rail	....	....
7046	Seagull Rash	....	....
7047	Seagull Rack	....	....
7048	Seagull Rafia	....	....
7049	Seagull Rap	....	....
7050	Seagull Lace	....	....
7051	Seagull Lad	....	....
7052	Seagull Lane	....	....
7053	Seagull Lamb	....	....
7054	Seagull Lair	....	....
7055	Seagull Lily	....	....
7056	Seagull Lash	....	....
7057	Seagull Lake	....	....
7058	Seagull Laugh	....	....
7059	Seagull Lab	....	....
7060	Seagull Chase	....	....
7061	Seagull Chat	....	....
7062	Seagull Chain	....	....
7063	Seagull Chime	....	....
7064	Seagull Chair	....	....
7065	Seagull Chill	....	....
7066	Seagull Chacha	....	....
7067	Seagull Check	....	....
7068	Seagull Chaff	....	....
7069	Seagull Chap	....	....
7070	Seagull Case	....	....
7071	Seagull Cat	....	....
7072	Seagull Can	....	....
7073	Seagull Cameo	....	....
7074	Seagull Car	....	....
7075	Seagull Call	....	....
7076	Seagull Cash	....	....
7077	Seagull Cake	....	....
7078	Seagull Café	....	....
7079	Seagull Cab	....	....
7080	Seagull Face	....	....
7081	Seagull Fat	....	....
7082	Seagull Fan	....	....
7083	Seagull Fame	....	....
7084	Seagull Fair	....	....
7085	Seagull Fall	....	....
7086	Seagull Fish	....	....
7087	Seagull Fake	....	....
7088	Seagull Fife	....	....
7089	Seagull Fab	....	....
7090	Seagull Base	....	....
7091	Seagull Bat	....	....
7092	Seagull Ban	....	....
7093	Seagull Bam!	....	....
7094	Seagull Bar	....	....
7095	Seagull Ball	....	....

NUMBER	SEM³	KEY WORD	IMAGE
7096	Seagull Bash	....	....
7097	Seagull Back	....	....
7098	Seagull Beef	....	....
7099	Seagull Baby	....	....
7100	Duck Zoo	....	....
7101	Duck Day	....	....
7102	Duck Noah	....	....
7103	Duck Ma	....	....
7104	Duck Rah	....	....
7105	Duck Law	....	....
7106	Duck Jaw	....	....
7107	Duck Key	....	....
7108	Duck Fee	....	....
7109	Duck Bay	....	....
7110	Duck Daze	....	....
7111	Duck Dad	....	....
7112	Duck Dan	....	....
7113	Duck Dam	....	....
7114	Duck Dare	....	....
7115	Duck Dale	....	....
7116	Duck Dash	....	....
7117	Duck Deck	....	....
7118	Duck Daffy	....	....
7119	Duck Dab	....	....
7120	Duck Nasa	....	....
7121	Duck Net	....	....
7122	Duck Nan	....	....
7123	Duck Name	....	....
7124	Duck Nero	....	....
7125	Duck Nail	....	....
7126	Duck Nash	....	....
7127	Duck Nag	....	....
7128	Duck Navy	....	....
7129	Duck Nab	....	....
7130	Duck Mace	....	....
7131	Duck Mat	....	....
7132	Duck Man	....	....
7133	Duck Ma'am	....	....
7134	Duck Mare	....	....
7135	Duck Mail	....	....
7136	Duck Mash	....	....
7137	Duck Mac	....	....
7138	Duck Mafia	....	....
7139	Duck Map	....	....
7140	Duck Race	....	....
7141	Duck Rat	....	....
7142	Duck Rain	....	....
7143	Duck Ram	....	....
7144	Duck Rare	....	....
7145	Duck Rail	....	....
7146	Duck Rash	....	....
7147	Duck Rack	....	....
7148	Duck Rafia	....	....
7149	Duck Rap	....	....

NUMBER	SEM[3]	KEY WORD	IMAGE
7150	Duck Lace	....	....
7151	Duck Lad	....	....
7152	Duck Lane	....	....
7153	Duck Lamb	....	....
7154	Duck Lair	....	....
7155	Duck Lily	....	....
7156	Duck Lash	....	....
7157	Duck Lake	....	....
7158	Duck Laugh	....	....
7159	Duck Lab	....	....
7160	Duck Chase	....	....
7161	Duck Chat	....	....
7162	Duck Chain	....	....
7163	Duck Chime	....	....
7164	Duck Chair	....	....
7165	Duck Chill	....	....
7166	Duck Chacha	....	....
7167	Duck Check	....	....
7168	Duck Chaff	....	....
7169	Duck Chap	....	....
7170	Duck Case	....	....
7171	Duck Cat	....	....
7172	Duck Can	....	....
7173	Duck Cameo	....	....
7174	Duck Car	....	....
7175	Duck Call	....	....
7176	Duck Cash	....	....
7177	Duck Cake	....	....
7178	Duck Café	....	....
7179	Duck Cab	....	....
7180	Duck Face	....	....
7181	Duck Fat	....	....
7182	Duck Fan	....	....
7183	Duck Fame	....	....
7184	Duck Fair	....	....
7185	Duck Fall	....	....
7186	Duck Fish	....	....
7187	Duck Fake	....	....
7188	Duck Fife	....	....
7189	Duck Fab	....	....
7190	Duck Base	....	....
7191	Duck Bat	....	....
7192	Duck Ban	....	....
7193	Duck Bam!	....	....
7194	Duck Bar	....	....
7195	Duck Ball	....	....
7196	Duck Bash	....	....
7197	Duck Back	....	....
7198	Duck Beef	....	....
7199	Duck Baby	....	....
7200	Nightingale Zoo	....	....
7201	Nightingale Day	....	....
7202	Nightingale Noah	....	....
7203	Nightingale Ma	....	....

NUMBER	SEM³	KEY WORD	IMAGE
7204	Nightingale Rah	....	....
7205	Nightingale Law	....	....
7206	Nightingale Jaw	....	....
7207	Nightingale Key	....	....
7208	Nightingale Fee	....	....
7209	Nightingale Bay	....	....
7210	Nightingale Daze	....	....
7211	Nightingale Dad	....	....
7212	Nightingale Dan	....	....
7213	Nightingale Dam	....	....
7214	Nightingale Dare	....	....
7215	Nightingale Dale	....	....
7216	Nightingale Dash	....	....
7217	Nightingale Deck	....	....
7218	Nightingale Daffy	....	....
7219	Nightingale Dab	....	....
7220	Nightingale Nasa	....	....
7221	Nightingale Net	....	....
7222	Nightingale Nan	....	....
7223	Nightingale Name	....	....
7224	Nightingale Nero	....	....
7225	Nightingale Nail	....	....
7226	Nightingale Nash	....	....
7227	Nightingale Nag	....	....
7228	Nightingale Navy	....	....
7229	Nightingale Nab	....	....
7230	Nightingale Mace	....	....
7231	Nightingale Mat	....	....
7232	Nightingale Man	....	....
7233	Nightingale Ma'am	....	....
7234	Nightingale Mare	....	....
7235	Nightingale Mail	....	....
7236	Nightingale Mash	....	....
7237	Nightingale Mac	....	....
7238	Nightingale Mafia	....	....
7239	Nightingale Map	....	....
7240	Nightingale Race	....	....
7241	Nightingale Rat	....	....
7242	Nightingale Rain	....	....
7243	Nightingale Ram	....	....
7244	Nightingale Rare	....	....
7245	Nightingale Rail	....	....
7246	Nightingale Rash	....	....
7247	Nightingale Rack	....	....
7248	Nightingale Rafia	....	....
7249	Nightingale Rap	....	....
7250	Nightingale Lace	....	....
7251	Nightingale Lad	....	....
7252	Nightingale Lane	....	....
7253	Nightingale Lamb	....	....
7254	Nightingale Lair	....	....
7255	Nightingale Lily	....	....
7256	Nightingale Lash	....	....
7257	Nightingale Lake	....	....

NUMBER	SEM³	KEY WORD	IMAGE
7258	Nightingale Laugh	....	....
7259	Nightingale Lab	....	....
7260	Nightingale Chase	....	....
7261	Nightingale Chat	....	....
7262	Nightingale Chain	....	....
7263	Nightingale Chime	....	....
7264	Nightingale Chair	....	....
7265	Nightingale Chill	....	....
7266	NightingaleChacha	....	....
7267	Nightingale Check	....	....
7268	Nightingale Chaff	....	....
7269	Nightingale Chap	....	....
7270	Nightingale Case	....	....
7271	Nightingale Cat	....	....
7272	Nightingale Can	....	....
7273	Nightingale Cameo	....	....
7274	Nightingale Car	....	....
7275	Nightingale Call	....	....
7276	Nightingale Cash	....	....
7277	Nightingale Cake	....	....
7278	Nightingale Café	....	....
7279	Nightingale Cab	....	....
7280	Nightingale Face	....	....
7281	Nightingale Fat	....	....
7282	Nightingale Fan	....	....
7283	Nightingale Fame	....	....
7284	Nightingale Fair	....	....
7285	Nightingale Fall	....	....
7286	Nightingale Fish	....	....
7287	Nightingale Fake	....	....
7288	Nightingale Fife	....	....
7289	Nightingale Fab	....	....
7290	Nightingale Base	....	....
7291	Nightingale Bat	....	....
7292	Nightingale Ban	....	....
7293	Nightingale Bam!	....	....
7294	Nightingale Bar	....	....
7295	Nightingale Ball	....	....
7296	Nightingale Bash	....	....
7297	Nightingale Back	....	....
7298	Nightingale Beef	....	....
7299	Nightingale Baby	....	....
7300	Magpie Zoo	....	....
7301	Magpie Day	....	....
7302	Magpie Noah	....	....
7303	Magpie Ma	....	....
7304	Magpie Rah	....	....
7305	Magpie Law	....	....
7306	Magpie Jaw	....	....
7307	Magpie Key	....	....
7308	Magpie Fee	....	....
7309	Magpie Bay	....	....
7310	Magpie Daze	....	....
7311	Magpie Dad	....	....

NUMBER	SEM[3]	KEY WORD	IMAGE
7312	Magpie Dan	....	....
7313	Magpie Dam	....	....
7314	Magpie Dare	....	....
7315	Magpie Dale	....	....
7316	Magpie Dash	....	....
7317	Magpie Deck	....	....
7318	Magpie Daffy	....	....
7319	Magpie Dab	....	....
7320	Magpie Nasa	....	....
7321	Magpie Net	....	....
7322	Magpie Nan	....	....
7323	Magpie Name	....	....
7324	Magpie Nero	....	....
7325	Magpie Nail	....	....
7326	Magpie Nash	....	....
7327	Magpie Nag	....	....
7328	Magpie Navy	....	....
7329	Magpie Nab	....	....
7330	Magpie Mace	....	....
7331	Magpie Mat	....	....
7332	Magpie Man	....	....
7333	Magpie Ma'am	....	....
7334	Magpie Mare	....	....
7335	Magpie Mail	....	....
7336	Magpie Mash	....	....
7337	Magpie Mac	....	....
7338	Magpie Mafia	....	....
7339	Magpie Map	....	....
7340	Magpie Race	....	....
7341	Magpie Rat	....	....
7342	Magpie Rain	....	....
7343	Magpie Ram	....	....
7344	Magpie Rare	....	....
7345	Magpie Rail	....	....
7346	Magpie Rash	....	....
7347	Magpie Rack	....	....
7348	Magpie Rafia	....	....
7349	Magpie Rap	....	....
7350	Magpie Lace	....	....
7351	Magpie Lad	....	....
7352	Magpie Lane	....	....
7353	Magpie Lamb	....	....
7354	Magpie Lair	....	....
7355	Magpie Lily	....	....
7356	Magpie Lash	....	....
7357	Magpie Lake	....	....
7358	Magpie Laugh	....	....
7359	Magpie Lab	....	....
7360	Magpie Chase	....	....
7361	Magpie Chat	....	....
7362	Magpie Chain	....	....
7363	Magpie Chime	....	....
7364	Magpie Chair	....	....
7365	Magpie Chill	....	....

NUMBER	SEM[3]	KEY WORD	IMAGE
7366	Magpie Chacha	....	....
7367	Magpie Check	....	....
7368	Magpie Chaff	....	....
7369	Magpie Chap	....	....
7370	Magpie Case	....	....
7371	Magpie Cat	....	....
7372	Magpie Can	....	....
7373	Magpie Cameo	....	....
7374	Magpie Car	....	....
7375	Magpie Call	....	....
7376	Magpie Cash	....	....
7377	Magpie Cake	....	....
7378	Magpie Café	....	....
7379	Magpie Cab	....	....
7380	Magpie Face	....	....
7381	Magpie Fat	....	....
7382	Magpie Fan	....	....
7383	Magpie Fame	....	....
7384	Magpie Fair	....	....
7385	Magpie Fall	....	....
7386	Magpie Fish	....	....
7387	Magpie Fake	....	....
7388	Magpie Fife	....	....
7389	Magpie Fab	....	....
7390	Magpie Base	....	....
7391	Magpie Bat	....	....
7392	Magpie Ban	....	....
7393	Magpie Bam!	....	....
7394	Magpie Bar	....	....
7395	Magpie Ball	....	....
7396	Magpie Bash	....	....
7397	Magpie Back	....	....
7398	Magpie Beef	....	....
7399	Magpie Baby	....	....
7400	Rooster Zoo	....	....
7401	Rooster Day	....	....
7402	Rooster Noah	....	....
7403	Rooster Ma	....	....
7404	Rooster Rah	....	....
7405	Rooster Law	....	....
7406	Rooster Jaw	....	....
7407	Rooster Key	....	....
7408	Rooster Fee	....	....
7409	Rooster Bay	....	....
7410	Rooster Daze	....	....
7411	Rooster Dad	....	....
7412	Rooster Dan	....	....
7413	Rooster Dam	....	....
7414	Rooster Dare	....	....
7415	Rooster Dale	....	....
7416	Rooster Dash	....	....
7417	Rooster Deck	....	....
7418	Rooster Daffy	....	....
7419	Rooster Dab	....	....

153

NUMBER	SEM[3]	KEY WORD	IMAGE
7420	Rooster Nasa		
7421	Rooster Net		
7422	Rooster Nan		
7423	Rooster Name		
7424	Rooster Nero		
7425	Rooster Nail		
7426	Rooster Nash		
7427	Rooster Nag		
7428	Rooster Navy		
7429	Rooster Nab		
7430	Rooster Mace		
7431	Rooster Mat		
7432	Rooster Man		
7433	Rooster Ma'am		
7434	Rooster Mare		
7435	Rooster Mail		
7436	Rooster Mash		
7437	Rooster Mac		
7438	Rooster Mafia		
7439	Rooster Map		
7440	Rooster Race		
7441	Rooster Rat		
7442	Rooster Rain		
7443	Rooster Ram		
7444	Rooster Rare		
7445	Rooster Rail		
7446	Rooster Rash		
7447	Rooster Rack		
7448	Rooster Rafia		
7449	Rooster Rap		
7450	Rooster Lace		
7451	Rooster Lad		
7452	Rooster Lane		
7453	Rooster Lamb		
7454	Rooster Lair		
7455	Rooster Lily		
7456	Rooster Lash		
7457	Rooster Lake		
7458	Rooster Laugh		
7459	Rooster Lab		
7460	Rooster Chase		
7461	Rooster Chat		
7462	Rooster Chain		
7463	Rooster Chime		
7464	Rooster Chair		
7465	Rooster Chill		
7466	Rooster Chacha		
7467	Rooster Check		
7468	Rooster Chaff		
7469	Rooster Chap		
7470	Rooster Case		
7471	Rooster Cat		
7472	Rooster Can		
7473	Rooster Cameo		

NUMBER	SEM[3]	KEY WORD	IMAGE
7474	Rooster Car	....	....
7475	Rooster Call	....	....
7476	Rooster Cash	....	....
7477	Rooster Cake	....	....
7478	Rooster Café	....	....
7479	Rooster Cab	....	....
7480	Rooster Face	....	....
7481	Rooster Fat	....	....
7482	Rooster Fan	....	....
7483	Rooster Fame	....	....
7484	Rooster Fair	....	....
7485	Rooster Fall	....	....
7486	Rooster Fish	....	....
7487	Rooster Fake	....	....
7488	Rooster Fife	....	....
7489	Rooster Fab	....	....
7490	Rooster Base	....	....
7491	Rooster Bat	....	....
7492	Rooster Ban	....	....
7493	Rooster Bam!	....	....
7494	Rooster Bar	....	....
7495	Rooster Ball	....	....
7496	Rooster Bash	....	....
7497	Rooster Back	....	....
7498	Rooster Beef	....	....
7499	Rooster Baby	....	....
7500	Lapwing Zoo	....	....
7501	Lapwing Day	....	....
7502	Lapwing Noah	....	....
7503	Lapwing Ma	....	....
7504	Lapwing Rah	....	....
7505	Lapwing Law	....	....
7506	Lapwing Jaw	....	....
7507	Lapwing Key	....	....
7508	Lapwing Fee	....	....
7509	Lapwing Bay	....	....
7510	Lapwing Daze	....	....
7511	Lapwing Dad	....	....
7512	Lapwing Dan	....	....
7513	Lapwing Dam	....	....
7514	Lapwing Dare	....	....
7515	Lapwing Dale	....	....
7516	Lapwing Dash	....	....
7517	Lapwing Deck	....	....
7518	Lapwing Daffy	....	....
7519	Lapwing Dab	....	....
7520	Lapwing Nasa	....	....
7521	Lapwing Net	....	....
7522	Lapwing Nan	....	....
7523	Lapwing Name	....	....
7524	Lapwing Nero	....	....
7525	Lapwing Nail	....	....
7526	Lapwing Nash	....	....
7527	Lapwing Nag	....	....

NUMBER	SEM³	KEY WORD	IMAGE
7528	Lapwing Navy	....	....
7529	Lapwing Nab	....	....
7530	Lapwing Mace	....	....
7531	Lapwing Mat	....	....
7532	Lapwing Man	....	....
7533	Lapwing Ma'am	....	....
7534	Lapwing Mare	....	....
7535	Lapwing Mail	....	....
7536	Lapwing Mash	....	....
7537	Lapwing Mac	....	....
7538	Lapwing Mafia	....	....
7539	Lapwing Map	....	....
7540	Lapwing Race	....	....
7541	Lapwing Rat	....	....
7542	Lapwing Rain	....	....
7543	Lapwing Ram	....	....
7544	Lapwing Rare	....	....
7545	Lapwing Rail	....	....
7546	Lapwing Rash	....	....
7547	Lapwing Rack	....	....
7548	Lapwing Rafia	....	....
7549	Lapwing Rap	....	....
7550	Lapwing Lace	....	....
7551	Lapwing Lad	....	....
7552	Lapwing Lane	....	....
7553	Lapwing Lamb	....	....
7554	Lapwing Lair	....	....
7555	Lapwing Lily	....	....
7556	Lapwing Lash	....	....
7557	Lapwing Lake	....	....
7558	Lapwing Laugh	....	....
7559	Lapwing Lab	....	....
7560	Lapwing Chase	....	....
7561	Lapwing Chat	....	....
7562	Lapwing Chain	....	....
7563	Lapwing Chime	....	....
7564	Lapwing Chair	....	....
7565	Lapwing Chill	....	....
7566	Lapwing Chacha	....	....
7567	Lapwing Check	....	....
7568	Lapwing Chaff	....	....
7569	Lapwing Chap	....	....
7570	Lapwing Case	....	....
7571	Lapwing Cat	....	....
7572	Lapwing Can	....	....
7573	Lapwing Cameo	....	....
7574	Lapwing Car	....	....
7575	Lapwing Call	....	....
7576	Lapwing Cash	....	....
7577	Lapwing Cake	....	....
7578	Lapwing Café	....	....
7579	Lapwing Cab	....	....
7580	Lapwing Face	....	....
7581	Lapwing Fat	....	....

NUMBER	SEM³	KEY WORD	IMAGE
7582	Lapwing Fan	....	....
7583	Lapwing Fame	....	....
7584	Lapwing Fair	....	....
7585	Lapwing Fall	....	....
7586	Lapwing Fish	....	....
7587	Lapwing Fake	....	....
7588	Lapwing Fife	....	....
7589	Lapwing Fab	....	....
7590	Lapwing Base	....	....
7591	Lapwing Bat	....	....
7592	Lapwing Ban	....	....
7593	Lapwing Bam!	....	....
7594	Lapwing Bar	....	....
7595	Lapwing Ball	....	....
7596	Lapwing Bash	....	....
7597	Lapwing Back	....	....
7598	Lapwing Beef	....	....
7599	Lapwing Baby	....	....
7600	Chaffinch Zoo	....	....
7601	Chaffinch Day	....	....
7602	Chaffinch Noah	....	....
7603	Chaffinch Ma	....	....
7604	Chaffinch Rah	....	....
7605	Chaffinch Law	....	....
7606	Chaffinch Jaw	....	....
7607	Chaffinch Key	....	....
7608	Chaffinch Fee	....	....
7609	Chaffinch Bay	....	....
7610	Chaffinch Daze	....	....
7611	Chaffinch Dad	....	....
7612	Chaffinch Dan	....	....
7613	Chaffinch Dam	....	....
7614	Chaffinch Dare	....	....
7615	Chaffinch Dale	....	....
7616	Chaffinch Dash	....	....
7617	Chaffinch Deck	....	....
7618	Chaffinch Daffy	....	....
7619	Chaffinch Dab	....	....
7620	Chaffinch Nasa	....	....
7621	Chaffinch Net	....	....
7622	Chaffinch Nan	....	....
7623	Chaffinch Name	....	....
7624	Chaffinch Nero	....	....
7625	Chaffinch Nail	....	....
7626	Chaffinch Nash	....	....
7627	Chaffinch Nag	....	....
7628	Chaffinch Navy	....	....
7629	Chaffinch Nab	....	....
7630	Chaffinch Mace	....	....
7631	Chaffinch Mat	....	....
7632	Chaffinch Man	....	....
7633	Chaffinch Ma'am	....	....
7634	Chaffinch Mare	....	....
7635	Chaffinch Mail	....	....

157

NUMBER	SEM³	KEY WORD	IMAGE
7636	Chaffinch Mash	....	....
7637	Chaffinch Mac	....	....
7638	Chaffinch Mafia	....	....
7639	Chaffinch Map	....	....
7640	Chaffinch Race	....	....
7641	Chaffinch Rat	....	....
7642	Chaffinch Rain	....	....
7643	Chaffinch Ram	....	....
7644	Chaffinch Rare	....	....
7645	Chaffinch Rail	....	....
7646	Chaffinch Rash	....	....
7647	Chaffinch Rack	....	....
7648	Chaffinch Rafia	....	....
7649	Chaffinch Rap	....	....
7650	Chaffinch Lace	....	....
7651	Chaffinch Lad	....	....
7652	Chaffinch Lane	....	....
7653	Chaffinch Lamb	....	....
7654	Chaffinch Lair	....	....
7655	Chaffinch Lily	....	....
7656	Chaffinch Lash	....	....
7657	Chaffinch Lake	....	....
7658	Chaffinch Laugh	....	....
7659	Chaffinch Lab	....	....
7660	Chaffinch Chase	....	....
7661	Chaffinch Chat	....	....
7662	Chaffinch Chain	....	....
7663	Chaffinch Chime	....	....
7664	Chaffinch Chair	....	....
7665	Chaffinch Chill	....	....
7666	Chaffinch Chacha	....	....
7667	Chaffinch Check	....	....
7668	Chaffinch Chaff	....	....
7669	Chaffinch Chap	....	....
7670	Chaffinch Case	....	....
7671	Chaffinch Cat	....	....
7672	Chaffinch Can	....	....
7673	Chaffinch Cameo	....	....
7674	Chaffinch Car	....	....
7675	Chaffinch Call	....	....
7676	Chaffinch Cash	....	....
7677	Chaffinch Cake	....	....
7678	Chaffinch Café	....	....
7679	Chaffinch Cab	....	....
7680	Chaffinch Face	....	....
7681	Chaffinch Fat	....	....
7682	Chaffinch Fan	....	....
7683	Chaffinch Fame	....	....
7684	Chaffinch Fair	....	....
7685	Chaffinch Fall	....	....
7686	Chaffinch Fish	....	....
7687	Chaffinch Fake	....	....
7688	Chaffinch Fife	....	....
7689	Chaffinch Fab	....	....

NUMBER	SEM³	KEY WORD	IMAGE
7690	Chaffinch Base	....	....
7691	Chaffinch Bat	....	....
7692	Chaffinch Ban	....	....
7693	Chaffinch Bam!	....	....
7694	Chaffinch Bar	....	....
7695	Chaffinch Ball	....	....
7696	Chaffinch Bash	....	....
7697	Chaffinch Back	....	....
7698	Chaffinch Beef	....	....
7699	Chaffinch Baby	....	....
7700	Eagle Zoo	....	....
7701	Eagle Day	....	....
7702	Eagle Noah	....	....
7703	Eagle Ma	....	....
7704	Eagle Rah	....	....
7705	Eagle Law	....	....
7706	Eagle Jaw	....	....
7707	Eagle Key	....	....
7708	Eagle Fee	....	....
7709	Eagle Bay	....	....
7710	Eagle Daze	....	....
7711	Eagle Dad	....	....
7712	Eagle Dan	....	....
7713	Eagle Dam	....	....
7714	Eagle Dare	....	....
7715	Eagle Dale	....	....
7716	Eagle Dash	....	....
7717	Eagle Deck	....	....
7718	Eagle Daffy	....	....
7719	Eagle Dab	....	....
7720	Eagle Nasa	....	....
7721	Eagle Net	....	....
7722	Eagle Nan	....	....
7723	Eagle Name	....	....
7724	Eagle Nero	....	....
7725	Eagle Nail	....	....
7726	Eagle Nash	....	....
7727	Eagle Nag	....	....
7728	Eagle Navy	....	....
7729	Eagle Nab	....	....
7730	Eagle Mace	....	....
7731	Eagle Mat	....	....
7732	Eagle Man	....	....
7733	Eagle Ma'am	....	....
7734	Eagle Mare	....	....
7735	Eagle Mail	....	....
7736	Eagle Mash	....	....
7737	Eagle Mac	....	....
7738	Eagle Mafia	....	....
7739	Eagle Map	....	....
7740	Eagle Race	....	....
7741	Eagle Rat	....	....
7742	Eagle Rain	....	....
7743	Eagle Ram	....	....

NUMBER	SEM³	KEY WORD	IMAGE
7744	Eagle Rare	....	....
7745	Eagle Rail	....	....
7746	Eagle Rash	....	....
7747	Eagle Rack	....	....
7748	Eagle Rafia	....	....
7749	Eagle Rap	....	....
7750	Eagle Lace	....	....
7751	Eagle Lad	....	....
7752	Eagle Lane	....	....
7753	Eagle Lamb	....	....
7754	Eagle Lair	....	....
7755	Eagle Lily	....	....
7756	Eagle Lash	....	....
7757	Eagle Lake	....	....
7758	Eagle Laugh	....	....
7759	Eagle Lab	....	....
7760	Eagle Chase	....	....
7761	Eagle Chat	....	....
7762	Eagle Chain	....	....
7763	Eagle Chime	....	....
7764	Eagle Chair	....	....
7765	Eagle Chill	....	....
7766	Eagle Chacha	....	....
7767	Eagle Check	....	....
7768	Eagle Chaff	....	....
7769	Eagle Chap	....	....
7770	Eagle Case	....	....
7771	Eagle Cat	....	....
7772	Eagle Can	....	....
7773	Eagle Cameo	....	....
7774	Eagle Car	....	....
7775	Eagle Call	....	....
7776	Eagle Cash	....	....
7777	Eagle Cake	....	....
7778	Eagle Café	....	....
7779	Eagle Cab	....	....
7780	Eagle Face	....	....
7781	Eagle Fat	....	....
7782	Eagle Fan	....	....
7783	Eagle Fame	....	....
7784	Eagle Fair	....	....
7785	Eagle Fall	....	....
7786	Eagle Fish	....	....
7787	Eagle Fake	....	....
7788	Eagle Fife	....	....
7789	Eagle Fab	....	....
7790	Eagle Base	....	....
7791	Eagle Bat	....	....
7792	Eagle Ban	....	....
7793	Eagle Bam!	....	....
7794	Eagle Bar	....	....
7795	Eagle Ball	....	....
7796	Eagle Bash	....	....
7797	Eagle Back	....	....

NUMBER	SEM³	KEY WORD	IMAGE
7798	Eagle Beef	....	....
7799	Eagle Baby	....	....
7800	Flamingo Zoo	....	....
7801	Flamingo Day	....	....
7802	Flamingo Noah	....	....
7803	Flamingo Ma	....	....
7804	Flamingo Rah	....	....
7805	Flamingo Law	....	....
7806	Flamingo Jaw	....	....
7807	Flamingo Key	....	....
7808	Flamingo Fee	....	....
7809	Flamingo Bay	....	....
7810	Flamingo Daze	....	....
7811	Flamingo Dad	....	....
7812	Flamingo Dan	....	....
7813	Flamingo Dam	....	....
7814	Flamingo Dare	....	....
7815	Flamingo Dale	....	....
7816	Flamingo Dash	....	....
7817	Flamingo Deck	....	....
7818	Flamingo Daffy	....	....
7819	Flamingo Dab	....	....
7820	Flamingo Nasa	....	....
7821	Flamingo Net	....	....
7822	Flamingo Nan	....	....
7823	Flamingo Name	....	....
7824	Flamingo Nero	....	....
7825	Flamingo Nail	....	....
7826	Flamingo Nash	....	....
7827	Flamingo Nag	....	....
7828	Flamingo Navy	....	....
7829	Flamingo Nab	....	....
7830	Flamingo Mace	....	....
7831	Flamingo Mat	....	....
7832	Flamingo Man	....	....
7833	Flamingo Ma'am	....	....
7834	Flamingo Mare	....	....
7835	Flamingo Mail	....	....
7836	Flamingo Mash	....	....
7837	Flamingo Mac	....	....
7838	Flamingo Mafia	....	....
7839	Flamingo Map	....	....
7840	Flamingo Race	....	....
7841	Flamingo Rat	....	....
7842	Flamingo Rain	....	....
7843	Flamingo Ram	....	....
7844	Flamingo Rare	....	....
7845	Flamingo Rail	....	....
7846	Flamingo Rash	....	....
7847	Flamingo Rack	....	....
7848	Flamingo Rafia	....	....
7849	Flamingo Rap	....	....
7850	Flamingo Lace	....	....
7851	Flamingo Lad	....	....

NUMBER	SEM³	KEY WORD	IMAGE
7852	Flamingo Lane	....	....
7853	Flamingo Lamb	....	....
7854	Flamingo Lair	....	....
7855	Flamingo Lily	....	....
7856	Flamingo Lash	....	....
7857	Flamingo Lake	....	....
7858	Flamingo Laugh	....	....
7859	Flamingo Lab	....	....
7860	Flamingo Chase	....	....
7861	Flamingo Chat	....	....
7862	Flamingo Chain	....	....
7863	Flamingo Chime	....	....
7864	Flamingo Chair	....	....
7865	Flamingo Chill	....	....
7866	Flamingo Chacha	....	....
7867	Flamingo Check	....	....
7868	Flamingo Chaff	....	....
7869	Flamingo Chap	....	....
7870	Flamingo Case	....	....
7871	Flamingo Cat	....	....
7872	Flamingo Can	....	....
7873	Flamingo Cameo	....	....
7874	Flamingo Car	....	....
7875	Flamingo Call	....	....
7876	Flamingo Cash	....	....
7877	Flamingo Cake	....	....
7878	Flamingo Cafe	....	....
7879	Flamingo Cab	....	....
7880	Flamingo Face	....	....
7881	Flamingo Fat	....	....
7882	Flamingo Fan	....	....
7883	Flamingo Fame	....	....
7884	Flamingo Fair	....	....
7885	Flamingo Fall	....	....
7886	Flamingo Fish	....	....
7887	Flamingo Fake	....	....
7888	Flamingo Fife	....	....
7889	Flamingo Fab	....	....
7890	Flamingo Base	....	....
7891	Flamingo Bat	....	....
7892	Flamingo Ban	....	....
7893	Flamingo Bam!	....	....
7894	Flamingo Bar	....	....
7895	Flamingo Ball	....	....
7896	Flamingo Bash	....	....
7897	Flamingo Back	....	....
7898	Flamingo Beef	....	....
7899	Flamingo Baby	....	....
7900	Peacock Zoo	....	....
7901	Peacock Day	....	....
7902	Peacock Noah	....	....
7903	Peacock Ma	....	....
7904	Peacock Rah	....	....
7905	Peacock Law	....	....

NUMBER	SEM³	KEY WORD	IMAGE
7906	Peacock Jaw	....	....
7907	Peacock Key	....	....
7908	Peacock Fee	....	....
7909	Peacock Bay	....	....
7910	Peacock Daze	....	....
7911	Peacock Dad	....	....
7912	Peacock Dan	....	....
7913	Peacock Dam	....	....
7914	Peacock Dare	....	....
7915	Peacock Dale	....	....
7916	Peacock Dash	....	....
7917	Peacock Deck	....	....
7918	Peacock Daffy	....	....
7919	Peacock Dab	....	....
7920	Peacock Nasa	....	....
7921	Peacock Net	....	....
7922	Peacock Nan	....	....
7923	Peacock Name	....	....
7924	Peacock Nero	....	....
7925	Peacock Nail	....	....
7926	Peacock Nash	....	....
7927	Peacock Nag	....	....
7928	Peacock Navy	....	....
7929	Peacock Nab	....	....
7930	Peacock Mace	....	....
7931	Peacock Mat	....	....
7932	Peacock Man	....	....
7933	Peacock Ma'am	....	....
7934	Peacock Mare	....	....
7935	Peacock Mail	....	....
7936	Peacock Mash	....	....
7937	Peacock Mac	....	....
7938	Peacock Mafia	....	....
7939	Peacock Map	....	....
7940	Peacock Race	....	....
7941	Peacock Rat	....	....
7942	Peacock Rain	....	....
7943	Peacock Ram	....	....
7944	Peacock Rare	....	....
7945	Peacock Rail	....	....
7946	Peacock Rash	....	....
7947	Peacock Rack	....	....
7948	Peacock Rafia	....	....
7949	Peacock Rap	....	....
7950	Peacock Lace	....	....
7951	Peacock Lad	....	....
7952	Peacock Lane	....	....
7953	Peacock Lamb	....	....
7954	Peacock Lair	....	....
7955	Peacock Lily	....	....
7956	Peacock Lash	....	....
7957	Peacock Lake	....	....
7958	Peacock Laugh	....	....
7959	Peacock Lab	....	....

NUMBER	SEM³	KEY WORD	IMAGE
7960	Peacock Chase	....	....
7961	Peacock Chat	....	....
7962	Peacock Chain	....	....
7963	Peacock Chime	....	....
7964	Peacock Chair	....	....
7965	Peacock Chill	....	....
7966	Peacock Chacha	....	....
7967	Peacock Check	....	....
7968	Peacock Chaff	....	....
7969	Peacock Chap	....	....
7970	Peacock Case	....	....
7971	Peacock Cat	....	....
7972	Peacock Can	....	....
7973	Peacock Cameo	....	....
7974	Peacock Car	....	....
7975	Peacock Call	....	....
7976	Peacock Cash	....	....
7977	Peacock Cake	....	....
7978	Peacock Café	....	....
7979	Peacock Cab	....	....
7980	Peacock Face	....	....
7981	Peacock Fat	....	....
7982	Peacock Fan	....	....
7983	Peacock Fame	....	....
7984	Peacock Fair	....	....
7985	Peacock Fall	....	....
7986	Peacock Fish	....	....
7987	Peacock Fake	....	....
7988	Peacock Fife	....	....
7989	Peacock Fab	....	....
7990	Peacock Base	....	....
7991	Peacock Bat	....	....
7992	Peacock Ban	....	.:.......................
7993	Peacock Bam!	....	....
7994	Peacock Bar	....	....
7995	Peacock Ball	....	....
7996	Peacock Bash	....	....
7997	Peacock Back	....	....
7998	Peacock Beef	....	....
7999	Peacock Baby	....	....

CHAPTER NINE

RAINBOW

NUMBER	SEM[3]	KEY WORD	IMAGE
8000	Red Zoo	....	....
8001	Red Day	....	....
8002	Red Noah	....	....
8003	Red Ma	....	....
8004	Red Rah	....	....
8005	Red Law	....	....
8006	Red Jaw	....	....
8007	Red Key	....	....
8008	Red Fee	....	....
8009	Red Bay	....	....
8010	Red Daze	....	....
8011	Red Dad	....	....
8012	Red Dan	....	....
8013	Red Dam	....	....
8014	Red Dare	....	....
8015	Red Dale	....	....
8016	Red Dash	....	....
8017	Red Deck	....	....
8018	Red Daffy	....	....
8019	Red Dab	....	....
8020	Red Nasa	....	....
8021	Red Net	....	....
8022	Red Nan	....	....
8023	Red Name	....	....
8024	Red Nero	....	....
8025	Red Nail	....	....
8026	Red Nash	....	....
8027	Red Nag	....	....
8028	Red Navy	....	....
8029	Red Nab	....	....
8030	Red Mace	....	....
8031	Red Mat	....	....
8032	Red Man	....	....
8033	Red Ma'am	....	....
8034	Red Mare	....	....
8035	Red Mail	....	....
8036	Red Mash	....	....
8037	Red Mac	....	....
8038	Red Mafia	....	....
8039	Red Map	....	....
8040	Red Race	....	....
8041	Red Rat	....	....

NUMBER	SEM³	KEY WORD	IMAGE
8042	Red Rain	....	....
8043	Red Ram	....	....
8044	Red Rare	....	....
8045	Red Rail	....	....
8046	Red Rash	....	....
8047	Red Rack	....	....
8048	Red Rafia	....	....
8049	Red Rap	....	....
8050	Red Lace	....	....
8051	Red Lad	....	....
8052	Red Lane	....	....
8053	Red Lamb	....	....
8054	Red Lair	....	....
8055	Red Lily	....	....
8056	Red Lash	....	....
8057	Red Lake	....	....
8058	Red Laugh	....	....
8059	Red Lab	....	....
8060	Red Chase	....	....
8061	Red Chat	....	....
8062	Red Chain	....	....
8063	Red Chime	....	....
8064	Red Chair	....	....
8065	Red Chill	....	....
8066	Red Chacha	....	....
8067	Red Check	....	....
8068	Red Chaff	....	....
8069	Red Chap	....	....
8070	Red Case	....	....
8071	Red Cat	....	....
8072	Red Can	....	....
8073	Red Cameo	....	....
8074	Red Car	....	....
8075	Red Call	....	....
8076	Red Cash	....	....
8077	Red Cake	....	....
8078	Red Café	....	....
8079	Red Cab	....	....
8080	Red Face	....	....
8081	Red Fat	....	....
8082	Red Fan	....	....
8083	Red Fame	....	....
8084	Red Fair	....	....
8085	Red Fall	....	....
8086	Red Fish	....	....
8087	Red Fake	....	....
8088	Red Fife	....	....
8089	Red Fab	....	....
8090	Red Base	....	....
8091	Red Bat	....	....
8092	Red Ban	....	....
8093	Red Bam!	....	....
8094	Red Bar	....	....
8095	Red Ball	....	....

NUMBER	SEM³	KEY WORD	IMAGE
8096	Red Bash	....	....
8097	Red Back	....	....
8098	Red Beef	....	....
8099	Red Baby	....	....
8100	Orange Zoo	....	....
8101	Orange Day	....	....
8102	Orange Noah	....	....
8103	Orange Ma	....	....
8104	Orange Rah	....	....
8105	Orange Law	....	....
8106	Orange Jaw	....	....
8107	Orange Key	....	....
8108	Orange Fee	....	....
8109	Orange Bay	....	....
8110	Orange Daze	....	....
8111	Orange Dad	....	....
8112	Orange Dan	....	....
8113	Orange Dam	....	....
8114	Orange Dare	....	....
8115	Orange Dale	....	....
8116	Orange Dash	....	....
8117	Orange Deck	....	....
8118	Orange Daffy	....	....
8119	Orange Dab	....	....
8120	Orange Nasa	....	....
8121	Orange Net	....	....
8122	Orange Nan	....	....
8123	Orange Name	....	....
8124	Orange Nero	....	....
8125	Orange Nail	....	....
8126	Orange Nash	....	....
8127	Orange Nag	....	....
8128	Orange Navy	....	....
8129	Orange Nab	....	....
8130	Orange Mace	....	....
8131	Orange Mat	....	....
8132	Orange Man	....	....
8133	Orange Ma'am	....	....
8134	Orange Mare	....	....
8135	Orange Mail	....	....
8136	Orange Mash	....	....
8137	Orange Mac	....	....
8138	Orange Mafia	....	....
8139	Orange Map	....	....
8140	Orange Race	....	....
8141	Orange Rat	....	....
8142	Orange Rain	....	....
8143	Orange Ram	....	....
8144	Orange Rare	....	....
8145	Orange Rail	....	....
8146	Orange Rash	....	....
8147	Orange Rack	....	....
8148	Orange Rafia	....	....
8149	Orange Rap	....	....

NUMBER	SEM³	KEY WORD	IMAGE
8150	Orange Lace	....	....
8151	Orange Lad	....	....
8152	Orange Lane	....	....
8153	Orange Lamb	....	....
8154	Orange Lair	....	....
8155	Orange Lily	....	....
8156	Orange Lash	....	....
8157	Orange Lake	....	....
8158	Orange Laugh	....	....
8159	Orange Lab	....	....
8160	Orange Chase	....	....
8161	Orange Chat	....	....
8162	Orange Chain	....	....
8163	Orange Chime	....	....
8164	Orange Chair	....	....
8165	Orange Chill	....	....
8166	Orange Chacha	....	....
8167	Orange Check	....	....
8168	Orange Chaff	....	....
8169	Orange Chap	....	....
8170	Orange Case	....	....
8171	Orange Cat	....	....
8172	Orange Can	....	....
8173	Orange Cameo	....	....
8174	Orange Car	....	....
8175	Orange Call	....	....
8176	Orange Cash	....	....
8177	Orange Cake	....	....
8178	Orange Café	....	....
8179	Orange Cab	....	....
8180	Orange Face	....	....
8181	Orange Fat	....	....
8182	Orange Fan	....	....
8183	Orange Fame	....	....
8184	Orange Fair	....	....
8185	Orange Fall	....	....
8186	Orange Fish	....	....
8187	Orange Fake	....	....
8188	Orange Fife	....	....
8189	Orange Fab	....	....
8190	Orange Base	....	....
8191	Orange Bat	....	....
8192	Orange Ban	....	....
8193	Orange Bam!	....	....
8194	Orange Bar	....	....
8195	Orange Ball	....	....
8196	Orange Bash	....	....
8197	Orange Back	....	....
8198	Orange Beef	....	....
8199	Orange Baby	....	....
8200	Yellow Zoo	....	....
8201	Yellow Day	....	....
8202	Yellow Noah	....	....
8203	Yellow Ma	....	....

168

NUMBER	SEM³	KEY WORD	IMAGE
8204	Yellow Rah	....	....
8205	Yellow Law	....	....
8206	Yellow Jaw	....	....
8207	Yellow Key	....	....
8208	Yellow Fee	....	....
8209	Yellow Bay	....	....
8210	Yellow Daze	....	....
8211	Yellow Dad	....	....
8212	Yellow Dan	....	....
8213	Yellow Dam	....	....
8214	Yellow Dare	....	....
8215	Yellow Dale	....	....
8216	Yellow Dash	....	....
8217	Yellow Deck	....	....
8218	Yellow Daffy	....	....
8219	Yellow Dab	....	....
8220	Yellow Nasa	....	....
8221	Yellow Net	....	....
8222	Yellow Nan	....	....
8223	Yellow Name	....	....
8224	Yellow Nero	....	....
8225	Yellow Nail	....	....
8226	Yellow Nash	....	....
8227	Yellow Nag	....	....
8228	Yellow Navy	....	....
8229	Yellow Nab	....	....
8230	Yellow Mace	....	....
8231	Yellow Mat	....	....
8232	Yellow Man	....	....
8233	Yellow Ma'am	....	....
8234	Yellow Mare	....	....
8235	Yellow Mail	....	....
8236	Yellow Mash	....	....
8237	Yellow Mac	....	....
8238	Yellow Mafia	....	....
8239	Yellow Map	....	....
8240	Yellow Race	....	....
8241	Yellow Rat	....	....
8242	Yellow Rain	....	....
8243	Yellow Ram	....	....
8244	Yellow Rare	....	....
8245	Yellow Rail	....	....
8246	Yellow Rash	....	....
8247	Yellow Rack	....	....
8248	Yellow Rafia	....	....
8249	Yellow Rap	....	....
8250	Yellow Lace	....	....
8251	Yellow Lad	....	....
8252	Yellow Lane	....	....
8253	Yellow Lamb	....	....
8254	Yellow Lair	....	....
8255	Yellow Lily	....	....
8256	Yellow Lash	....	....
8257	Yellow Lake	....	....

NUMBER	SEM³	KEY WORD	IMAGE
8258	Yellow Laugh	....	....
8259	Yellow Lab	....	....
8260	Yellow Chase	....	....
8261	Yellow Chat	....	....
8262	Yellow Chain	....	....
8263	Yellow Chime	....	....
8264	Yellow Chair	....	....
8265	Yellow Chill	....	....
8266	Yellow Chacha	....	....
8267	Yellow Check	....	....
8268	Yellow Chaff	....	....
8269	Yellow Chap	....	....
8270	Yellow Case	....	....
8271	Yellow Cat	....	....
8272	Yellow Can	....	....
8273	Yellow Cameo	....	....
8274	Yellow Car	....	....
8275	Yellow Call	....	....
8276	Yellow Cash	....	....
8277	Yellow Cake	....	....
8278	Yellow Café	....	....
8279	Yellow Cab	....	....
8280	Yellow Face	....	....
8281	Yellow Fat	....	....
8282	Yellow Fan	....	....
8283	Yellow Fame	....	....
8284	Yellow Fair	....	....
8285	Yellow Fall	....	....
8286	Yellow Fish	....	....
8287	Yellow Fake	....	....
8288	Yellow Fife	....	....
8289	Yellow Fab	....	....
8290	Yellow Base	....	....
8291	Yellow Bat	....	....
8292	Yellow Ban	....	....
8293	Yellow Bam!	....	....
8294	Yellow Bar	....	....
8295	Yellow Ball	....	....
8296	Yellow Bash	....	....
8297	Yellow Back	....	....
8298	Yellow Beef	....	....
8299	Yellow Baby	....	....
8300	Green Zoo	....	....
8301	Green Day	....	....
8302	Green Noah	....	....
8303	Green Ma	....	....
8304	Green Rah	....	....
8305	Green Law	....	....
8306	Green Jaw	....	....
8307	Green Key	....	....
8308	Green Fee	....	....
8309	Green Bay	....	....
8310	Green Daze	....	....
8311	Green Dad	....	....

NUMBER	SEM[3]	KEY WORD	IMAGE
8312	Green Dan	....	....
8313	Green Dam	....	....
8314	Green Dare	....	....
8315	Green Dale	....	....
8316	Green Dash	....	....
8317	Green Deck	....	....
8318	Green Daffy	....	....
8319	Green Dab	....	....
8320	Green Nasa	....	....
8321	Green Net	....	....
8322	Green Nan	....	....
8323	Green Name	....	....
8324	Green Nero	....	....
8325	Green Nail	....	....
8326	Green Nash	....	....
8327	Green Nag	....	....
8328	Green Navy	....	....
8329	Green Nab	....	....
8330	Green Mace	....	....
8331	Green Mat	....	....
8332	Green Man	....	....
8333	Green Ma'am	....	....
8334	Green Mare	....	....
8335	Green Mail	....	....
8336	Green Mash	....	....
8337	Green Mac	....	....
8338	Green Mafia	....	....
8339	Green Map	....	....
8340	Green Race	....	....
8341	Green Rat	....	....
8342	Green Rain	....	....
8343	Green Ram	....	....
8344	Green Rare	....	....
8345	Green Rail	....	....
8346	Green Rash	....	....
8347	Green Rack	....	....
8348	Green Rafia	....	....
8349	Green Rap	....	....
8350	Green Lace	....	....
8351	Green Lad	....	....
8352	Green Lane	....	....
8353	Green Lamb	....	....
8354	Green Lair	....	....
8355	Green Lily	....	....
8356	Green Lash	....	....
8357	Green Lake	....	....
8358	Green Laugh	....	....
8359	Green Lab	....	....
8360	Green Chase	....	....
8361	Green Chat	....	....
8362	Green Chain	....	....
8363	Green Chime	....	....
8364	Green Chair	....	....
8365	Green Chill	....	....

NUMBER	SEM³	KEY WORD	IMAGE
8366	Green Chacha	....	....
8367	Green Check	....	....
8368	Green Chaff	....	....
8369	Green Chap	....	....
8370	Green Case	....	....
8371	Green Cat	....	....
8372	Green Can	....	....
8373	Green Cameo	....	....
8374	Green Car	....	....
8375	Green Call	....	....
8376	Green Cash	....	....
8377	Green Cake	....	....
8378	Green Café	....	....
8379	Green Cab	....	....
8380	Green Face	....	....
8381	Green Fat	....	....
8382	Green Fan	....	....
8383	Green Fame	....	....
8384	Green Fair	....	....
8385	Green Fall	....	....
8386	Green Fish	....	....
8387	Green Fake	....	....
8388	Green Fife	....	....
8389	Green Fab	....	....
8390	Green Base	....	....
8391	Green Bat	....	....
8392	Green Ban	....	....
8393	Green Bam!	....	....
8394	Green Bar	....	....
8395	Green Ball	....	....
8396	Green Bash	....	....
8397	Green Back	....	....
8398	Green Beef	....	....
8399	Green Baby	....	....
8400	Blue Zoo	....	....
8401	Blue Day	....	....
8402	Blue Noah	....	....
8403	Blue Ma	....	....
8404	Blue Rah	....	....
8405	Blue Law	....	....
8406	Blue Jaw	....	....
8407	Blue Key	....	....
8408	Blue Fee	....	....
8409	Blue Bay	....	....
8410	Blue Daze	....	....
8411	Blue Dad	....	....
8412	Blue Dan	....	....
8413	Blue Dam	....	....
8414	Blue Dare	....	....
8415	Blue Dale	....	....
8416	Blue Dash	....	....
8417	Blue Deck	....	....
8418	Blue Daffy	....	....
8419	Blue Dab	....	....

NUMBER	SEM³	KEY WORD	IMAGE
8420	Blue Nasa	....	....
8421	Blue Net	....	....
8422	Blue Nan	....	....
8423	Blue Name	....	....
8424	Blue Nero	....	....
8425	Blue Nail	....	....
8426	Blue Nash	....	....
8427	Blue Nag	....	....
8428	Blue Navy	....	....
8429	Blue Nab	....	....
8430	Blue Mace	....	....
8431	Blue Mat	....	....
8432	Blue Man	....	....
8433	Blue Ma'am	....	....
8434	Blue Mare	....	....
8435	Blue Mail	....	....
8436	Blue Mash	....	....
8437	Blue Mac	....	....
8438	Blue Mafia	....	....
8439	Blue Map	....	....
8440	Blue Race	....	....
8441	Blue Rat	....	....
8442	Blue Rain	....	....
8443	Blue Ram	....	....
8444	Blue Rare	....	....
8445	Blue Rail	....	....
8446	Blue Rash	....	....
8447	Blue Rack	....	....
8448	Blue Rafia	....	....
8449	Blue Rap	....	....
8450	Blue Lace	....	....
8451	Blue Lad	....	....
8452	Blue Lane	....	....
8453	Blue Lamb	....	....
8454	Blue Lair	....	....
8455	Blue Lily	....	....
8456	Blue Lash	....	....
8457	Blue Lake	....	....
8458	Blue Laugh	....	....
8459	Blue Lab	....	....
8460	Blue Chase	....	....
8461	Blue Chat	....	....
8462	Blue Chain	....	....
8463	Blue Chime	....	....
8464	Blue Chair	....	....
8465	Blue Chill	....	....
8466	Blue Chacha	....	....
8467	Blue Check	....	....
8468	Blue Chaff	....	....
8469	Blue Chap	....	....
8470	Blue Case	....	....
8471	Blue Cat	....	....
8472	Blue Can	....	....
8473	Blue Cameo	....	....

NUMBER	SEM³	KEY WORD	IMAGE
8474	Blue Car	....	....
8475	Blue Call	....	....
8476	Blue Cash	....	....
8477	Blue Cake	....	....
8478	Blue Café	....	....
8479	Blue Cab	....	....
8480	Blue Face	....	....
8481	Blue Fat	....	....
8482	Blue Fan	....	....
8483	Blue Fame	....	....
8484	Blue Fair	....	....
8485	Blue Fall	....	....
8486	Blue Fish	....	....
8487	Blue Fake	....	....
8488	Blue Fife	....	....
8489	Blue Fab	....	....
8490	Blue Base	....	....
8491	Blue Bat	....	....
8492	Blue Ban	....	....
8493	Blue Bam!	....	....
8494	Blue Bar	....	....
8495	Blue Ball	....	....
8496	Blue Bash	....	....
8497	Blue Back	....	....
8498	Blue Beef	....	....
8499	Blue Baby	....	....
8500	Indigo Zoo	....	....
8501	Indigo Day	....	....
8502	Indigo Noah	....	....
8503	Indigo Ma	....	....
8504	Indigo Rah	....	....
8505	Indigo Law	....	....
8506	Indigo Jaw	....	....
8507	Indigo Key	....	....
8508	Indigo Fee	....	....
8509	Indigo Bay	....	....
8510	Indigo Daze	....	....
8511	Indigo Dad	....	....
8512	Indigo Dan	....	....
8513	Indigo Dam	....	....
8514	Indigo Dare	....	....
8515	Indigo Dale	....	....
8516	Indigo Dash	....	....
8517	Indigo Deck	....	....
8518	Indigo Daffy	....	....
8519	Indigo Dab	....	....
8520	Indigo Nasa	....	....
8521	Indigo Net	....	....
8522	Indigo Nan	....	....
8523	Indigo Name	....	....
8524	Indigo Nero	....	....
8525	Indigo Nail	....	....
8526	Indigo Nash	....	....
8527	Indigo Nag	....	....

174

NUMBER	SEM[3]	KEY WORD	IMAGE
8528	Indigo Navy	....	....
8529	Indigo Nab	....	....
8530	Indigo Mace	....	....
8531	Indigo Mat	....	....
8532	Indigo Man	....	....
8533	Indigo Ma'am	....	....
8534	Indigo Mare	....	....
8535	Indigo Mail	....	....
8536	Indigo Mash	....	....
8537	Indigo Mac	....	....
8538	Indigo Mafia	....	....
8539	Indigo Map	....	....
8540	Indigo Race	....	....
8541	Indigo Rat	....	....
8542	Indigo Rain	....	....
8543	Indigo Ram	....	....
8544	Indigo Rare	....	....
8545	Indigo Rail	....	....
8546	Indigo Rash	....	....
8547	Indigo Rack	....	....
8548	Indigo Rafia	....	....
8549	Indigo Rap	....	....
8550	Indigo Lace	....	....
8551	Indigo Lad	....	....
8552	Indigo Lane	....	....
8553	Indigo Lamb	....	....
8554	Indigo Lair	....	....
8555	Indigo Lily	....	....
8556	Indigo Lash	....	....
8557	Indigo Lake	....	....
8558	Indigo Laugh	....	....
8559	Indigo Lab	....	....
8560	Indigo Chase	....	....
8561	Indigo Chat	....	....
8562	Indigo Chain	....	....
8563	Indigo Chime	....	....
8564	Indigo Chair	....	....
8565	Indigo Chill	....	....
8566	Indigo Chacha	....	....
8567	Indigo Check	....	....
8568	Indigo Chaff	....	....
8569	Indigo Chap	....	....
8570	Indigo Case	....	....
8571	Indigo Cat	....	....
8572	Indigo Can	....	....
8573	Indigo Cameo	....	....
8574	Indigo Car	....	....
8575	Indigo Call	....	....
8576	Indigo Cash	....	....
8577	Indigo Cake	....	....
8578	Indigo Café	....	....
8579	Indigo Cab	....	....
8580	Indigo Face	....	....
8581	Indigo Fat	....	....

NUMBER	SEM³	KEY WORD	IMAGE
8582	Indigo Fan	....	....
8583	Indigo Fame	....	....
8584	Indigo Fair	....	....
8585	Indigo Fall	....	....
8586	Indigo Fish	....	....
8587	Indigo Fake	....	....
8588	Indigo Fife	....	....
8589	Indigo Fab	....	....
8590	Indigo Base	....	....
8591	Indigo Bat	....	....
8592	Indigo Ban	....	....
8593	Indigo Bam!	....	....
8594	Indigo Bar	....	....
8595	Indigo Ball	....	....
8596	Indigo Bash	....	....
8597	Indigo Back	....	....
8598	Indigo Beef	....	....
8599	Indigo Baby	....	....
8600	Violet Zoo	....	....
8601	Violet Day	....	....
8602	Violet Noah	....	....
8603	Violet Ma	....	....
8604	Violet Rah	....	....
8605	Violet Law	....	....
8606	Violet Jaw	....	....
8607	Violet Key	....	....
8608	Violet Fee	....	....
8609	Violet Bay	....	....
8610	Violet Daze	....	....
8611	Violet Dad	....	....
8612	Violet Dan	....	....
8613	Violet Dam	....	....
8614	Violet Dare	....	....
8615	Violet Dale	....	....
8616	Violet Dash	....	....
8617	Violet Deck	....	....
8618	Violet Daffy	....	....
8619	Violet Dab	....	....
8620	Violet Nasa	....	....
8621	Violet Net	....	....
8622	Violet Nan	....	....
8623	Violet Name	....	....
8624	Violet Nero	....	....
8625	Violet Nail	....	....
8626	Violet Nash	....	....
8627	Violet Nag	....	....
8628	Violet Navy	....	....
8629	Violet Nab	....	....
8630	Violet Mace	....	....
8631	Violet Mat	....	....
8632	Violet Man	....	....
8633	Violet Ma'am	....	....
8634	Violet Mare	....	....
8635	Violet Mail	....	....

NUMBER	SEM³	KEY WORD	IMAGE
8636	Violet Mash	....	....
8637	Violet Mac	....	....
8638	Violet Mafia	....	....
8639	Violet Map	....	....
8640	Violet Race	....	....
8641	Violet Rat	....	....
8642	Violet Rain	....	....
8643	Violet Ram	....	....
8644	Violet Rare	....	....
8645	Violet Rail	....	....
8646	Violet Rash	....	....
8647	Violet Rack	....	....
8648	Violet Rafia	....	....
8649	Violet Rap	....	....
8650	Violet Lace	....	....
8651	Violet Lad	....	....
8652	Violet Lane	....	....
8653	Violet Lamb	....	....
8654	Violet Lair	....	....
8655	Violet Lily	....	....
8656	Violet Lash	....	....
8657	Violet Lake	....	....
8658	Violet Laugh	....	....
8659	Violet Lab	....	....
8660	Violet Chase	....	....
8661	Violet Chat	....	....
8662	Violet Chain	....	....
8663	Violet Chime	....	....
8664	Violet Chair	....	....
8665	Violet Chill	....	....
8666	Violet Chacha	....	....
8667	Violet Check	....	....
8668	Violet Chaff	....	....
8669	Violet Chap	....	....
8670	Violet Case	....	....
8671	Violet Cat	....	....
8672	Violet Can	....	....
8673	Violet Cameo	....	....
8674	Violet Car	....	....
8675	Violet Call	....	....
8676	Violet Cash	....	....
8677	Violet Cake	....	....
8678	Violet Café	....	....
8679	Violet Cab	....	....
8680	Violet Face	....	....
8681	Violet Fat	....	....
8682	Violet Fan	....	....
8683	Violet Fame	....	....
8684	Violet Fair	....	....
8685	Violet Fall	....	....
8686	Violet Fish	....	....
8687	Violet Fake	....	....
8688	Violet Fife	....	....
8689	Violet Fab	....	....

NUMBER	SEM³	KEY WORD	IMAGE
8690	Violet Base	....	....
8691	Violet Bat	....	....
8692	Violet Ban	....	....
8693	Violet Bam!	....	....
8694	Violet Bar	....	....
8695	Violet Ball	....	....
8696	Violet Bash	....	....
8697	Violet Back	....	....
8698	Violet Beef	....	....
8699	Violet Baby	....	....
8700	Black Zoo	....	....
8701	Black Day	....	....
8702	Black Noah	....	....
8703	Black Ma	....	....
8704	Black Rah	....	....
8705	Black Law	....	....
8706	Black Jaw	....	....
8707	Black Key	....	....
8708	Black Fee	....	....
8709	Black Bay	....	....
8710	Black Daze	....	....
8711	Black Dad	....	....
8712	Black Dan	....	....
8713	Black Dam	....	....
8714	Black Dare	....	....
8715	Black Dale	....	....
8716	Black Dash	....	....
8717	Black Deck	....	....
8718	Black Daffy	....	....
8719	Black Dab	....	....
8720	Black Nasa	....	....
8721	Black Net	....	....
8722	Black Nan	....	....
8723	Black Name	....	....
8724	Black Nero	....	....
8725	Black Nail	....	....
8726	Black Nash	....	....
8727	Black Nag	....	....
8728	Black Navy	....	....
8729	Black Nab	....	....
8730	Black Mace	....	....
8731	Black Mat	....	....
8732	Black Man	....	....
8733	Black Ma'am	....	....
8734	Black Mare	....	....
8735	Black Mail	....	....
8736	Black Mash	....	....
8737	Black Mac	....	....
8738	Black Mafia	....	....
8739	Black Map	....	....
8740	Black Race	....	....
8741	Black Rat	....	....
8742	Black Rain	....	....
8743	Black Ram	....	....

NUMBER	SEM[3]	KEY WORD	IMAGE
8744	Black Rare	....	....
8745	Black Rail	....	....
8746	Black Rash	....	....
8747	Black Rack	....	....
8748	Black Rafia	....	....
8749	Black Rap	....	....
8750	Black Lace	....	....
8751	Black Lad	....	....
8752	Black Lane	....	....
8753	Black Lamb	....	....
8754	Black Lair	....	....
8755	Black Lily	....	....
8756	Black Lash	....	....
8757	Black Lake	....	....
8758	Black Laugh	....	....
8759	Black Lab	....	....
8760	Black Chase	....	....
8761	Black Chat	....	....
8762	Black Chain	....	....
8763	Black Chime	....	....
8764	Black Chair	....	....
8765	Black Chill	....	....
8766	Black Chacha	....	....
8767	Black Check	....	....
8768	Black Chaff	....	....
8769	Black Chap	....	....
8770	Black Case	....	....
8771	Black Cat	....	....
8772	Black Can	....	....
8773	Black Cameo	....	....
8774	Black Car	....	....
8775	Black Call	....	....
8776	Black Cash	....	....
8777	Black Cake	....	....
8778	Black Café	....	....
8779	Black Cab	....	....
8780	Black Face	....	....
8781	Black Fat	....	....
8782	Black Fan	....	....
8783	Black Fame	....	....
8784	Black Fair	....	....
8785	Black Fall	....	....
8786	Black Fish	....	....
8787	Black Fake	....	....
8788	Black Fife	....	....
8789	Black Fab	....	....
8790	Black Base	....	....
8791	Black Bat	....	....
8792	Black Ban	....	....
8793	Black Bam!	....	....
8794	Black Bar	....	....
8795	Black Ball	....	....
8796	Black Bash	....	....
8797	Black Back	....	....

179

NUMBER	SEM[3]	KEY WORD	IMAGE
8798	Black Beef	....	....
8799	Black Baby	....	....
8800	Grey Zoo	....	....
8801	Grey Day	....	....
8802	Grey Noah	....	....
8803	Grey Ma	....	....
8804	Grey Rah	....	....
8805	Grey Law	....	....
8806	Grey Jaw	....	....
8807	Grey Key	....	....
8808	Grey Fee	....	....
8809	Grey Bay	....	....
8810	Grey Daze	....	....
8811	Grey Dad	....	....
8812	Grey Dan	....	....
8813	Grey Dam	....	....
8814	Grey Dare	....	....
8815	Grey Dale	....	....
8816	Grey Dash	....	....
8817	Grey Deck	....	....
8818	Grey Daffy	....	....
8819	Grey Dab	....	....
8820	Grey Nasa	....	....
8821	Grey Net	....	....
8822	Grey Nan	....	....
8823	Grey Name	....	....
8824	Grey Nero	....	....
8825	Grey Nail	....	....
8826	Grey Nash	....	....
8827	Grey Nag	....	....
8828	Grey Navy	....	....
8829	Grey Nab	....	....
8830	Grey Mace	....	....
8831	Grey Mat	....	....
8832	Grey Man	....	....
8833	Grey Ma'am	....	....
8834	Grey Mare	....	....
8835	Grey Mail	....	....
8836	Grey Mash	....	....
8837	Grey Mac	....	....
8838	Grey Mafia	....	....
8839	Grey Map	....	....
8840	Grey Race	....	....
8841	Grey Rat	....	....
8842	Grey Rain	....	....
8843	Grey Ram	....	....
8844	Grey Rare	....	....
8845	Grey Rail	....	....
8846	Grey Rash	....	....
8847	Grey Rack	....	....
8848	Grey Rafia	....	....
8849	Grey Rap	....	....
8850	Grey Lace	....	....
8851	Grey Lad	....	....

NUMBER	SEM³	KEY WORD	IMAGE
8852	Grey Lane	....	....
8853	Grey Lamb	....	....
8854	Grey Lair	....	....
8855	Grey Lily	....	....
8856	Grey Lash	....	....
8857	Grey Lake	....	....
8858	Grey Laugh	....	....
8859	Grey Lab	....	....
8860	Grey Chase	....	....
8861	Grey Chat	....	....
8862	Grey Chain	....	....
8863	Grey Chime	....	....
8864	Grey Chair	....	....
8865	Grey Chill	....	....
8866	Grey Chacha	....	....
8867	Grey Check	....	....
8868	Grey Chaff	....	....
8869	Grey Chap	....	....
8870	Grey Case	....	....
8871	Grey Cat	....	....
8872	Grey Can	....	....
8873	Grey Cameo	....	....
8874	Grey Car	....	....
8875	Grey Call	....	....
8876	Grey Cash	....	....
8877	Grey Cake	....	....
8878	Grey Café	....	....
8879	Grey Cab	....	....
8880	Grey Face	....	....
8881	Grey Fat	....	....
8882	Grey Fan	....	....
8883	Grey Fame	....	....
8884	Grey Fair	....	....
8885	Grey Fall	....	....
8886	Grey Fish	....	....
8887	Grey Fake	....	....
8888	Grey Fife	....	....
8889	Grey Fab	....	....
8890	Grey Base	....	....
8891	Grey Bat	....	....
8892	Grey Ban	....	....
8893	Grey Bam!	....	....
8894	Grey Bar	....	....
8895	Grey Ball	....	....
8896	Grey Bash	....	....
8897	Grey Back	....	....
8898	Grey Beef	....	....
8899	Grey Baby	....	....
8900	White Zoo	....	....
8901	White Day	....	....
8902	White Noah	....	....
8903	White Ma	....	....
8904	White Rah	....	....
8905	White Law	....	....

NUMBER	SEM³	KEY WORD	IMAGE
8906	White Jaw	....	....
8907	White Key	....	....
8908	White Fee	....	....
8909	White Bay	....	....
8910	White Daze	....	....
8911	White Dad	....	....
8912	White Dan	....	....
8913	White Dam	....	....
8914	White Dare	....	....
8915	White Dale	....	....
8916	White Dash	....	....
8917	White Deck	....	....
8918	White Daffy	....	....
8919	White Dab	....	....
8920	White Nasa	....	....
8921	White Net	....	....
8922	White Nan	....	....
8923	White Name	....	....
8924	White Nero	....	....
8925	White Nail	....	....
8926	White Nash	....	....
8927	White Nag	....	....
8928	White Navy	....	....
8929	White Nab	....	....
8930	White Mace	....	....
8931	White Mat	....	....
8932	White Man	....	....
8933	White Ma'am	....	....
8934	White Mare	....	....
8935	White Mail	....	....
8936	White Mash	....	....
8937	White Mac	....	....
8938	White Mafia	....	....
8939	White Map	....	....
8940	White Race	....	....
8941	White Rat	....	....
8942	White Rain	....	....
8943	White Ram	....	....
8944	White Rare	....	....
8945	White Rail	....	....
8946	White Rash	....	....
8947	White Rack	....	....
8948	White Rafia	....	....
8949	White Rap	....	....
8950	White Lace	....	....
8951	White Lad	....	....
8952	White Lane	....	....
8953	White Lamb	....	....
8954	White Lair	....	....
8955	White Lily	....	....
8956	White Lash	....	....
8957	White Lake	....	....
8958	White Laugh	....	....
8959	White Lab	....	....

NUMBER	SEM³	KEY WORD	IMAGE
8960	White Chase	....	....
8961	White Chat	....	....
8962	White Chain	....	....
8963	White Chime	....	....
8964	White Chair	....	....
8965	White Chill	....	....
8966	White Chacha	....	....
8967	White Check	....	....
8968	White Chaff	....	....
8969	White Chap	....	....
8970	White Case	....	....
8971	White Cat	....	....
8972	White Can	....	....
8973	White Cameo	....	....
8974	White Car	....	....
8975	White Call	....	....
8976	White Cash	....	....
8977	White Cake	....	....
8978	White Café	....	....
8979	White Cab	....	....
8980	White Face	....	....
8981	White Fat	....	....
8982	White Fan	....	....
8983	White Fame	....	....
8984	White Fair	....	....
8985	White Fall	....	....
8986	White Fish	....	....
8987	White Fake	....	....
8988	White Fife	....	....
8989	White Fab	....	....
8990	White Base	....	....
8991	White Bat	....	....
8992	White Ban	....	....
8993	White Bam!	....	....
8994	White Bar	....	....
8995	White Ball	....	....
8996	White Bash	....	....
8997	White Back	....	....
8998	White Beef	....	....
8999	White Baby	....	....

CHAPTER TEN

THE SOLAR SYSTEM

NUMBER	SEM³	KEY WORD	IMAGE
9000	Sun Zoo	....	....
9001	Sun Day	....	....
9002	Sun Noah	....	....
9003	Sun Ma	....	....
9004	Sun Rah	....	....
9005	Sun Law	....	....
9006	Sun Jaw	....	....
9007	Sun Key	....	....
9008	Sun Fee	....	....
9009	Sun Bay	....	....
9010	Sun Daze	....	....
9011	Sun Dad	....	....
9012	Sun Dan	....	....
9013	Sun Dam	....	....
9014	Sun Dare	....	....
9015	Sun Dale	....	....
9016	Sun Dash	....	....
9017	Sun Deck	....	....
9018	Sun Daffy	....	....
9019	Sun Dab	....	....
9020	Sun Nasa	....	....
9021	Sun Net	....	....
9022	Sun Nan	....	....
9023	Sun Name	....	....
9024	Sun Nero	....	....
9025	Sun Nail	....	....
9026	Sun Nash	....	....
9027	Sun Nag	....	....
9028	Sun Navy	....	....
9029	Sun Nab	....	....
9030	Sun Mace	....	....
9031	Sun Mat	....	....
9032	Sun Man	....	....
9033	Sun Ma'am	....	....
9034	Sun Mare	....	....
9035	Sun Mail	....	....
9036	Sun Mash	....	....
9037	Sun Mac	....	....
9038	Sun Mafia	....	....
9039	Sun Map	....	....
9040	Sun Race	....	....
9041	Sun Rat	....	....

NUMBER	SEM[3]	KEY WORD	IMAGE
9042	Sun Rain	....	....
9043	Sun Ram	....	....
9044	Sun Rare	....	....
9045	Sun Rail	....	....
9046	Sun Rash	....	....
9047	Sun Rack	....	....
9048	Sun Rafia	....	....
9049	Sun Rap	....	....
9050	Sun Lace	....	....
9051	Sun Lad	....	....
9052	Sun Lane	....	....
9053	Sun Lamb	....	....
9054	Sun Lair	....	....
9055	Sun Lily	....	....
9056	Sun Lash	....	....
9057	Sun Lake	....	....
9058	Sun Laugh	....	....
9059	Sun Lab	....	....
9060	Sun Chase	....	....
9061	Sun Chat	....	....
9062	Sun Chain	....	....
9063	Sun Chime	....	....
9064	Sun Chair	....	....
9065	Sun Chill	....	....
9066	Sun Chacha	....	....
9067	Sun Check	....	....
9068	Sun Chaff	....	....
9069	Sun Chap	....	....
9070	Sun Case	....	....
9071	Sun Cat	....	....
9072	Sun Can	....	....
9073	Sun Cameo	....	....
9074	Sun Car	....	....
9075	Sun Call	....	....
9076	Sun Cash	....	....
9077	Sun Cake	....	....
9078	Sun Café	....	....
9079	Sun Cab	....	....
9080	Sun Face	....	....
9081	Sun Fat	....	....
9082	Sun Fan	....	....
9083	Sun Fame	....	....
9084	Sun Fair	....	....
9085	Sun Fall	....	....
9086	Sun Fish	....	....
9087	Sun Fake	....	....
9088	Sun Fife	....	....
9089	Sun Fab	....	....
9090	Sun Base	....	....
9091	Sun Bat	....	....
9092	Sun Ban	....	....
9093	Sun Bam!	....	....
9094	Sun Bar	....	....
9095	Sun Ball	....	....

NUMBER	SEM[3]	KEY WORD	IMAGE
9096	Sun Bash	....	....
9097	Sun Back	....	....
9098	Sun Beef	....	....
9099	Sun Baby	....	....
9100	Mercury Zoo	....	....
9101	Mercury Day	....	....
9102	Mercury Noah	....	....
9103	Mercury Ma	....	....
9104	Mercury Rah	....	....
9105	Mercury Law	....	....
9106	Mercury Jaw	....	....
9107	Mercury Key	....	....
9108	Mercury Fee	....	....
9109	Mercury Bay	....	....
9110	Mercury Daze	....	....
9111	Mercury Dad	....	....
9112	Mercury Dan	....	....
9113	Mercury Dam	....	....
9114	Mercury Dare	....	....
9115	Mercury Dale	....	....
9116	Mercury Dash	....	....
9117	Mercury Deck	....	....
9118	Mercury Daffy	....	....
9119	Mercury Dab	....	....
9120	Mercury Nasa	....	....
9121	Mercury Net	....	....
9122	Mercury Nan	....	....
9123	Mercury Name	....	....
9124	Mercury Nero	....	....
9125	Mercury Nail	....	....
9126	Mercury Nash	....	....
9127	Mercury Nag	....	....
9128	Mercury Navy	....	....
9129	Mercury Nab	....	....
9130	Mercury Mace	....	....
9131	Mercury Mat	....	....
9132	Mercury Man	....	....
9133	Mercury Ma'am	....	....
9134	Mercury Mare	....	....
9135	Mercury Mail	....	....
9136	Mercury Mash	....	....
9137	Mercury Mac	....	....
9138	Mercury Mafia	....	....
9139	Mercury Map	....	....
9140	Mercury Race	....	....
9141	Mercury Rat	....	....
9142	Mercury Rain	....	....
9143	Mercury Ram	....	....
9144	Mercury Rare	....	....
9145	Mercury Rail	....	....
9146	Mercury Rash	....	....
9147	Mercury Rack	....	....
9148	Mercury Rafia	....	....
9149	Mercury Rap	....	....

NUMBER	SEM[3]	KEY WORD	IMAGE
9150	Mercury Lace	....	....
9151	Mercury Lad	....	....
9152	Mercury Lane	....	....
9153	Mercury Lamb	....	....
9154	Mercury Lair	....	....
9155	Mercury Lily	....	....
9156	Mercury Lash	....	....
9157	Mercury Lake	....	....
9158	Mercury Laugh	....	....
9159	Mercury Lab	....	....
9160	Mercury Chase	....	....
9161	Mercury Chat	....	....
9162	Mercury Chain	....	....
9163	Mercury Chime	....	....
9164	Mercury Chair	....	....
9165	Mercury Chill	....	....
9166	Mercury Chacha	....	....
9167	Mercury Check	....	....
9168	Mercury Chaff	....	....
9169	Mercury Chap	....	....
9170	Mercury Case	....	....
9171	Mercury Cat	....	....
9172	Mercury Can	....	....
9173	Mercury Cameo	....	....
9174	Mercury Car	....	....
9175	Mercury Call	....	....
9176	Mercury Cash	....	....
9177	Mercury Cake	....	....
9178	Mercury Café	....	....
9179	Mercury Cab	....	....
9180	Mercury Face	....	....
9181	Mercury Fat	....	....
9182	Mercury Fan	....	....
9183	Mercury Fame	....	....
9184	Mercury Fair	....	....
9185	Mercury Fall	....	....
9186	Mercury Fish	....	....
9187	Mercury Fake	....	....
9188	Mercury Fife	....	....
9189	Mercury Fab	....	....
9190	Mercury Base	....	....
9191	Mercury Bat	....	....
9192	Mercury Ban	....	....
9193	Mercury Bam!	....	....
9194	Mercury Bar	....	....
9195	Mercury Ball	....	....
9196	Mercury Bash	....	....
9197	Mercury Back	....	....
9198	Mercury Beef	....	....
9199	Mercury Baby	....	....
9200	Venus Zoo	....	....
9201	Venus Day	....	....
9202	Venus Noah	....	....
9203	Venus Ma	....	....

NUMBER	SEM[3]	KEY WORD	IMAGE
9204	Venus Rah	....	....
9205	Venus Law	....	....
9206	Venus Jaw	....	....
9207	Venus Key	....	....
9208	Venus Fee	....	....
9209	Venus Bay	....	....
9210	Venus Daze	....	....
9211	Venus Dad	....	....
9212	Venus Dan	....	....
9213	Venus Dam	....	....
9214	Venus Dare	....	....
9215	Venus Dale	....	....
9216	Venus Dash	....	....
9217	Venus Deck	....	....
9218	Venus Daffy	....	....
9219	Venus Dab	....	....
9220	Venus Nasa	....	....
9221	Venus Net	....	....
9222	Venus Nan	....	....
9223	Venus Name	....	....
9224	Venus Nero	....	....
9225	Venus Nail	....	....
9226	Venus Nash	....	....
9227	Venus Nag	....	....
9228	Venus Navy	....	....
9229	Venus Nab	....	....
9230	Venus Mace	....	....
9231	Venus Mat	....	....
9232	Venus Man	....	....
9233	Venus Ma'am	....	....
9234	Venus Mare	....	....
9235	Venus Mail	....	....
9236	Venus Mash	....	....
9237	Venus Mac	....	....
9238	Venus Mafia	....	....
9239	Venus Map	....	....
9240	Venus Race	....	....
9241	Venus Rat	....	....
9242	Venus Rain	....	....
9243	Venus Ram	....	....
9244	Venus Rare	....	....
9245	Venus Rail	....	....
9246	Venus Rash	....	....
9247	Venus Rack	....	....
9248	Venus Rafia	....	....
9249	Venus Rap	....	....
9250	Venus Lace	....	....
9251	Venus Lad	....	....
9252	Venus Lane	....	....
9253	Venus Lamb	....	....
9254	Venus Lair	....	....
9255	Venus Lily	....	....
9256	Venus Lash	....	....
9257	Venus Lake	....	....

NUMBER	SEM³	KEY WORD	IMAGE
9258	Venus Laugh	....	....
9259	Venus Lab	....	....
9260	Venus Chase	....	....
9261	Venus Chat	....	....
9262	Venus Chain	....	....
9263	Venus Chime	....	....
9264	Venus Chair	....	....
9265	Venus Chill	....	....
9266	Venus Chacha	....	....
9267	Venus Check	....	....
9268	Venus Chaff	....	....
9269	Venus Chap	....	....
9270	Venus Case	....	....
9271	Venus Cat	....	....
9272	Venus Can	....	....
9273	Venus Cameo	....	....
9274	Venus Car	....	....
9275	Venus Call	....	....
9276	Venus Cash	....	....
9277	Venus Cake	....	....
9278	Venus Café	....	....
9279	Venus Cab	....	....
9280	Venus Face	....	....
9281	Venus Fat	....	....
9282	Venus Fan	....	....
9283	Venus Fame	....	....
9284	Venus Fair	....	....
9285	Venus Fall	....	....
9286	Venus Fish	....	....
9287	Venus Fake	....	....
9288	Venus Fife	....	....
9289	Venus Fab	....	....
9290	Venus Base	....	....
9291	Venus Bat	....	....
9292	Venus Ban	....	....
9293	Venus Bam!	....	....
9294	Venus Bar	....	....
9295	Venus Ball	....	....
9296	Venus Bash	....	....
9297	Venus Back	....	....
9298	Venus Beef	....	....
9299	Venus Baby	....	....
9300	Earth Zoo	....	....
9301	Earth Day	....	....
9302	Earth Noah	....	....
9303	Earth Ma	....	....
9304	Earth Rah	....	....
9305	Earth Law	....	....
9306	Earth Jaw	....	....
9307	Earth Key	....	....
9308	Earth Fee	....	....
9309	Earth Bay	....	....
9310	Earth Daze	....	....
9311	Earth Dad	....	....

NUMBER	SEM³	KEY WORD	IMAGE
9312	Earth Dan	....	....
9313	Earth Dam	....	....
9314	Earth Dare	....	....
9315	Earth Dale	....	....
9316	Earth Dash	....	....
9317	Earth Deck	....	....
9318	Earth Daffy	....	....
9319	Earth Dab	....	....
9320	Earth Nasa	....	....
9321	Earth Net	....	....
9322	Earth Nan	....	....
9323	Earth Name	....	....
9324	Earth Nero	....	....
9325	Earth Nail	....	....
9326	Earth Nash	....	....
9327	Earth Nag	....	....
9328	Earth Navy	....	....
9329	Earth Nab	....	....
9330	Earth Mace	....	....
9331	Earth Mat	....	....
9332	Earth Man	....	....
9333	Earth Ma'am	....	....
9334	Earth Mare	....	....
9335	Earth Mail	....	....
9336	Earth Mash	....	....
9337	Earth Mac	....	....
9338	Earth Mafia	....	....
9339	Earth Map	....	....
9340	Earth Race	....	....
9341	Earth Rat	....	....
9342	Earth Rain	....	....
9343	Earth Ram	....	....
9344	Earth Rare	....	....
9345	Earth Rail	....	....
9346	Earth Rash	....	....
9347	Earth Rack	....	....
9348	Earth Rafia	....	....
9349	Earth Rap	....	....
9350	Earth Lace	....	....
9351	Earth Lad	....	....
9352	Earth Lane	....	....
9353	Earth Lamb	....	....
9354	Earth Lair	....	....
9355	Earth Lily	....	....
9356	Earth Lash	....	....
9357	Earth Lake	....	....
9358	Earth Laugh	....	....
9359	Earth Lab	....	....
9360	Earth Chase	....	....
9361	Earth Chat	....	....
9362	Earth Chain	....	....
9363	Earth Chime	....	....
9364	Earth Chair	....	....
9365	Earth Chill	....	....

190

NUMBER	SEM³	KEY WORD	IMAGE
9366	Earth Chacha	....	....
9367	Earth Check	....	....
9368	Earth Chaff	....	....
9369	Earth Chap	....	....
9370	Earth Case	....	....
9371	Earth Cat	....	....
9372	Earth Can	....	....
9373	Earth Cameo	....	....
9374	Earth Car	....	....
9375	Earth Call	....	....
9376	Earth Cash	....	....
9377	Earth Cake	....	....
9378	Earth Café	....	....
9379	Earth Cab	....	....
9380	Earth Face	....	....
9381	Earth Fat	....	....
9382	Earth Fan	....	....
9383	Earth Fame	....	....
9384	Earth Fair	....	....
9385	Earth Fall	....	....
9386	Earth Fish	....	....
9387	Earth Fake	....	....
9388	Earth Fife	....	....
9389	Earth Fab	....	....
9390	Earth Base	....	....
9391	Earth Bat	....	....
9392	Earth Ban	....	....
9393	Earth Bam!	....	....
9394	Earth Bar	....	....
9395	Earth Ball	....	....
9396	Earth Bash	....	....
9397	Earth Back	....	....
9398	Earth Beef	....	....
9399	Earth Baby	....	....
9400	Mars Zoo	....	....
9401	Mars Day	....	....
9402	Mars Noah	....	....
9403	Mars Ma	....	....
9404	Mars Rah	....	....
9405	Mars Law	....	....
9406	Mars Jaw	....	....
9407	Mars Key	....	....
9408	Mars Fee	....	....
9409	Mars Bay	....	....
9410	Mars Daze	....	....
9411	Mars Dad	....	....
9412	Mars Dan	....	....
9413	Mars Dam	....	....
9414	Mars Dare	....	....
9415	Mars Dale	....	....
9416	Mars Dash	....	....
9417	Mars Deck	....	....
9418	Mars Daffy	....	....
9419	Mars Dab	....	....

191

NUMBER	SEM[3]	KEY WORD	IMAGE
9420	Mars Nasa	....	....
9421	Mars Net	....	....
9422	Mars Nan	....	....
9423	Mars Name	....	....
9424	Mars Nero	....	....
9425	Mars Nail	....	....
9426	Mars Nash	....	....
9427	Mars Nag	....	....
9428	Mars Navy	....	....
9429	Mars Nab	....	....
9430	Mars Mace	....	....
9431	Mars Mat	....	....
9432	Mars Man	....	....
9433	Mars Ma'am	....	....
9434	Mars Mare	....	....
9435	Mars Mail	....	....
9436	Mars Mash	....	....
9437	Mars Mac	....	....
9438	Mars Mafia	....	....
9439	Mars Map	....	....
9440	Mars Race	....	....
9441	Mars Rat	....	....
9442	Mars Rain	....	....
9443	Mars Ram	....	....
9444	Mars Rare	....	....
9445	Mars Rail	....	....
9446	Mars Rash	....	....
9447	Mars Rack	....	....
9448	Mars Rafia	....	....
9449	Mars Rap	....	....
9450	Mars Lace	....	....
9451	Mars Lad	....	....
9452	Mars Lane	....	....
9453	Mars Lamb	....	....
9454	Mars Lair	....	....
9455	Mars Lily	....	....
9456	Mars Lash	....	....
9457	Mars Lake	....	....
9458	Mars Laugh	....	....
9459	Mars Lab	....	....
9460	Mars Chase	....	....
9461	Mars Chat	....	....
9462	Mars Chain	....	....
9463	Mars Chime	....	....
9464	Mars Chair	....	....
9465	Mars Chill	....	....
9466	Mars Chacha	....	....
9467	Mars Check	....	....
9468	Mars Chaff	....	....
9469	Mars Chap	....	....
9470	Mars Case	....	....
9471	Mars Cat	....	....
9472	Mars Can	....	....
9473	Mars Cameo	....	....

NUMBER	SEM[3]	KEY WORD	IMAGE
9474	Mars Car	....	....
9475	Mars Call	....	....
9476	Mars Cash	....	....
9477	Mars Cake	....	....
9478	Mars Café	....	....
9479	Mars Cab	....	....
9480	Mars Face	....	....
9481	Mars Fat	....	....
9482	Mars Fan	....	....
9483	Mars Fame	....	....
9484	Mars Fair	....	....
9485	Mars Fall	....	....
9486	Mars Fish	....	....
9487	Mars Fake	....	....
9488	Mars Fife	....	....
9489	Mars Fab	....	....
9490	Mars Base	....	....
9491	Mars Bat	....	....
9492	Mars Ban	....	....
9493	Mars Bam!	....	....
9494	Mars Bar	....	....
9495	Mars Ball	....	....
9496	Mars Bash	....	....
9497	Mars Back	....	....
9498	Mars Beef	....	....
9499	Mars Baby	....	....
9500	Jupiter Zoo	....	....
9501	Jupiter Day	....	....
9502	Jupiter Noah	....	....
9503	Jupiter Ma	....	....
9504	Jupiter Rah	....	....
9505	Jupiter Law	....	....
9506	Jupiter Jaw	....	....
9507	Jupiter Key	....	....
9508	Jupiter Fee	....	....
9509	Jupiter Bay	....	....
9510	Jupiter Daze	....	....
9511	Jupiter Dad	....	....
9512	Jupiter Dan	....	....
9513	Jupiter Dam	....	....
9514	Jupiter Dare	....	....
9515	Jupiter Dale	....	....
9516	Jupiter Dash	....	....
9517	Jupiter Deck	....	....
9518	Jupiter Daffy	....	....
9519	Jupiter Dab	....	....
9520	Jupiter Nasa	....	....
9521	Jupiter Net	....	....
9522	Jupiter Nan	....	....
9523	Jupiter Name	....	....
9524	Jupiter Nero	....	....
9525	Jupiter Nail	....	....
9526	Jupiter Nash	....	....
9527	Jupiter Nag	....	....

NUMBER	SEM³	KEY WORD	IMAGE
9528	Jupiter Navy	....	....
9529	Jupiter Nab	....	....
9530	Jupiter Mace	....	....
9531	Jupiter Mat	....	....
9532	Jupiter Man	....	....
9533	Jupiter Ma'am	....	....
9534	Jupiter Mare	....	....
9535	Jupiter Mail	....	....
9536	Jupiter Mash	....	....
9537	Jupiter Mac	....	....
9538	Jupiter Mafia	....	....
9539	Jupiter Map	....	....
9540	Jupiter Race	....	....
9541	Jupiter Rat	....	....
9542	Jupiter Rain	....	....
9543	Jupiter Ram	....	....
9544	Jupiter Rare	....	....
9545	Jupiter Rail	....	....
9546	Jupiter Rash	....	....
9547	Jupiter Rack	....	....
9548	Jupiter Rafia	....	....
9549	Jupiter Rap	....	....
9550	Jupiter Lace	....	....
9551	Jupiter Lad	....	....
9552	Jupiter Lane	....	....
9553	Jupiter Lamb	....	....
9554	Jupiter Lair	....	....
9555	Jupiter Lily	....	....
9556	Jupiter Lash	....	....
9557	Jupiter Lake	....	....
9558	Jupiter Laugh	....	....
9559	Jupiter Lab	....	....
9560	Jupiter Chase	....	....
9561	Jupiter Chat	....	....
9562	Jupiter Chain	....	....
9563	Jupiter Chime	....	....
9564	Jupiter Chair	....	....
9565	Jupiter Chill	....	....
9566	Jupiter Chacha	....	....
9567	Jupiter Check	....	....
9568	Jupiter Chaff	....	....
9569	Jupiter Chap	....	....
9570	Jupiter Case	....	....
9571	Jupiter Cat	....	....
9572	Jupiter Can	....	....
9573	Jupiter Cameo	....	....
9574	Jupiter Car	....	....
9575	Jupiter Call	....	....
9576	Jupiter Cash	....	....
9577	Jupiter Cake	....	....
9578	Jupiter Café	....	....
9579	Jupiter Cab	....	....
9580	Jupiter Face	....	....
9581	Jupiter Fat	....	....

NUMBER	SEM³	KEY WORD	IMAGE
9582	Jupiter Fan	....	....
9583	Jupiter Fame	....	....
9584	Jupiter Fair	....	....
9585	Jupiter Fall	....	....
9586	Jupiter Fish	....	....
9587	Jupiter Fake	....	....
9588	Jupiter Fife	....	....
9589	Jupiter Fab	....	....
9590	Jupiter Base	....	....
9591	Jupiter Bat	....	....
9592	Jupiter Ban	....	....
9593	Jupiter Bam!	....	....
9594	Jupiter Bar	....	....
9595	Jupiter Ball	....	....
9596	Jupiter Bash	....	....
9597	Jupiter Back	....	....
9598	Jupiter Beef	....	....
9599	Jupiter Baby	....	....
9600	Saturn Zoo	....	....
9601	Saturn Day	....	....
9602	Saturn Noah	....	....
9603	Saturn Ma	....	....
9604	Saturn Rah	....	....
9605	Saturn Law	....	....
9606	Saturn Jaw	....	....
9607	Saturn Key	....	....
9608	Saturn Fee	....	....
9609	Saturn Bay	....	....
9610	Saturn Daze	....	....
9611	Saturn Dad	....	....
9612	Saturn Dan	....	....
9613	Saturn Dam	....	....
9614	Saturn Dare	....	....
9615	Saturn Dale	....	....
9616	Saturn Dash	....	....
9617	Saturn Deck	....	....
9618	Saturn Daffy	....	....
9619	Saturn Dab	....	....
9620	Saturn Nasa	....	....
9621	Saturn Net	....	....
9622	Saturn Nan	....	....
9623	Saturn Name	....	....
9624	Saturn Nero	....	....
9625	Saturn Nail	....	....
9626	Saturn Nash	....	....
9627	Saturn Nag	....	....
9628	Saturn Navy	....	....
9629	Saturn Nab	....	....
9630	Saturn Mace	....	....
9631	Saturn Mat	....	....
9632	Saturn Man	....	....
9633	Saturn Ma'am	....	....
9634	Saturn Mare	....	....
9635	Saturn Mail	....	....

NUMBER	SEM³	KEY WORD	IMAGE
9636	Saturn Mash	....	....
9637	Saturn Mac	....	....
9638	Saturn Mafia	....	....
9639	Saturn Map	....	....
9640	Saturn Race	....	....
9641	Saturn Rat	....	....
9642	Saturn Rain	....	....
9643	Saturn Ram	....	....
9644	Saturn Rare	....	....
9645	Saturn Rail	....	....
9646	Saturn Rash	....	....
9647	Saturn Rack	....	....
9648	Saturn Rafia	....	....
9649	Saturn Rap	....	....
9650	Saturn Lace	....	....
9651	Saturn Lad	....	....
9652	Saturn Lane	....	....
9653	Saturn Lamb	....	....
9654	Saturn Lair	....	....
9655	Saturn Lily	....	....
9656	Saturn Lash	....	....
9657	Saturn Lake	....	....
9658	Saturn Laugh	....	....
9659	Saturn Lab	....	....
9660	Saturn Chase	....	....
9661	Saturn Chat	....	....
9662	Saturn Chain	....	....
9663	Saturn Chime	....	....
9664	Saturn Chair	....	....
9665	Saturn Chill	....	....
9666	Saturn Chacha	....	....
9667	Saturn Check	....	....
9668	Saturn Chaff	....	....
9669	Saturn Chap	....	....
9670	Saturn Case	....	....
9671	Saturn Cat	....	....
9672	Saturn Can	....	....
9673	Saturn Cameo	....	....
9674	Saturn Car	....	....
9675	Saturn Call	....	....
9676	Saturn Cash	....	....
9677	Saturn Cake	....	....
9678	Saturn Café	....	....
9679	Saturn Cab	....	....
9680	Saturn Face	....	....
9681	Saturn Fat	....	....
9682	Saturn Fan	....	....
9683	Saturn Fame	....	....
9684	Saturn Fair	....	....
9685	Saturn Fall	....	....
9686	Saturn Fish	....	....
9687	Saturn Fake	....	....
9688	Saturn Fife	....	....
9689	Saturn Fab	....	....

NUMBER	SEM[3]	KEY WORD	IMAGE
9690	Saturn Base	....	....
9691	Saturn Bat	....	....
9692	Saturn Ban	....	....
9693	Saturn Bam!	....	....
9694	Saturn Bar	....	....
9695	Saturn Ball	....	....
9696	Saturn Bash	....	....
9697	Saturn Back	....	....
9698	Saturn Beef	....	....
9699	Saturn Baby	....	....
9700	Uranus Zoo	....	....
9701	Uranus Day	....	....
9702	Uranus Noah	....	....
9703	Uranus Ma	....	....
9704	Uranus Rah	....	....
9705	Uranus Law	....	....
9706	Uranus Jaw	....	....
9707	Uranus Key	....	....
9708	Uranus Fee	....	....
9709	Uranus Bay	....	....
9710	Uranus Daze	....	....
9711	Uranus Dad	....	....
9712	Uranus Dan	....	....
9713	Uranus Dam	....	....
9714	Uranus Dare	....	....
9715	Uranus Dale	....	....
9716	Uranus Dash	....	....
9717	Uranus Deck	....	....
9718	Uranus Daffy	....	....
9719	Uranus Dab	....	....
9720	Uranus Nasa	....	....
9721	Uranus Net	....	....
9722	Uranus Nan	....	....
9723	Uranus Name	....	....
9724	Uranus Nero	....	....
9725	Uranus Nail	....	....
9726	Uranus Nash	....	....
9727	Uranus Nag	....	....
9728	Uranus Navy	....	....
9729	Uranus Nab	....	....
9730	Uranus Mace	....	....
9731	Uranus Mat	....	....
9732	Uranus Man	....	....
9733	Uranus Ma'am	....	....
9734	Uranus Mare	....	....
9735	Uranus Mail	....	....
9736	Uranus Mash	....	....
9737	Uranus Mac	....	....
9738	Uranus Mafia	....	....
9739	Uranus Map	....	....
9740	Uranus Race	....	....
9741	Uranus Rat	....	....
9742	Uranus Rain	....	....
9743	Uranus Ram	....	....

NUMBER	SEM³	KEY WORD	IMAGE
9744	Uranus Rare	....	....
9745	Uranus Rail	....	....
9746	Uranus Rash	....	....
9747	Uranus Rack	....	....
9748	Uranus Rafia	....	....
9749	Uranus Rap	....	....
9750	Uranus Lace	....	....
9751	Uranus Lad	....	....
9752	Uranus Lane	....	....
9753	Uranus Lamb	....	....
9754	Uranus Lair	....	....
9755	Uranus Lily	....	....
9756	Uranus Lash	....	....
9757	Uranus Lake	....	....
9758	Uranus Laugh	....	....
9759	Uranus Lab	....	....
9760	Uranus Chase	....	....
9761	Uranus Chat	....	....
9762	Uranus Chain	....	....
9763	Uranus Chime	....	....
9764	Uranus Chair	....	....
9765	Uranus Chill	....	....
9766	Uranus Chacha	....	....
9767	Uranus Check	....	....
9768	Uranus Chaff	....	....
9769	Uranus Chap	....	....
9770	Uranus Case	....	....
9771	Uranus Cat	....	....
9772	Uranus Can	....	....
9773	Uranus Cameo	....	....
9774	Uranus Car	....	....
9775	Uranus Call	....	....
9776	Uranus Cash	....	....
9777	Uranus Cake	....	....
9778	Uranus Café	....	....
9779	Uranus Cab	....	....
9780	Uranus Face	....	....
9781	Uranus Fat	....	....
9782	Uranus Fan	....	....
9783	Uranus Fame	....	....
9784	Uranus Fair	....	....
9785	Uranus Fall	....	....
9786	Uranus Fish	....	....
9787	Uranus Fake	....	....
9788	Uranus Fife	....	....
9789	Uranus Fab	....	....
9790	Uranus Base	....	....
9791	Uranus Bat	....	....
9792	Uranus Ban	....	....
9793	Uranus Bam!	....	....
9794	Uranus Bar	....	....
9795	Uranus Ball	....	....
9796	Uranus Bash	....	....
9797	Uranus Back	....	....

NUMBER	SEM[3]	KEY WORD	IMAGE
9798	Uranus Beef	....	....
9799	Uranus Baby	....	....
9800	Neptune Zoo	....	....
9801	Neptune Day	....	....
9802	Neptune Noah	....	....
9803	Neptune Ma	....	....
9804	Neptune Rah	....	....
9805	Neptune Law	....	....
9806	Neptune Jaw	....	....
9807	Neptune Key	....	....
9808	Neptune Fee	....	....
9809	Neptune Bay	....	....
9810	Neptune Daze	....	....
9811	Neptune Dad	....	....
9812	Neptune Dan	....	....
9813	Neptune Dam	....	....
9814	Neptune Dare	....	....
9815	Neptune Dale	....	....
9816	Neptune Dash	....	....
9817	Neptune Deck	....	....
9818	Neptune Daffy	....	....
9819	Neptune Dab	....	....
9820	Neptune Nasa	....	....
9821	Neptune Net	....	....
9822	Neptune Nan	....	....
9823	Neptune Name	....	....
9824	Neptune Nero	....	....
9825	Neptune Nail	....	....
9826	Neptune Nash	....	....
9827	Neptune Nag	....	....
9828	Neptune Navy	....	....
9829	Neptune Nab	....	....
9830	Neptune Mace	....	....
9831	Neptune Mat	....	....
9832	Neptune Man	....	....
9833	Neptune Ma'am	....	....
9834	Neptune Mare	....	....
9835	Neptune Mail	....	....
9836	Neptune Mash	....	....
9837	Neptune Mac	....	....
9838	Neptune Mafia	....	....
9839	Neptune Map	....	....
9840	Neptune Race	....	....
9841	Neptune Rat	....	....
9842	Neptune Rain	....	....
9843	Neptune Ram	....	....
9844	Neptune Rare	....	....
9845	Neptune Rail	....	....
9846	Neptune Rash	....	....
9847	Neptune Rack	....	....
9848	Neptune Rafia	....	....
9849	Neptune Rap	....	....
9850	Neptune Lace	....	....
9851	Neptune Lad	....	....

NUMBER	SEM[3]	KEY WORD	IMAGE
9852	Neptune Lane	....	....
9853	Neptune Lamb	....	....
9854	Neptune Lair	....	....
9855	Neptune Lily	....	....
9856	Neptune Lash	....	....
9857	Neptune Lake	....	....
9858	Neptune Laugh	....	....
9859	Neptune Lab	....	....
9860	Neptune Chase	....	....
9861	Neptune Chat	....	....
9862	Neptune Chain	....	....
9863	Neptune Chime	....	....
9864	Neptune Chair	....	....
9865	Neptune Chill	....	....
9866	Neptune Chacha	....	....
9867	Neptune Check	....	....
9868	Neptune Chaff	....	....
9869	Neptune Chap	....	....
9870	Neptune Case	....	....
9871	Neptune Cat	....	....
9872	Neptune Can	....	....
9873	Neptune Cameo	....	....
9874	Neptune Car	....	....
9875	Neptune Call	....	....
9876	Neptune Cash	....	....
9877	Neptune Cake	....	....
9878	Neptune Cafe	....	....
9879	Neptune Cab	....	....
9880	Neptune Face	....	....
9881	Neptune Fat	....	....
9882	Neptune Fan	....	....
9883	Neptune Fame	....	....
9884	Neptune Fair	....	....
9885	Neptune Fall	....	....
9886	Neptune Fish	....	....
9887	Neptune Fake	....	....
9888	Neptune Fife	....	....
9889	Neptune Fab	....	....
9890	Neptune Base	....	....
9891	Neptune Bat	....	....
9892	Neptune Ban	....	....
9893	Neptune Bam!	....	....
9894	Neptune Bar	....	....
9895	Neptune Ball	....	....
9896	Neptune Bash	....	....
9897	Neptune Back	....	....
9898	Neptune Beef	....	....
9899	Neptune Baby	....	....
9900	Pluto Zoo	....	....
9901	Pluto Day	....	....
9902	Pluto Noah	....	....
9903	Pluto Ma	....	....
9904	Pluto Rah	....	....
9905	Pluto Law	....	....

NUMBER	SEM³	KEY WORD	IMAGE
9906	Pluto Jaw	....	....
9907	Pluto Key	....	....
9908	Pluto Fee	....	....
9909	Pluto Bay	....	....
9910	Pluto Daze	....	....
9911	Pluto Dad	....	....
9912	Pluto Dan	....	....
9913	Pluto Dam	....	....
9914	Pluto Dare	....	....
9915	Pluto Dale	....	....
9916	Pluto Dash	....	....
9917	Pluto Deck	....	....
9918	Pluto Daffy	....	....
9919	Pluto Dab	....	....
9920	Pluto Nasa	....	....
9921	Pluto Net	....	....
9922	Pluto Nan	....	....
9923	Pluto Name	....	....
9924	Pluto Nero	....	....
9925	Pluto Nail	....	....
9926	Pluto Nash	....	....
9927	Pluto Nag	....	....
9928	Pluto Navy	....	....
9929	Pluto Nab	....	....
9930	Pluto Mace	....	....
9931	Pluto Mat	....	....
9932	Pluto Man	....	....
9933	Pluto Ma'am	....	....
9934	Pluto Mare	....	....
9935	Pluto Mail	....	....
9936	Pluto Mash	....	....
9937	Pluto Mac	....	....
9938	Pluto Mafia	....	....
9939	Pluto Map	....	....
9940	Pluto Race	....	....
9941	Pluto Rat	....	....
9942	Pluto Rain	....	....
9943	Pluto Ram	....	....
9944	Pluto Rare	....	....
9945	Pluto Rail	....	....
9946	Pluto Rash	....	....
9947	Pluto Rack	....	....
9948	Pluto Rafia	....	....
9949	Pluto Rap	....	....
9950	Pluto Lace	....	....
9951	Pluto Lad	....	....
9952	Pluto Lane	....	....
9953	Pluto Lamb	....	....
9954	Pluto Lair	....	....
9955	Pluto Lily	....	....
9956	Pluto Lash	....	....
9957	Pluto Lake	....	....
9958	Pluto Laugh	....	....
9959	Pluto Lab	....	....

NUMBER	SEM³	KEY WORD	IMAGE
9960	Pluto Chase	....	....
9961	Pluto Chat	....	....
9962	Pluto Chain	....	....
9963	Pluto Chime	....	....
9964	Pluto Chair	....	....
9965	Pluto Chill	....	....
9966	Pluto Chacha	....	....
9967	Pluto Check	....	....
9968	Pluto Chaff	....	....
9969	Pluto Chap	....	....
9970	Pluto Case	....	....
9971	Pluto Cat	....	....
9972	Pluto Can	....	....
9973	Pluto Cameo	....	....
9974	Pluto Car	....	....
9975	Pluto Call	....	....
9976	Pluto Cash	....	....
9977	Pluto Cake	....	....
9978	Pluto Café	....	....
9979	Pluto Cab	....	....
9980	Pluto Face	....	....
9981	Pluto Fat	....	....
9982	Pluto Fan	....	....
9983	Pluto Fame	....	....
9984	Pluto Fair	....	....
9985	Pluto Fall	....	....
9986	Pluto Fish	....	....
9987	Pluto Fake	....	....
9988	Pluto Fife	....	....
9989	Pluto Fab	....	....
9990	Pluto Base	....	....
9991	Pluto Bat	....	....
9992	Pluto Ban	....	....
9993	Pluto Bam!	....	....
9994	Pluto Bar	....	....
9995	Pluto Ball	....	....
9996	Pluto Bash	....	....
9997	Pluto Back	....	....
9998	Pluto Beef	....	....
9999	Pluto Baby	....	....

APPENDIX

Tony Buzan

Tony Buzan is the originator of Mind Maps, the SEM^3 (Self-Enhancing Master Memory Matrix), the Group/Family Work/Mind Map Study Technique, and new concepts in brain functioning relating to the process of Change and Metapositive Thinking. He is also the Founder of the International Brain Clubs and Buzan Centres.

Tony Buzan was born in London in 1942, emigrated to Vancouver in 1954 and graduated from the University of British Columbia in 1964, achieving double Honours in Psychology, English, Mathematics and the General Sciences. Returning to England in 1966, he worked on Fleet Street, also editing the International Journal of MENSA (the high IQ society).

Since then he has published ten books (nine on the brain and learning and one volume of poetry). His books have now been published in fifty countries and translated into twenty languages. *Use Your Head* has surpassed worldwide sales of a million, and is a standard introductory text for the Open University.

Tony Buzan has featured in, presented and co-produced many television, video and radio programmes, both national and international, including the record-breaking *Use Your Head* series (BBC TV); the *Open Mind* series (ITV); *The Enchanted Loom*, a one-hour feature documentary on the brain; and numerous talk shows. His latest video series, *Buzan Business Training*, is a three-part training package introducing the major elements of his work to the international business community.

He is advisor to royalty, governments, multi-national organisations, including IBM, BP, Barclays International, Digital Equipment Corporation, Buzan Mast, Management Centre Europe, General Motors, Bell Telephone, AT&T, Rank Xerox, and Nabisco, and is a regular lecturer at the leading international universities and schools.

He is a Fellow of the Institute of Training and Development, the Jamaican Institute of Management and the Swedish Management Group, and is an elected member of the International Faculty of the Young Presidents' Organisation and the International Council of Psychologists. A Member of the Institute of Directors, and a Freeman of the City of London, he is also advisor to the British Olympic Rowing Squad.

Products

Audio tapes

Learning and Memory – produced for *Psychology Today* magazine
The Intelligence Revolution (set of 3 tapes)
Tony Buzan on Memory and Advanced Mind Mapping.
Make the Most of Your Mind – based on the book of the same name,
and *Harnessing the ParaBrain*.
Supercreativity and Mind Mapping – a comprehensive introduction to
the workings of your brain, and the theory and use of Mind Mapping
(with manuallette).

Video tapes

Use Your Head – the original nine part BBC TV series attractively
presented with updated facilitator's manual and *Use Your Head* and
Use Your Memory books.
The Enchanted Loom – documentary on the brain featuring inter-
views with the world's major contributors to the field devised and
presented by Tony Buzan.
Buzan Business Training – complete business training course
emphasising the application of Mind Mapping, Memory and
Information Management to business.
Family Genius Training – complete video series based on *Use Your
Head* and *Make the Most of Your Mind*, which guides the family
through the latest information on brain and brain training.

Poster

'*Body and Soul*' Master Mind Map poster
A limited edition poster depicting, in a surrealist manner, all the
principles taught by Tony Buzan. This beautiful picture is called
'Body and Soul' and each numbered copy is signed by the Swedish
artist, Ulf Ekberg.

Mind Map Kits

Specially designed A3 and A4 pads and pens

Master Your Memory Matrix 0–10,000

Laminated 0–99 and 100 to 10,000 Matrix plus full instructions to
assist the *Master Your Memory* reader. To order, contact

The Buzan Centre
Suite 2, Cardigan House,
37 Waterloo Road
Winton
Dorset BH9 1BD

Telephone enquiries to: 0202 533593
Fax: 0202 534572

The Brain Club

The Brain Club is an international organisation designed to help you increase your mental, physical and spiritual awareness. This is done by waking that sleeping giant, your brain, and teaching you how to access its vast intelligences, first by learning how to learn and then by developing specific skills in areas that you choose.

You can do this by studying in your own home, or meeting regularly with others who also wish to expand their vast range of mental skills as outlined in *Master Your Memory*.

Join these 'mental gymnasiums' and improve your following skill areas:

a. Memorising
b. Range/Speed Reading
c. Mind Mapping and Creative Thinking
d. Learning and Studying
e. I.Q.
f. Mathematics
g. The Arts
h. Physical Performance
i. Vocabulary Building/Language Learning
j. Communicating
k. Personality Development
l. Games Skills
m. Special Skills

Each area within The Brain Club will be graded and certificates awarded as you reach advancing levels of competence.

> For details of the nearest cell of the Brain Club, contact
>
> The Buzan Centre
> Suite 2, Cardigan House,
> 37 Waterloo Road
> Winton
> Dorset BH9 1BD
>
> Telephone enquiries to: 0202 533593
> Fax: 0202 534572

The Universal Personal Organiser (UPO)

This **new** and **unique** approach to time and self-management is a diary system, based on the techniques created and taught by Tony Buzan.

The Universal Personal Organiser is a living system that **grows** with you, and that provides a comprehensive perspective on your life, your desires, and your business and family functions.

The Universal Personal Organiser is the first diary system to use the principles that Leonardo da Vinci discovered in the Italian Renaissance: that images and colour enhance both **creativity** and **memory**, as well as being more **enjoyable** and **easier** than regular diary systems.

The Universal Personal Organiser **reflects you,** and gives you the **freedom** to perform at your Highest Potential. The Universal Personal Organiser is made of materials that are of the **highest quality**, using the best leathers and paper available.

The Universal Personal Organiser is designed to help you manage the four main areas of life: **health** (mental, physical and emotional); **happiness (family), creativity and wealth.**

The Universal Personal Organiser, in so doing, allows you to **organise** your past, present and future in a manner that is both **enjoyable** and **fun.**

The Universal Personal Organiser's pages and partitions have been designed to enable you to get a comprehensive perspective on your **yearly plan,** your **monthly** and **weekly plans,** and your **daily plan,** using the new **twenty-four hour clock, mind mapping,** and *Master Your Memory* systems.

For further information on:

* Training courses based on Tony Buzan's methods
* Co-ordination of the Brain Club
* Supportive books, tapes and educational products

Contact

The Buzan Centre
Suite 2, Cardigan House
37 Waterloo Road
Winton
Dorset BH9 1BD

Telephone enquiries to: 0202 533593
Fax: 0202 534572

* Please send a stamped, self-addressed envelope for your reply.

Buzan Training Courses

Courses are prepared for:
* Governments
* Corporations
* Schools and universities
* Private groups and organisations
* Foundations
* Children
* Families
* Senior citizens

The courses are based on the following books by Tony Buzan:
* Make the Most of Your Mind
* Master Your Memory
* Speed (and Range) Reading
* Use Your Head
* Use Your Memory
* The Brain User's Guide
* Harnessing the ParaBrain
* Universal Personal Organiser

The courses emphasise:
* Mind mapping
* Memory skills – advanced
* Speed reading – advanced
* Learning to learn
* Creativity
* Presentation skills
* Work/study skills
* Corporate and family brain training
* The ageing brain
* Managing change
* Personal and time management
* Especially tailored courses

For enquiries, contact

The Buzan Centre
Suite 2, Cardigan House
37 Waterloo Road
Winton
Dorset BH9 1BD

Telephone enquiries to: 0202 533593
Fax: 0202 534572